Collected Works of
Professor B. R. Grover
Vol. V

Mughal Land Revenue Apparatus

Collected Works of
Professor B. R. Grover
Vol. V

Mughal Land Revenue Apparatus

Edited by
Miss Amrita Grover
Dr. Anju Grover Chaudhary
Dr. J.C. Dua

Originals
Delhi-110052

First Published 2010

ISBN 978-81-8454-080-2 (Vol. 5)

Published by
Originals
A-6, Nimri Commercial Centre,
Ashok Vihar Phase-IV, Delhi-110052
Phones: 27302453
e-mail: info@Lppindia.com
visit us at: www.Lppindia.com

Printed at
D K Fine Art Press P Ltd.
Delhi-110052

PRINTED IN INDIA

Dedicated to the Memory of my
Esteemed Brother
Professor B.R. Grover

Amrita Grover

Table of Contents

About the Author

(b. 1923- d. 2001)

Professor B.R. Grover, former Chairman of the Indian Council of Historical Research, with an academic and administrative career spanning more than 55 years, has left an indelible mark as one of India's most eminent and dedicated historians. He has left behind a massive wealth of historical research based on original Persian, Urdu, Ottoman Turkish, Punjabi and English sources. Known for doing intensive research in the archives and libraries of India, several European countries and the United States of America, Professor Grover had carved out a distinct position for himself as a moving encyclopaedia of source material on agrarian history of the Mughals, especially the land revenue administration.

Upon his death on May 10, 2001, the then Prime Minister Atal Behari Vajpayee paid him a rich tribute, stating: šHe would always be remembered for his formidable legacy of excellence, erudition, and dedication to historical research and academic administration.› Dr. Murli Manohar Joshi, then Minister of Human Resources and Scientific Research, paid him a personal homage and called him a real šKarma Yogi›. He said, šHe lived like a Yogi and died like a Yogi.› Former Vice President of India, Justice Hidayatullah, had also applauded him for his research. His colleagues described him as ša man of sterling qualities of head and heart›; and ša dynamic and objective head of country's premier historical Institute who has left a rich legacy of his outstanding achievements in the world of historical research,› among other things.

Born on February 10, 1923, Professor Grover started his career in teaching in 1946 in Lahore and later taught at the University of Punjab and various universities in Delhi until 1974, including Delhi University, Jawahar Lal Nehru University and Jamia Milia Islamia, where he also served as head of the Department of Indian History and Culture. In 1974, he was called upon to join as Director cum Member-Secretary of the newly established Indian Council of Historical Research (ICHR), a premier historical research Institute, where he served from 1974 to 1985 as Director and was later appointed as Chairman in 1999. For his long association with ICHR, his colleague, Prof. A.R. Khan, wrote in his obituary: šOn account of his long association with the Council and the services rendered by him to it, Professor Grover became an institution by himself and he and the Council became a synonymy, as the latter came to be identified, both in India and abroad, with Professor Grover, even when he was not holding any office in the Council.

Initially having received training at Paris under the auspices of UNESCO for the promotion of history as a means of international understanding, Professor Grover wrote and published books in British history. Later, because of his deep interest in the study of original sources and his proficiency in Persian language, his research interests shifted to the medieval period of Indian history. His interest later widened to the study and research in regard to the social, cultural and economic impact of the Indian immigrants in West Asia and East European countries. As an avid researcher, Professor Grover wrote and published copiously on various aspects of the Mughal Agrarian System, Patterns of Rural Trade, The Concept of Village Community and a host of other topics. His writings, mostly published in prestigious journals, like the journals of the Delhi School of Economics and the proceedings of various conferences, became nodal points for the scholars of his generation. His published writings in

The Indian Economic and Social History Review, Proceedings of the Indian Historical Records Commission, Indian Archives, Proceedings of the Punjab History Conference, Punjab Past and Present and *The Proceedings of the Indian History Congress,* among others, brought him national and international recognition. At an early stage of Professor Grover's career, Prof. M.M. Pearson of Pennsylvania University, U.S.A., wrote about his Mughal Agrarian writings as š...an impressive start...brilliant, which makes fundamental contribution in this area.› Prof. C.A. Bailey of Cambridge University, complimented him for šcomprehensive listing of materials› and šexcellent bibliographies.›

Because of his expertise in historical manuscripts/documents and objects, Professor Grover was nominated by the Government of India for several honorary positions such as member of the Indian Historical Records Commission, member of the Historical Documents Purchase Committee of the National Archives of India, member of the Committee on Preservation and Development of Cultural Heritage of Delhi, and an expert member of the Verification Committee of National Museum, India. Professor Grover was also a member of the Publication Committee of the šComprehensive History of India›. For the Indian History Congress, he served intermittently as a Joint Secretary, a Treasurer and Sectional President (Medieval India). Professor Grover also edited the well-known Time Capsule in 1978, and advised the Government to display it in the National Museum instead of inserting it again underground. He also served on the Editorial Board constituted by the Government of India for the production of documentaries on šFreedom Struggle for India's Independence, 1984-2001.› Under this scheme, more than 75 documentaries were published by the Films Division, Ministry of Information and Broadcasting.

Professor Grover represented India at several international organizations, including UNESCO in 1951; Indian delegate to West Germany, 1957; delegate to the International Conference in History, Bucharest, 1980; delegate to the International Conference on the Bulgarian Studies, Sofia, 1986; and delegate to the World Archaeological Congress, Croatia, 1998, among others. Besides participating in numerous Indo-European cultural exchange programmes, presiding over innumerable regional/national/international seminars and conferences and contributing papers to various national/international seminars and conferences, he also lectured widely in West Germany (1957), Bulgaria (1986), Zagreb (1998), UK (1998), Holland (1998), and United States (1998 and 2000).

Professor Grover received several honours and awards for his historical research. For his writings on Georgi Dimitrov, the šRole of the Indian Immigrants in the Culture and Economy of the West Asian and East

European Countries During the Medieval Age,› and šThe Social, Religious and Agrarian Aspects in East Europe, especially Bulgaria under the Ottoman-Turkish Rule (14th-19th centuries),› he was awarded Georgi Dimitrov Gold Medal by the Peoples Republic of Bulgaria. For his work on Punjab History, Professor Grover was awarded Saropa Roll of Honour by the Punjabi University, Patiala, in 1996. A life-long scholar of medieval and Islamic India, Professor Grover again came in limelight in 2001 when (upon the demolition of Buddhist statues at Bamiyan by the Taliban government), his expert opinion was sought by the Indian media to determine whether there was any parallel between Bamiyan and Ayodhya.

As a distinguished historian and a scholar with an integrated and scientific approach to the analysis of the historical process, Professor Grover, being a liberal thinker, was a great believer in the social cohesion and national integration in India and made an immense contribution in this regard.

Preface

This is the fifth volume of *The Collected Works of Professor B.R. Grover* which deals with the administrative units of the Mughal Empire as it developed in India. For the purposes of administration, the Mughal Empire was divided into *Subahs*. As far as possible, the effort was to make the *Subahs* more or less of equal dimensions keeping in view the administrative convenience and the natural frontier of the units. Each *Subah* was divided into *Sarkars*, each *Sarkar* into *Parganas* and *Mahals*, each *Pargana* into *Tappas*, and each *Tappa* into *Mauzas*. This volume is, in fact, an in-depth and critical study of the entire Mughal land revenue apparatus.

Professor Grover was of the view that success of the fiscal policy of the State, howsoever well intentioned and enlightened, rests mainly on the administrative apparatus set-up by the State and the manner in which the land revenue administration is operated. Known for his expertise in the various aspects of medieval land revenue system, Professor Grover made a very critical and valuable assessment of the various revenue and administrative officials in this regard. Though written in the late 1950s and early 1960s, the views expressed are still relevant and useful for the scholars of history. Amongst the Papers included in the Volume, two Papers, viz. '*Diwan-i-Sarkar* in the Mughal Administration' (*Indian Historical records Commission*, 1962) and 'The Position of Desai in the *Pargana* Administration of *Subah* Gujarat under the Mughals' (*Indian History Congress*, 1961) are published and were very well received when presented. The views expressed therein are still valued by the scholars of the agrarian system of the Mughals.

In order to cope with the pressing administrative problems, the Mughal rulers, from Akbar to Aurangzeb, keeping also in view the changing circumstances, introduced the required reforms in the territorial circles as well as changes in the functions of the local officials both in *Sarkar* and *Pargana* administration. These changes were meticulously highlighted by Professor Grover upon an examination of contemporary and near contemporary original Persian documents found in libraries and Archives in India and other countries. As highlighted by him, these changes were necessary to have more effective control over the local administration, and for the batterment of its machinery of land revenue collection. These changes were especially essential in the case of realization of revenues from the *Zur-talab* areas.

The papers published in the present Volume show that Professor Grover seriously thought that there was a real need for a complete re-orientation of the existing theories and viewpoints in order to get a comprehensive picture of administrative jurisdiction and duties of the officials of various categories and in order to understand the detailed working of the Mughal land revenue administration. If the information available in the well-known sources was not sufficient, he explored for further evidence in the original documents scattered throughout various libraries and Archives in India and abroad. To illustrate the above viewpoint, Professor Grover for the first time highlighted that a *Chakla* division as a distinct territorial revenue-cum-administrative circle had become more or less a uniform feature of the Mughal provinces, more especially from the reign of Shahjahan onwards. The details given in the Papers point out that the administration of *Chakla* was similar to that of the *Sarkar*. Also, as per the 17th century evidence, a *Pargana* existed in a duel capacity, as a part of *Sarkar* for the maintenance of revenue accounts and as a part of a specified *Chakla* for revenue administration. Again, contrary to the then belief that the office of *Diwan* existed at the central and provincial headquarters, Professor Grover for the first time produced direct contemporary evidence proving the existence of the office of *Diwan* as finance-cum-revenue officer at the headquarters of the *Sarkar* division as well. The *Diwans* of the centre and provinces were designated as *Diwaniyan-i-Azaam* and that of the *Sarkars* simply as *Diwaniyan*.

Professor Grover based his critical and convincing analysis about the administrative divisions, especially *Sarkar*, *Chakla*, *Pargana* and *Zillah* as well as the land revenue apparatus of the Mughal Age after a critical examination of the original contemporary source material in Persian, Urdu and other regional languages available in various libraries and Archives. The main officials whose position, function and duties have been critically analysed include *Diwan-i-Sarkar*, *Faujdar*, *Bitikchi*, *Shiqdar*, *Amal Guzar* or *Karori*, *Qanungo*, *Amin*, *Chaudhari*, *Desai*, *Karkun*, *Fotehdar/ Khazanahdar* and *Thanahdar*.

The editors hope that this Volume of the collection of Professor B. R. Grover's works, like previous four volumes, will also prove valuable for scholars interested in the economic history of the Mughal age.

The editors also express their thanks to Shri Pradeep Mittal, proprietor, Originals, for the excellent production of this work.

New Delhi

Ms. Amrita Grover
Dr. Anju Grover Chaudhary
Dr. J. C. Dua

Introduction

Professor B. R. Grover, a well-known scholar of history, particularly Agrarian history of India, was an untiring researcher who spent his whole life in search of un-tapped sources in several libraries and Archives of India and abroad as well as in the private collections of erstwhile Chiefs in order to get a clear and correct picture of the agrarian aspects of medieval Indian history. This is the precise reason why his unpublished writings are far more than the published ones. Nevertheless, the quality and quantity of his published works attracted great admiration of the academicians all over the world. Besides, there are perhaps very few historians who had the privilege of holding so many different posts and receiving so much honours as Professor B. R. Grover. I was lucky to have such a master as my 'guru'.

It is a great privilege for me to write an Introduction to one of the Volumes of *The Collected Works of Professor B.R. Grover*. I had the opportunity of having a very close academic relationship with Professor Grover since December 1961 when I was in my 1st year of B.A. (Hons.) History. My first introduction to the writing of history was when he gave me the dictation of the Paper, 'The Position of *Desai* in the *Pargana* Administration of *Subah* Gujarat under the Mughals' to be presented in the then forthcoming Delhi session of *Indian History Congress*, incidently being published in the current volume of this Collection.

Professor Grover's major areas of concern were to examine and re-examine the working of land revenue system, agrarian economy, rural, social and economic structure and above all, a systematic study of *Zamindars* and *Jagirdars*. Without having any particular ideological bias or subscribing to any particular school of thought, he contributed his writings on the above subjects by making an objective and analytical study of a large number of the primary sources in Persian, Urdu, English and other languages. His writings, without any exception, were widely appreciated by the scholars of India and abroad.

The theme of the present Volume, the fifth in the series of *The Collected Works of Professor B. R. Grover*, is basically the administrative apparatus and the way the land revenue administration was worked out in practice during the Mughal rule. Through his Papers, being presented in this volume, Professor Grover has given a clear and comprehensive picture of administrative jurisdiction, duties of the officials and the details of the working of the land revenue administration. These Papers were written during the period 1950s and early 1 960s. As such, the views of some of the then prominent historians such as Moreland, P. Saran, I. H. Qureshi and Noman Siddiqi have been critically examined in this volume. Professor Irfan Habib's book was yet to be published.

The important topics covered in the Volume include a critical evaluation of the administrative divisions especially *Sarkar*, *Chakla*, *Pargana* and *Zillah* as well as the land revenue apparatus of the Mughal Age, including *Diwan-i-Sarkar*, *Faujdar*, *Bitikchi*, *Shiqdar*, *Amal Guzar* or *Karori*, *Qanungo*, *Amin*, *Chaudhari*, *Desai*, *Karkun*, *Fotedar/Khazanahdar* and *Thanahdar.*

The Mughal administration was essentially dynamic in character and changes in the territorial circles and functions of the local officials in the *Sarkar* and *Pargana* administration to cope with the changing circumstances was an accepted practice. One such change was the creation of the *Chakla*, having a separate revenue administration. It was formed with a view to having better machinery of land revenue collection, especially in certain *Zor Talab* areas. A *Chakla* could have inter-*Sarkar* jurisdiction over numerous *Parganas* drawn from a few adjoining *Sarkars* of the same *Subah*, and at the same time, a group of hill or border *Parganas* in a *Subah* could form an independent *Chakla*. However, the term *Chakla* was applied both as an administrative territorial circle comprising a few *Parganas* and as a fiscal unit of a *Pargana*.

Unlike *Chakla*, the territorial jurisdiction of a *Zillah* was by no means fixed. Usually, it meant a territorial circle comprising of a few *Parganas*, or it appears to have been a fiscal territorial unit of a *Sarkar* division. But it never acquired the character of a regular administrative unit of a *Subah* administration during the Mughal rule.

Setting the misconception about the jurisdiction and duties of an important functionary, *Faujdar*, to rest, Professor Grover concluded that a *Faujdar* may be appointed for the territorial jurisdiction of a *Sarkar*, a few *Parganas* of a *Sarkar* or a single *Pargana*. Moreover, the term '*Faujdari-i-Sarkar*' may also imply the appointment of a *Faujdar* in a portion of a *Sarkar 's* division and not necessarily for the entire division of the *Sarkar*. As the head of the administrative division comprising numerous *Parganas*, whether inter-*Sarkar* or of a full *Sarkar* or a still lesser territorial jurisdiction, he represented the *Subahadar* and exercised multifarious powers viz, military, police, revenue and judicial.

However, there were certain factors that led to a deviation from the rigid application of a fixed *Faujdari*-cum-revenue circles within a *Chakla* or *Sarkar*. In the event of a *Mansabdar* rendering special services to the State he may ask for an additional grant of *Faujdari* of particular *Parganas*. In case of *Zor Talab* areas, the grant of such rights could have simultaneous jurisdiction in areas under more than a *Sarkar*. At the same time, a *Mansabdar* having *Faujdari* rights of various *Parganas* situated at different places and even in different *Sarkars* appointed his own *Gumashtas* even when assisted by a *Naib-Faujdar* in his *Faujdari Parganas*. Professor Grover held that the *Faujdar* with any jurisdiction dealt with the same territorial units as earmarked for fiscal purposes. This certainly helped in an integrated administration both for *Faujdari* and revenue purposes.

Most of the historians held that the office of *Diwan* was the finance-cum-revenue minister that existed in the central and provincial headquarters. Professor Grover unearthed some documents that provided evidence which proved that the office of *Diwan* also existed in the headquarters of the *Sarkar's* division. Moreover, there was a *Diwan* in every *Chakla* and invariably the offices of the *Diwan* and *Faujdar* were combined in the same person. The *Diwans* at the centre and the provinces were designated as *Diwaniayan-i-Aazam* and that of the *sarkars* simply as *Diwaniayan*.

With regard to the *pargana* administration, Professor Grover critically examined the views expressed especially by Saran and Qureshi. He was of the view that the *Ain-i-Amal Guzar* narrates the functions of *Amal Guzar* and the other technical staff for survey and assessment as well as the revenue officials of the *Pargana* serving under his general supervision. As the *Shiqdar* was the revenue officer of the *Pargana* representing the *Amal Guzar*, many of the functions stated in *Ain-i-Amal Guzar* had to be performed by him. That was the precise reason for the absence of a separate code of instructions for the *Shiqdars* in the *Ain-i Akbari* and akinness of various duties of the *Shiqdar* narrated in *Ain-i Bitikchi* and *Ain-i Khazanadar*.

The office of *Desai* had not received any attention in the relevant respective works of noted historians like Sir J. N. Sarkar, Moreland, P. Saran and S. R. Sharma. After studying the Persian records related to Deccan and other areas and the *English Factory Records*, Professor Grover, in his Paper on the subject, made an assessment of the position and responsibilities of this important official in the context of the fiscal administration of Mughal India. The *Desai* was appointed by *parwana* issued by the provincial authorities and had territorial jurisdiction over a circle of villages or at times over a full *Pargana*. His status in the *Pargana* was next to that of the *Shiqdar* but higher than the other revenue officials like *Muqaddams*, *Chaudharies* and the *Qanungos* who worked under him. In coordination with the *Muqaddams* under him, the *Desai* was responsible for proper collection of land revenue and advancing of *Taqavi* to the deserving *Ryots*. Moreover, the *Desai* also had a jurisdiction over the commercial dealings in his territorial circle.

At the time when Professor Grover made a detailed critical assessment of the place of *Chaudhari* in the *Pargana* administration under the Mughals, the then prominent historians viz. Moreland, P. Saran and Qureshi had either given no attention or an inadequate attention to this important official connected with the land revenue administration. However, with the help of newly discovered revenue literature and various *Dastur ul Amls*, Professor Grover attempted to make a reliable and comprehensive picture about the position and obligations of *Chaudhari*.

Professor Grover viewed that a *Chaudhari* was a generic term. There was a *Chaudhari* of every individual mint, a *Chaudhari* of a *Ganj* (market) in a port, a city, *Pargana* or *Qasba*, who was responsible for recording all the sale-proceeds, customs and commercial transactions in his jurisdiction. However, as the land revenue official in the *Pargana*, he was head of the village *Muqaddams*, and had multifarious revenue duties. There was the chief *Chaudhari* for the entire *Pargana*, who had under him a few field *Chaudharis* for a group of villages. A field *Chaudhari* was in charge of a circle each. The practice was to appoint a *Chaudhari* for one full *Tappah* and a group of villages from another *Tappah* or a group of named villages drawn from two different *Tappahs*. He was legally bound by his appointment order and a yearly deed to collect the land revenue in his area. He was also supposed to attest all legal transactions concerning sale or mortgage of the land as well as any remission on account of drought, trampling of the crops and natural calamity. He had special responsibility of the advancement of *Taqavi* to the cultivators and their recovery in regular installments. The authorities would always keep him informed about any *Jagir* or *Zamindari* assignments in his jurisdiction. He, along with the *Patwari*, *Qanungos* and *Malguzar* had to attest their assignment *Chaknamahs* and relevant documents. However, the *Qanungo* was essentially a technical expert in all revenue matters and keeper of revenue records in his jurisdiction over which the *Chaudhari* had no jurisdiction.

In the detailed critical discussion on an important *Pargana* functionary, *Amalguzar/Karori*, Professor Grover made an evaluation of various Persian sources available in archives/libraries of India and abroad, *The English Factories in India* and the works on the subject already done, especially those of the prominent historians like Moreland, P. Saran and Qureshi. A *Karori* would have the territorial jurisdiction over a circle comprising usually of two to four *Parganas* and even sometimes on a single exclusive *Khalsa Pargana* with large revenues. The territorial jurisdiction of every *Karori* was by no means uniform as it would essentially depend upon the approximate amount of the land revenue of the area in one circle as well as on the administrative convenience necessitated by the geographical features of the revenue circles.

A *Karori* was responsible for the general superintendence of the land revenue administration of his circle and the *Shiqdars* and other *Pargana* and village officials pertaining to the circle worked under his directions. If the circle happened to be one large *Pargana*, he was the ex-officio head of the *Pargana* administration while the *Shiqdar* and other area officials acted as his subordinates. The *Karori* was responsible for the collection of the land revenue on the basis of *Tumar Jama Bandi* prepared by the *Bitikchi* and his staff. He had to see that the assessment was done with extreme caution and moderation in accordance with the regulations. He was not to allow the realisation of any illegal cesses or customary dues from anybody. Moreover, he was to be held accountable in case the cultivators deserted their lands due to oppression. The deserted *ryots* had to be exempted from the payment of the revenues. The *Karori* along with his staff had to tour every village to take note of the condition of the cultivators and to see that that the fields were sown according to the understanding and that no cultivable land was left uncultivated.

Refuting the views expressed by Moreland and Saran that there was only one *Qanungo* in the *Pargana*, Professor Grover, on the basis of fresh interpretation of many an original record, viewed that every *Pargana* had a chief *Qanungo* known as *Qanungo-i-Pargana* and had under him a few other field *Qanungos*, each being in-charge of a division in the *Pargana*. Moreover, apart from the *Qanungo* for land revenue administration, another office of *Qanungo* for grain market also existed. Unlike the *Muqaddam*, the *Patwari* and the *Chaudhari*, the *Qanungo* was regarded as a full-fledged government servant and was appointed for life. Certainly, his tenure had to be consistent with efficiency and proper discharge of duties. Technically, his office was not hereditary though it invariably passed on to the male successor on petition from the candidate, subject to the approval by the Emperor.

A *Qanungo* had to deal with the land revenue administration right from the survey to the assessment and collection of the revenues, preparation and the preservation of their respective documents in his office. Moreover, along with the *Chaudhari*, he had to work for the realization of the land revenue from the *Khalsa* lands, dues from *Jagirdars* and *Peshkash* from the *Zamindars* in his jurisdiction. For any mortgage or sale transaction, the *Qanungo's* evidence and attestation in the court of the *qazi* was essential. The office of the *Qanungo* continued in the 18th century with more or less the same status, duties and obligations.

Another important official related to the land revenue administration researched upon by Professor Grover is the *Amin*. The *Amin 's* office existed at the two-fold level, namely the provincial and the *Pargana*. At the provincial level, *Amin* was in-charge of the assessment returns of the entire *Subah* and worked in coordination with the *Diwan-i-Subah*. At the *Pargana* level, the *Amin* was in charge of the survey and the lower staff. Professor Grover noted that under Akbar and Jahangir, the office of the *Amin* as the local assessment officer of the *Pargana* did not exist. Islam Khan, the *Diwan-i Ala* during Shahjahan's reign, instituted the *Amin's* office in the local administration on permanent basis. With the creation of the *Chaklas* as large revenue circles in a *Subah*, the *Faujdari* and *Amini* powers were combined in the same officer who acted as administrator of the *Chakla*.

In the Paper on *Thanahdar*, Professor Grover concluded that the said official was the representative of the central government and subordinate to the *Faujdar* of his division. Apart from being the custodian of law and order, he also safeguarded the revenue interests of the State in the *Pargana* administration. Besides, he ensured the smooth working of the local administration and exercised a check against any unauthorized financial practice on the part of the *Jagirdar*. He especially protected the interests of the *ryots* against any illegal realization of the *abwab* (cesses).

Though written nearly five decades ago and despite the fact that considerable work on the Mughal land revenue has been done during the intervening period, Professor Grover's writings remain singularly distinctive and relevant even today. I wish he had published all these writings years ago. It would have been a great inspiration for the students and researchers on the subject. Even as it is, Professor Grover will always be known as a distinguished and dedicated researcher in the area.

In view of the demand from scholars on the subject and the tremendous positive response from them on the release of the first four volumes in the series, the Editors were encouraged to bring out further unpublished and valuable writings of Professor Grover. We are sure that like the earlier four volumes, this volume would also be appreciated and prove to be of great benefit to the scholars on the subject.

New Delhi — Dr. J. C. Dua

29th December 2008

I. An Introduction to Mughal Land Revenue Apparatus

The success of the fiscal policy of a State, howsoever well intentioned and enlightened, rests on the administrative apparatus and the way the land revenue administration is worked out in practice. Never was any enlightened medieval monarch more conscious than Akbar was of the modern concept that the soundest principle of public finance is good public administration. Among the Muslim rulers of India, Sher Shah was the first to base his administration directed towards the welfare of the cultivators. This inherited ideal was realised to full fruition by Akbar in the course of his nearly half a century's stable reign with an expanded, consolidated and unified Empire. Akbar and his ministers were fully conscious of the two-fold ends – the good of the State with strong administrative machinery as well as the welfare of the *ryots*. In his theoretical concept of public finance embroiled in *Ain-i-Khazina-abadi*, Abul Fazl finds ethical-cum-political basis of administration and comments, "the best way of worshipping God is allaying the distress of the times and improving the condition of man. All this depends on the intelligent management of the revenues and public expenditure."[1] The administration, thus set up, bore a completely non-sectarian and secular outlook.

Having inherited the Afghan revenue administrative setup, Akbar modified and improved upon it considerably in accordance with local agrarian and political needs of the country. Through a consistent policy of trials and errors and introduction of reforms after repeated experiments, his expert revenue ministers[2] were able to raise upon it a highly developed superstructure which became the basis of the Mughal Empire. Though tempered in some aspects and details by his successors due to exigencies of the Government policy and needs of the time, the sound system of land revenue administration built by Akbar and his expert ministers, remained the same in all its essential characteristics right till the reign of Aurangzeb. Eminent scholars like Saran and Moreland have dealt with the topic of land revenue administration quite at length. Still their views are contradictory to each other and various lacuna leave much room for reaffirmation and reinterpretation of various aspects of the administration of Akbar's and more especially those of his successors' reigns. This is still more true of the local administration, which, in view of many of the so far unutilised manuscripts and newly discovered documents, needs a complete reorientation for a comprehensive picture of administrative jurisdiction, duties of the officials and the very details of the working of the land revenue administration.

1. Administrative Territorial Divisions Under Akbar And Jahangir

For the purposes of administration, the Empire under Akbar was divided into fifteen *Subahs*[3] and every *Subah* had uniform fiscal territorial pattern for land revenue administration.[4] *Ain* mentions the creation of twelve *Subahs* in 1580 and states that three *Subahs* were added subsequently.[5] Each *Subah* was further divided into *Sarkars*, each *Sarkar* into *Parganas* and *Mahals*, each *Pargana* into *Tappas* and each *Tappa* into *Mauzas*. Though *Ain* mentions the divisions of the *Subah* into *Sarkars*, *Parganas*, and *Mahals*,[6] their further subdivisions can be known from the official *Pargana* and village documents, both contemporary and those of the reign of Aurangzeb.[7] The territorial divisions of both the *Sarkar* and *Pargana* were already known to the Sur administration but as to how their territorial boundaries inevitably came to be reshuffled with the expansion of the Empire under Akbar cannot be stated with precision.

On the basis of Sir Thomas Roe's report entitled, "*The Kingdoms and Provinces Subject to the Great Mogoll*",[8] Moreland concludes that within the *Subah*, there were two separate and completely distinct territorial divisions – one *Sarkar* for purely fiscal purposes and the second *Faujdari* for general administration under the charge of *Faujdar*.[9]

As against 105 fiscal territorial divisions of *Sarkars* noted in *Ain*, Moreland suggests that the Empire under Akbar was divided into 59 *Faujdari* charges and that the latter's number increased to 60 during the reigns of Jahangir and Shah Jahan.[10] On the contrary, Saran has categorically rejected Moreland's theory of separate *Faujdari* charges as district from the *Sarkars* within the same *Subha* and holds that the territorial division of *Sarkar* was as much for fiscal purposes as for general administration.[11] Saran in his discussion has challenged the very authenticity *of Reo's* information due to serious omissions in his report wherein the country between Agra and Bihar and the major part of Rajputana are not mentioned at all.[12] Apart from it, Saran in support of his contention, has advanced various other arguments (a) There is much discrepancy in *Reo's* list and Moreland's version of territorial divisions.[13] (b) As according to Moreland's calculation, the area of a *Faujdari* would generally be larger than a *Sarkar*, many of the *Sarkars* would fall partly under the jurisdiction of one *Faujdar*, and partly that of another, and thus the *Amal Guzar* (whom Saran thinks to be a full-fledged *Sarkar* official) would be thrown on the mercy of more than one *Faujdar* in the execution of his duties.[14] (c) Abul Fazl could not have ignored such an important fact of administrative organisation while he took care to describe the revenue, military and other departments so minutely. Nor is it mentioned by any other contemporary source.[15] (d) Qaziwini in *PadShahnama* mentions the appointment of *Faujdars* of *Sarkars* and refers to the term '*Faujdari-i-Sarkar*'. Neither Qaziwini nor any other contemporary writer referred to any other kind of administrative divisions. The term *Faujdari* as an official name for any executive territorial jurisdiction is nowhere used.[16] (e) The term '*Naheti*' used in *Ain* as identified by Moreland with *Faujdari* charge, denotes the formal designation of the officer appointed by the '*Farman-Sabti*' rather than an "administrative charge" under the *Faujdar*.[17]

A careful analysis of the above controversy shows that, though some of Saran's objections (Nos. b and d) are rather weak, his refutation of Moreland's thesis of two-fold divisions of the *subah*-fiscal and administrative is rather justified. As to point (b), Saran is not right in assigning *Amal Guzar* as the officer of the full division of *Sarkar*.[18] As for point (d), quoted from Qaziwini, in the context of the general language used by the chroniclers, the term '*Faujdari-i-Sarkar*' may also imply the appointment of a *Faujdar* in a portion of *Sarkar's* division and not necessarily for the entire division of the *Sarkar*.[19] Notwithstanding these faults, Saran's conclusion seems to be correct and can be further substantiated with more cogent and direct evidence.

(1) Moreland's version of *Faujdari* divisions cannot be supported by any of the chronicles or administrative literature of the Mughal age.[20] It is surprising that the numerous detailed and comprehensive *Dasturulamls* of the reigns of Shah Jahan and Aurangzeb should have omitted this important fact.

(2) Moreland's view is based on the misunderstanding of the nature of *Faujdari*, the jurisdiction and the duties of the *Faujdar*. The term *Faujdari* does not stand for territorial division. It is rather an act of administration in contrast to *Amaldari* or *Man Amal* or *Diwani* or *Karori* for an act of revenue administration – all these terms being affixed to a territorial unit whether *Sarkar Parganas* or a single *Pargana*.[21]

(3) Mohammad Warris and Abdul Hamid Lahori, writers of Shah Jahan's reign, clearly state that every *Subah* was divided into *Sarkars*, *Parganas* and *Dehat*.[22] This is equally confirmed by the later authors.[23]

(4) A later examination of the jurisdiction and duties of the *Faujdar* clearly shows that a *Faujdar* may be appointed for the territorial jurisdiction of a *Sarkar*, a few *Parganas* of the *Sarkar* or a single *Pargana* – a fact which is true for every reign from Akbar to Aurangzeb.

(5) As to his duties, apart from his police and military powers, a *Faujdar* was in-charge of overall administration inclusive of the revenue

department. The *Shiqdar* of a *Pargana* and *Karori* of *Parganas* were as much responsible to him for the realisation of land revenue as to the *Diwan*.

(6) The fact that from the reign of Jahangir, the office of the *Faujdar* was at times combined with that of the *Amin* or *Diwan* or *Karori* crosses out the theory of separate *Faujdari* circles. How could the *Faujdari* and fiscal offices of the two separate territorial circles be combined in the same person?

(7) There was sufficient laxity in the jurisdiction of the *Faujdar* especially in the reign of Aurangzeb where '*Thanas*' and *Parganas* would be added to the jurisdiction of a *Faujdar* just at random. There are instances when a *Faujdar's* jurisdiction would comprise few *Parganas* from one *Sarkar* and a few other *Parganas* or *Thanas* from another *Sarkar*. Though otherwise quite misleading, this would not point towards any set Faujdari circles and can be explained on the reasons of administrative expediency and laxity.[24]

The foregoing facts of evidence rule out the possibility of separate *Faujdari* charges as distinct from the *Sarkars* and *Parganas*. Even if Moreland's version were to be conceded, his calculation of 59 *Faujdari* charges as against 105 *Sarkars* recorded in *Ain* for Akbar's reign would give an area of one '*Faujdari charge*' much larger in extent than those of the *Parganas* making at least one *Sarkar* and that the surplus territory would be covered from the *Parganas* of other *Sarkars* or a *Sarkar* as needed for the territorial extent of each '*Faujdari* charge'. It is evident from the entire range of Mughal literature that the designation of *Faujdar* is rather generic. It is equally applicable to the jurisdiction over a group of *Parganas* smaller than a *Sarkar* or a single *Pargana*.[25] Thus whatever be the largest circle of a *Faujdar's* jurisdiction – whether the so-called *Faujdari* charge composed of numerous *Pargana* of more than one *Sarkar* or a *Sarkar* comprising various *Parganas*, the unit of administration was the *Pargana*, which, for administration purposes was divided into *Thanas*. The *Pargana* was a common unit both to the *Faujdari* jurisdiction and fiscal division. Even a grouping of few *Parganas* in a division lesser than a *Sarkar*, both for administrative and fiscal purposes is on record.[26] This alone can account for the general supervisory powers of the *Faujdar* over the revenue administration and also the fact of combining the *Faujdar's* office with either *Amin* or *Karori*. Regardless of the jurisdiction of the largest circle for *Faujdari* purposes, the *Faujdar* of a group of few *Parganas* or a *Pargana* dealt with the same territorial units as earmarked for fiscal purposes, which is an ample proof of an integrated administration both for *Faujdari* and revenue purposes.

References

1. *Ain*: Hamilton I, fol. 5a-5b.
2. The important stages of revenue reforms were carried out by Itmad Khan; Muzaffar Khan; Shahabuddin Ahmad Khan; Shah Mansur; Todar Mal; and Fathullak Shirazi.
3. *Ain*: Hamilton I, fol. 150b; B.M. Add. 6552, fol. 158b. Also Saran, p. 70.
4. The twelve Provinces created in 1580 stated in reference No.:8 had uniformity of administration but for the sake of administrative convenience, Khandesh, Berar and Ahmadnagar were constituted into a single vice royalty of the Deccan. See Saran, p. 71.
5. *Ain*: Hamilton I, fol. 150b; B.M. Add. 6552, fol. 158b. "When the ten year settlement was made (i.e. in 1580)……His Majesty apportioned the Empire into twelve divisions, to each of which he gave the name of *subah* and distinguished them by the appellation of the tract of the country or its capital city. They were Allahabad, Agra, Oudh, Ajmer, Kabul, Lahore, Multan, Malwah, and when Berar, Khandesh and Ahmadnagar were conquered, their number was fixed at fifteen." Jarrett, p. 129. Also see Saran '*Provincial Government*, p. 70.
6. *Ain*: Hamilton I, fols. 136a-258b; B.M. Add. 7652 fols. 174a-296a. The division of every *Subah* into *Sarkars*, *Parganas* and *Mahals* is given in the account of Twelve Subahs and is confirmed by numerous *Dasturulamls* of the 17th century. In its introduction to the 'Account of the twelve Subahs', *Ain* puts the number of *Sarkars* and *Qasbas* at 105 and 2737 respectively as prevalent in 1594. Here a *Qasba* denotes a *Pargana*. Technically, a *Qasba* was a town and mostly the headquarters seat of *Pargana* which was named after it but which had also various other *Mauzas* within its jurisdiction. But here by metaphorical association, Abul Fazl has put the number of *Qasbas* which stand for *Parganas*.
7. See discussion on *Raqba-bandi* documents of Akbar's reign and Jaipur records of Aurangzeb's reign, '*Raqba-Bandi* Documents of Akbar's Reign', *I.H.R.C.*, 1961; *Land Rights, Landed Hierarchy and Village Community During the Mughal Age, Collected Works of Professor B.R. Grover*, Vol. I, ed. Amrita Grover, et. al., New Delhi, 2005, pp. 299-306.
8. The Embassi of Sir Thomas Reo to India, edited by Sir William Foster, p. 489. Edward Terry and other European travellers who followed each other have given similar lists which differ from each other. Also see Saran, p. 88.
9. Moreland: J.I.H. (Madras), Vol. VI, Pt. II, p. 1. Moreland commenting on Reo's list of administrative divisions suggests, the list in question consists of general administrative divisions … while a *Faujdar* was sometimes in-charge of the area of a *Sarkar.* The relation was by no means invariable, so that the local unit of general administration within the Province could be described only as a *Faujdari*, while the *Sarkar* must be regarded as belonging, definitely to the Revenue Department.
10. *Ibid.*, p. 2.
11. Saran, pp. 88-109.
12. *Ibid.*, p. 91.

13. *Ibid.*, p. 95.
14. *Ibid.*, p. 97.
15. *Ibid.*, p. 97.
16. *Ibid.*, pp. 98-99.
17. *Ibid.*, p. 100.
18. See for discussion on jurisdiction and duties of the *Faujdar*, see chapter on *Faujdar*.
19. *Ibid.*
20. A few important of these are *Khullasul Sayaq Makhzan-i-Ihtsab Marauf Dasturulaml*; *Sayaq Nama*; *Zawabit-i-Almgiri*.
21. *Mirat-i-Alm*. fol. *Amla-i-sarkar*; Original letters. Supply. Pers. 2052 N.B. Paris; *Man Amal-i-Sarkar Chouderi*: *Mirat,* p. 335; *Amal-i-Liwani*, Qazwini's *Padshahnama*, p. 544; *Karorai-i-Mahal*: *Mirat,* p. 404.
22. Mohd. Warris: *Pad Shahnama*, fol. 347a-347b.
23. MalumatulUfaq, fol. 174a; Shafiq; Haqiqat Hai Hindustan, fol. 90a.
24. For full discussioj on the jurisdiction of *Faujdar*, see chapter on *Faujdar*.
25. *Ibid.*
26. *Ibid.*

2. Administrative Modifications Under Shahjahan And Aurangzeb

Akbar's land revenue administrative structure underwent considerable modification in Shahjahan's reign. The Mughal administration was never static but essentially dynamic in character so as to evolve itself with changing circumstances. In order to cope with pressing administrative problems, changes were effected in both in the territorial circles and functions of the local officials in the *Sarkar* administration. It is evident from the revenue literature of the reigns of Shahjahan and Aurangzeb that the *Pargana* units of the *Sarkar* divisions of the *Subahs* do not essentially fit in with the description found in the *Ain-i Akbari*. Due to the absence of any consolidated account like the *Ain*, it is not possible to draw a full comparison of the *Pargana* territorial changes which took place in the 17th century. But the scattered evidence of varied nature for many a *Subah* does suggest some of the changes in this respect. In north India, the divisions of Thatta and Kashmir were respectively detached from the *subahs* of Multan and Kabul and were created as full-fledged *Subahs* of the Empire.[1] As regards the reshuffling of the *Pargana* units in a *Sarkar*, *Mahzar-i Shahjahani* in its detailed account of the *Parganas* in the *Sarkars* of Sehwan (*Subah* Thatta) and Bhakhar (*Subah* Multan) gives a clear view of the change in the number of the *Parganas*, the disappearance of some of the old ones and the creation of the new ones consequent on their territorial regrouping during the course of nearly four decades since the compilation of the *Ain* in Akbar's reign.[2] Similar changes for many a *Pargana* are discernable from the revenue literature of the 17th century for the *Subahs* of Ajmer, Malwa, Agra, Delhi and Gujrat.[3] *Mirat-i Ahmadi* affords another detailed illustration of such changes in the *Subah* of Gujrat from Akbar's period to the fifth decade of the 18th century.[4]

The Chakla Division

The major change in the *Subah* administration under Shahjahan was the creation of the *Chakla* divisions. Literally speaking, a *Chakla* would mean a composite geographical block.[5] It seems that in some of the *Subahs*, it had been understood as a revenue circle ever since Akbar's reign.[6] For a few territories of *Subah* Bengal, *Baharistan* makes a clear reference to the existence of *Chaklas* as revenue circles.[7] Each *Chakla* had separate revenue administration with clearly defined revenues accruing from its circle. The territorial extent of a *Chakla* comprised numerous *Parganas* but it is difficult to establish its regular relationship with the *Sarkar* divisions of the *Subah*. From the reign of Shahjahan, a *Chakla* division as a distinct territorial revenue-cum-administrative circle became more or less a uniform feature of the Mughal Provinces.[8] With the present contemporary evidence in hand, excepting the Gujrat *Subah*,[9] the *Chakla* division can be traced for practically all the *Subahs*. As regards the exact nature of the territorial jurisdiction of a *Chakla* as a revenue and administrative unit, four-fold evidence is available for the reigns of Shahjahan and Aurangzeb. Firstly, a *Chakla* though comprising numerous *Parganas* was a smaller unit than a *Sarkar* and formed a regular unit of the latter. Secondly, it could as well be co-terminous in territory with the *Sarkar* division. Thirdly, it could have inter-*Sarkar* jurisdiction over numerous *Parganas* drawn from a few adjoining *Sarkars* of the same *Subah*. And lastly, a group of hill or border *Parganas* in a *Subah* could form an independent *Chakla* unattached with any *Sarkar* of the *Subah*.

According to *Khulasatu-s Siyaq*, the creation of *Chakla* Circle was an administrative innovation of Sadullah Khan in Shahjahan's reign.[10] As the concept of a *Chakla* was already known to some of the territories, it may well be conceded that under Sadullah Khan's administration, a *Chakla* as a well-defined revenue circle became more or less a regular feature of the local administration throughout the Mughal territories. As regards its territorial jurisdiction, the *Khulasatu-s Siyaq* makes only a general statement that a few *Parganas* constituted a *Chakla*[11] and does not mention its exact relationship to the *Sarkar* divisions of a *Subah*. But it is possible to construct a reliable picture about the role of the *Chakla* division in the revenue administration of the *Subah*. For *Subah* Delhi, Chander Bhan Brahaman states that there were forty *Chaklas* in the territories of Doab, *Sarkar* Hissar and *Chakla* Sirhind.[12] As in Shahjahan's reign, there were 12 *Sarkars* in the *Subah* of Delhi, this would render a *Chakla* circle much smaller in territorial jurisdiction than a *Sarkar* in *Subah* Delhi.[13] Abul Fazl Mamuri mentions that after the annexation of Cooch Bihar to the Imperial territories in the 4th Regnal year of Aurangzeb's reign, eighty nine *Parganas* of the *Sarkar* of Cooch Bihar (alias Alamgirnagar) were grouped into five *Chaklas* for the purposes of administration.[14] Thus the *Sarkar* division was divided into well defined *Chaklas* whose number would vary from one *Sarkar* to another depending on the total number of the *Parganas* in the *Sarkar*. When the number of *Parganas* in an erstwhile *Sarkar* was comparatively small or otherwise needed no further division, this was by itself considered as a *Chakla* for revenue administration[15] though for the purposes of revenue records, it still carried the title of a *Sarkar*. In such cases *Chaklas* and *Sarkars* are synonymous. Thus an erstwhile small *Sarkar* may by itself constitute a *Chakla* or a large *Sarkar* may be its own *Chakla*, divisions ranging approximately from one to five.[16] In the process of formation of *Chaklas* in a large *Sarkar*, the headquarters of the erstwhile *Sarkar* also constituted as one of the Circles.

If the number of *Parganas* attached to the headquarters Circle of the *Sarkar* comprised larger number of *Parganas* than assigned to its *Chakla* divisions, the former continued to be termed as *Sarkar* as distinct from the latter.[17] But on the other hand, if the number of the *Parganas* attached to the headquarters Circle was not larger than needed for a *Chakla*, this by itself constituted a *Chakla* named *Chakla Haveli*.[18] At times, a group of border or hill *Parganas* constituted a separate *Chakla* unrelated to any of the *Sarkars* of the *Subah*. Thus for *Subah* Lahore, *Tohka Dapan* (?) with 15 *Mahals* was always treated as a *Chakla* quite distinct from the five *Sarkars*[19] which had their own *Chakla* Circles.[20] In various *Subahs*, a *Chakla* comprised numerous inter-*Sarkar Parganas* and formed quite a distinct revenue circle than a *Sarkar* division.[21] In such cases, a few *Parganas* each belonging to different *Sarkars* were included in one *Chakla* so as to form one compact geographical administrative division.[22] Conversely speaking, different *Parganas* of one *Sarkar* could be assigned to more than one *Chakla* which could cover a few *Parganas* each from a few *Sarkars*.[23] Ordinarily, a number of inter-*Sarkar Parganas* were included in any of the *Sarkars* of the *Subah*. It is quite evident from the 17th century evidence that a *Pargana* had dual relation, as a part of a *Sarkar* for the maintenance of revenue accounts and also as a part of specified *Chakla* for revenue administration.[24] An 18th century evidence suggests that in accordance with the continued practice, a *Chakla* could cover in its jurisdiction a few *Parganas* each drawn from as many as four *Sarkars*.[25] Of course, such a number would vary with every *Chakla*.[26] Notwithstanding the formation of *Chaklas* for executive and revenue administration, the documentation of the revenue records of the *Parganas* continued with status quo under the title of the main *Sarkar*. Thus for the purposes of revenue income (*Jama*), a *Chakla* was always considered as an attached unit of the main *Sarkar*[27] division and its *Parganas* formed a regular part of the main *Sarkar*.[28]

Apart from this, a *Chakla* was also a fiscal unit of a *Pargana* under the charge of a *Chakladar* for the purposes of revenue collection. Such a notion of a *Chakla* is available throughout the Mughal age.[29] The term *Chakla* stood both as an administrative territorial circle comprising a few *Parganas* and as a fiscal unit of a *Pargana*. The meaning of the term in either sense has to be read in the context of description. The creation of *Chaklas* as revenue circles in the *Subah* administration under Shahjahan was a vital change from Akbar's administration. It was essentially an act of revenue administration, more especially for the realisation of land revenue from the *Khalsa Parganas* of a *Subah*.[30] The end in view was to have more effective control over the local administration, the betterment of its machinery of land revenue collection and above all, realisation of revenues from the recalcitrant territories.[31] Most likely, pressing problem of the turbulence of certain recalcitrant (*Zur Talba*) areas had demanded territorial administrative reshuffling resulting in the formation of more compact and coherent block of *Parganas* into a *Chakla* within any *Sarkar* with numerous unwieldy *Parganas*.[32] But even for normal administration, the *Chakla* division became a regular feature throughout the Mughal territories. The main treasury (*Khazana*) of the district came to be essentially located at the *Chakla* headquarters and all the sub-treasuries (*Fotah Khanas*) of the *Parganas* in its jurisdiction were governed by it.[33]

The administration of a *Chakla* was similar to that of the *Sarkar*. The executive head of the *Chakla* was the *Faujdar*[34] whereas the revenue powers were vested in the *Diwan* who also exercised powers of the *Amin*.[35] Invariably, the *Faujdari*, *Diwani* and *Amini* powers were combined in the same person[36] though usually he was designated as the *Faujdar* and *Amin* of the *Chakla*.[37] As the head of the administration, he exercised full control over the *Faujdars*, *Karories* and *Amins* of the 'ad hoc' *Pargana* Circles in the *Chakla* division.[38] In revenue matters, he exercised the same powers and owed similar obligations as explained for the *Diwan-i Sarkar*.[39] The *Chakla* administration was responsible to the *Subah* authorities.[40] The officer-in-charge of the treasury of the *Chakla* was the *Khazanchi* who was responsible for the maintenance of the accounts of all the income and expenditure of the *Parganas* in the *Chakla*.[41] The *Khazanchi* had full control over the *Fotahdars* and the *Fotah Khanas* (sub-treasuries) wherein the revenues of the villages of *Parganas* were initially deposited.[42] As regards himself, the *Khazanchi* was responsible to the *Diwan* or the *Amin* of the *Chakla*.

References

1. *Ain* puts *Thatta* (*Sindh*) with five *Sarkars* as an attached division of *Subah* Multan (vide Br. M. Add. 7652, fols. 266b-270a, tr. J. II. pp. 329-42). It also shows Kashmir as a *Sarkar* of *Subah* Kabul (*Ibid.*, Tonk 2011, fols. 215a-219b; Nawal Kishor ed. Pp. 167-76. Ms. Br. M. Add. 7652, fols. 279a-283a puts it as a *Sarkar* but under the General title names it as *Subah* Kashmir. Also tr. J. II. pp. 351-70. It is not clear as to when they were declared as full-fledged *Subahs*. But it is certain that by 5th R.Y. of Shahjahan's reign, Kashmir was a full *Subah*. (vide Qazvini, Br. M. Copy Aligh, p. 509; Amal Salih I, p. 544) *Thatta* is shown as a *Subah* in various *Dasturulamls* dealing with the revenues of the Mughal Empire under Shahjahan and Aurangzeb (vide *Intkhab-i Dasturulaml- Badshahi*, Ms. Edinburgh, fols. 1b-11b; *Intkhab-i Dasturulaml-i Alamgiri*, Br. M. fols. 131a-132a; Kh.S. N.A.I., pp. 119-32, Ms. Aligh, fols. 29a-37b. F.K. Aligh, fols. 19a-20b, Ms. Fraser, Bod. Oxfd., fols. 57b-61b. Also see Saran's *Provincial Government*, pp. 65-70, Dr. Saran's criticism of Sarkar's view (vide *India of Aurangzeb*, Topography, etc., 1901, pp. XXV, XXVI for having counted Thatta and Kashmir as *Subahs* under Akbar.
2. M.S. pp. 55-81, gives details of 11 *Parganas* in *Sarkar* Sehwan while *Ain* (tr. J. II. p. 342) mentions only 9 *Mahals*. The *Parganas* of Nairun (*Wahi*), Nairun (*Kolab*) and San do not find any mention in the *Ain*. Similarly, for *Sarkar* Bhakkar (*Subah* Multan), *Mahzar-i Shah Jahani* (pp. 5-17) counts 8 *Parganas* while the *Ain* (J. II. p. 336) mentions 12 *Mahals*. Apart from the *Parganas* mentioned in common, the *Parganas* of Matila, Lasta Kakan, Chandoka and Takkar described in M.S. do not find mention in the *Ain*. On the other hand, the *Mahals* of Sankar, Siwi, Fathpur, found in the latter are not mentioned in M.S.
3. R.A.J. for the reigns of Shahjahan and Aurangzeb mention various *Parganas* which are not traceable in the *Ain*. Similarly, M.S. Suppl. 482 B.M. Paris mentions many *Parganas* of *Subah* Gujrat not found in the *Ain*.
4. Compare the relevant pages of *Mirat* Suppl. with the *Ain*, tr. J. II. pp. 258-64.
5. B.G. Ms. B.N. Paris, fol. 285b uses *Chaklas* in terms of geographical divisions.
6. *Haqiqat-Hai Hindustan*, Ms. No. 100 Aligh, fols. 90a-96a while explaining the 19th R.Y.'s *Karori* experiment of Akbar's reign states that a *Karori* was entrusted with the realisation of one *Kror dams* of revenues to be collected in territorially demarcated *Khalsa* lands constituting one *Chakla*. But this version of a *Chakla* Circle is not borne out by any other source. (For discussion on *Karori* experiment see chapter on *Karori*). In fact, other sources use the term *Chakla* in a general territorial sense. Darjul Nafais, no. 464 Rampur in its account of 34th R.Y. of Akbar's reign associates *Chakla* with the Nandimarg territory in Kashmir.
7. B.G. Ms. B.N. Paris, fol. 312b gives 7 laks of Rupees as the *Khalsa* revenues of *Chakla* Akbar Nagar (*Subah* Bengal). That every *Chakla* had distinct administration is clear from the fact that in course of quarrel between Mir Safi, the Diwan and Shaykh Kamal, the *Sardar* of *Sarkar* Kuch Bihar, Mirza

Nathan refused to intervene on the plea that he belonged to the *Chakla* of Dakhinkul (South) and the former officers belonged to the *Chakla* of Uttarkul (North) (*Ibid.*, fol. 285b). Dr. Ray Chaudhuri's suggestion that a *Karori* was put as in-charge of a *Chakla* is incorrect (Bengal under Akbar and Jahangir, p. 27). In fact, a *Chakla* was large revenue circle wherein a few *Karories* were appointed.

8. *Kh. S.*, N.A.I., p. 32; *Ibriya*, Continuation Bod. Oxfd., fol. 110b; *Mufidul Insha*, Bod. Oxfd., fol. 16a, 23b, 71b, 86b-87a; *Ahkam*, Printed text, p. 222/2.
9. *Mirat* bears no evidence for the existence of *Chaklas* as revenue circles. It rather puts *Chaklas* as the wards into which a city was divided for police administration. Thus the city of Ahmadabad had 17 *Chaklas* (Mirat. Suppl. pp. 26-27).
10. *Kh. S.*, N.A.I., p. 32; Ms. Berlin, fol. 159a-b; Ms. Br. M. fol. 34a; Ms. Aligh, fol. 16a.
11. *Ibid.*
12. *Char Chaman*, Ms. Aligh, fol. 46a.
13. Kh. S., N.A.I., pp. 119-20; Ms. Aligh, fols. 29a-b, mentions 12 *Sarkars*. *Ain* (tr. J. II. pp. 291-301) gives only 8 *Sarkars*. Evidently, four *Sarkars* had been added till Aurangzeb's reign. Also M. or quart 259, Berlin, fols. 36a-37a gives 12 *Sarkars*. At the same time, for *Sarkar* Haveli Shahjahan and its *Chaklas*, it counts 49 *Mahals*. Evidently, in the *Sarkar* of Shahjahanabad, the jurisdiction of one *Chakla* was lesser than the entire *Sarkar*. Thus it is possible that in all the twelve *Sarkars* of *Subah* Delhi, there were forty *Chaklas*. An 18th Cent. Dictionary (Ms. Br. M. Add. 6603, fols. 58a, 65b) quotes a traditional practice that a grouping of 21 *Parganas* would make one *Chakla* and a circle of 22 *Parganas* or more would make a *Sarkar*. This may be true only in some regions as there are various *Sarkars* on record which had less than 22 *Mahals* and *Chaklas* which had more than 21 *Parganas*. For example, in *Subah* Delhi, *Sarkar* Hissar had 16 *Mahals*, Faizabad 12 *Mahals*, Srinagar 7 *Mahals*, Kamaon 6 *Mahals*, Narnaul 14 *Mahals* (vide Khs. S. Alogh, fols. 29a-b. Ms. Or. quart 259 Berlin, fols. 36a-b). For *Chaklas*, see Ms. Or. quart 259 Berlin, fols. 52a-54b.
14. Mamuri, Ms. 2093 Rampur, pp. 436-37; also Khwafi II, p. 137.
15. For *Chakla* Hissar, see *Maktubat-i Khanjahan*, Br. M. fols. 37a-b, 47b-48a, 52a, 62b; *R.A.J. Akhbarat* dated 4th Jamada 44th R.Y. (Aurangzeb); 8th Jamada II, 44th R.Y. (*Ibid*). *Chakla* Jodhpur, see *Waqai R*, pp. 173, 175; *Chakla* Sirhind, see R.A.J. *Akhbarat* reg. No. 1560/2 dated 11th Rajab 23rd R.Y. (Aurangzeb). *Chakla* Gwalior, *Maktubat-i Khan Jahan*, fols. 2a-b; R.A.J. *Akhbarat*, dated 25th Zilqada 10th R.Y. (Aurangzeb) *Chakla* Narnol vide R.A.J. category no. 4, reg. No. 895 dated 4th Zilhaj A.H. 1130/1718 A.D. For the *Sarkars* of Hissar Firozah, Jodhpur Narnol and Gwalior *Ain* (tr. J. II. pp. 299, 281, 204, 198) mentions 27, 22, 16 and 13 *Mahals* respectively.
16. Cooch Bihar comprising 89 *Parganas* was divided into 5 *Chaklas*. For the *Sarkar* of Agra, two *Chaklas* viz. Mathura and Etawah are on record. (vide R.A.J. case no. 756 dated A.H. 1106, 39th R.Y. Aurangzeb; *Maktubat-i Khanjahan*, fol. 47b respectively). One *Chakla* of Bareli can be traced for

Sarkar Badaon (*Subah* Delhi) vide R.A.J. *Akhbarat* reg. no. 1612 dated 13th Shahban A.H. 1123.

17. For *Sarkar* Ranthambhor (*Subah* Ajmer), see *Waqai. R.*, pp. 19, 79, 179, 371, 414, 422, 454 for *Chakla* Ranthambhor, see R.A.J. *Vakil* Report reg. no. 866/651 dated 20th *Shahban* A.H. 1106/26th March 1695 A.D.
18. *Nigar Nama*, Bod. Oxfd., fol. 79a *Chakla* Haveli Kora and *Chakla* Kanauj. Ms. N.A.I. fol. 62a.
19. Kh. S., N.A.I., pp. 121-31, Ms. Aligh, fols. 30a-b; Ms. Or. quart 259 Berlin, fols. 38b-39b.
20. *Ahkam*, p. 423.
21. R.A.J. category no. 4 regd. no. 149 (Aurangzeb's reign) states that owing to the disturbance caused by the *Jats*, Raja Bishen Singh was entrusted with the realisation of revenues from the *Khalsa* and *Paibaqi Parganas* of *Chakla* Mathura which comprised *Parganas* both from *Sarkar* Kol and *Sarkar* Islamabad. (Mathura). Also 'Maharaja's Letters' case no. 756 dated 39th R.Y. A.H. 1106/ *Chakla* Mewat comprised inter-*Sarkar Parganas* in *Subah* Ajmer. (vide R.A.J. letter on behalf of Nawab Muzaffar Khan to Maharaja of Amber dated 1136 Fasli). An 18th Cent. *Dasturulaml* Ms. Or. quart 259 Berlin, fols. 52a-54b gives details of the 13 *Chaklas* incorporating 34 *Sarkars* of *Subah* Bengal. Also Ms. Or. quart 258 Berlin, fol. 150b.
22. *Ibid.*
23. For example, for *Subah* Bengal, Ms. Or. quart 259 Berlin, fols. 52a-54b states that *Chakla* Bardwan comprised *Parganas* from 5 *Sarkars*, *Chakla* Hijli from 3 *Sarkars*, *Chakla* Hugli from 5 *Sarkars*, *Chakla* Ghora Ghat from 9 *Sarkars* and so on, Mirat-i Aftab Numa, Ms. Aligh, fol. 337a mentions that *Chakla* Gwalior (*Subah* Agra) with *Parganas* from 4 *Sarkars*. Also *Hadiqul-Aqalim*, Ms. 637 Patna, fol. 267a.
24. See f.n. 27. Also for Deccan *Subahs*, see S.D.A.R., pp. 69, 79.
25. See f.n. 23.
26. *Ibid.*
27. Ms. Suppl. Persan 2052, B.N. Paris. An original letter quotes news communicated by Sheikh Saiduddin Qazi of *Chakla* Fatehpur in early Aurangzeb's reign. It puts *Chakla* Fatehpur amla *Sarkar* Cooch Bihar. R.A.J. category no. 3 reg. No. 925 dated 2nd Rabi I 3rd R.Y. (Aurangzeb) shows the amount of an assigned *Jagir* in '*Pargana* Sikanderpur *Sarkar* Kol mutaliqa *Chakla* Islamabad' (*Subah* Agra). *Siyaq Nama*, fol. 50b in an example shows the revenues of *Pargana* Fatehpur, *Sarkar* Faizabad to be deposited in the treasury of *Chakla* Faizabad.
28. For the revenues of the *Parganas* and *Sarkars*, also see Khs. N.A.I., pp. 119-32, Ms. Aligh, fols. 29a-37b, F.K. Aligh, fols. 19a-20b; *Intkhab-i Dasturulaml-i Alamgiri*, Br. M. fols. 131s-132a; *Intkhab-i Dasturulaml-i Badshahi*, Edinburgh, fols. 1b-11b.
29. M.I. Berlin, fols. 6a-b; *Malumat Ufaq*, Ms. 249, Edinburgh, fol. 9a; Ms. Or. quart 259, Berlin, fol. 36a.
30. An 18th century source Ms. Or. quart 258, Berlin, fol. 150 b suggests that in the *Subah* of Bengal 13 *Chaklas* were created for the realisation of revenues

and administration of the *Khalsa Parganas* and each *Chakla* was put under the charge of a *Sarishtadar*.

31. *Lubbut – tawarikh-i Hindi* by Bindra Ban, Ms. 954/15 Aligh fol. 84b makes a general statement of such aims for the improvement of administration under Shahjahan.
32. *Siyaq Nama*, fols. 52a-53b clearly stresses the role of the *Faujdar* of the *Chakla* in this respect. Also *Maktubat-i Khan Jahan*, fols. 2a-b, 11a-b, 47a-48a, 55b-57a, 63a-b, 113b-114a, 115a.
33. *Ibid.*, fols. 50a-51b, 73a-75b, 81b-82a, 199a-b, 202b-204a; *Maktubat-i Khan Jahan*, fols. 37a-b, 39b-40a.
34. *Kh. S.*, vide f.n. 10; *Maktubat-i Khan Jahan*, fols. 2a-b; *Siyaq Nama*, fols. 52a-53a; *R.A.J. Akhbarat* dated 20th Zilhaj 4th R.Y. (Aurangzeb) shows Mir Khan as the *Faujdar* of *Chakla* Mewat with the rank of 2000 Z 500 S and additional 500 S; (*Ibid*) quotes the transfer of Mohammad Khan, the *Faujdar* of *Chakla* Mewat to Kohari with the rank of 3000 Z 2000 S with additional 500 S Do Aspa 300 S; *Ibid*. reg. no. 1560/2 dated 11th Rajab 23rd R.Y. (*Ibid*).
35. *R.A.J. Akhbarat* dated 25th Zilqada 10th R.Y. (*Ibid*); also Mamuri, pp. 437, 449-50.
36. *Maktubat-i Khan Jahan*, fols. 52a, 100a.
37. *Ibid.*, fols. 62a-b; also see Kh. S. (vide f.n. 10), also *R.A.J. Akhbarat* reg. no. 2726 dated 4th Zilqada A.H. 1127/18th Oct. 1715; For Amin-i *Chakla*, see R.A.J. *Akhbarat* 36th R.Y. (Aurangzeb)/6th November 1693 A.D.
38. Kh. S. vide f.n. 10, also Siyaq Nama, fols. 52a-53b.
39. See chapter on *Diwan-i Sarkar*.
40. See f.n. 36.
41. *Siyaq Nama*, fols. 50a-51b, 73a-75b, 81b-82a, 199a-b, 202b-204a.
42. *Ibid.*

3. Intorudction of The Office of *Bar–Amad Nawis*

Another important administrative innovation in Shahjahan's reign was the institution of the office of *Bar-Amad Nawis* (Accounts officer). This office was created by Rai Rayan Jaswant Rai, '*Peshkar*' (Personal Assistant), the *Diwan-i Ala* with a view to tighten control over the land reforms accounts of the *Parganas* and to have a proper audit check over the *Karori*, the *Fotahdar* and the subordinate staff of each *Pargana*. *Daroghas* and *Mushrifs* were appointed to this office.[1] A *Bar Amad Nawis* was in fact an Accounts and Audit officer of the *Parganas* and his territorial jurisdiction ran concurrently with the *Karori* of a circle. He took cognisance of *Tumar* documents pertaining to the realisations made and expenditure incurred by the *Karori* of the circle and *Fotahdar*, *Shiqdar*, *Karkun* and other revenue staff of a *Pargana*.[2] The documents of Income and expenditure in the office of the Bar and *Nawis* were recorded from the original documents of the *Patwari* (*Kaghaz Khana-i Patwari*) and that of the *Chaudharies* and the *Qanungos*.[3] For this purpose, the village revenue documents maintained by the *Patwari*, *Chaudharies* and the *Qanungos* were translated from the local language into Persian.[4] The latter officials had to certify the true copies of these documents and also to execute a bond (*muchalka*) that nothing whatever had been concealed.[5] Most detailed accounts for the villages of a *Pargana* were prepared in respect of realisations of land reforms, income from orchards and authorised cesses (*Sai-i Jihat*).[6] On the expenditure side, full records were prepared for the customary collection charges of the semi officials and the officials of a *Pargana* and the *Karori*, the expenditure on the agents and office of the *Amin*, the exchange rate of the currency, the entertainment charges of the *Muqaddam's* guests, *Qanungos*, *Chaudharies* daily allowances of the underlings and *Paiyadas* (*Khitmatghars*) employed for the collection of the revenues and the alms given in charity.[7] Therefore, the entire *Sarasari* (the ledger of assessment, income and expenditure) account of each *Pargana* were prepared.[8] Such accounts gave detailed account of every official, clerk or a servant from *Karori* of a circle to a *Patwari* or a petty underling of a village and left practically no chance of any illegal exaction or misappropriation on the part of any revenue official. All these documents were forwarded to the higher authorities of the *Diwan's* office.[9] For the purposes of the perusal and inspection, the *Bar Amad Nawis* could summon the *Qanungo* documents relating to the detailed list of the villages, '*Muawazana Deh Sala*' (Ten yr. revenue) and *Nalbandi* tribute from the *Zandians*) documents, *Dasturulaml* (schedule of regulations) of the *Pargana*, the income of the *Fotah* (sub-treasury), *Tumar Jama* (revenue assessment), the *Awrija* (ledger) of the present and the past arrears of revenue, *Jama wasulbaqi*, the *Nankar* and the *muqaddami* charges, the list of *madad-i maash* assignees, *Mahsul-i Saoi* (income from cesses), the security documents for the payment of revenues.[10] Apart from this, the clerks (*Muharrars*) of the office of the *Bar Amad Nawis*, would keep their own records of the copies of the documents pertaining to the original documents of every village (*Khaghaz-i Khami Asli Delhi Badehi*), the *Bar amad* documents and their translations (in Persian) attested by the *Chaudharies*, *Qanungos* and the *Patwaries*, the price list attested by the *Muhtsib* (Police officer), the bonds (*muchalkas*) of the *Muqaddams* and the *Patwaries* of every village duly certified by the *Qazi*.[11]

References

1. *Kh.S.*, N.A.I., p. 59; Ms. Aligh, fol. 26b.
2. *Ibid.*
3. *Ibid.*, also *S.N.* Hydbd., fols. 58a-b.
4. *Ibid.*
5. *S.N.* Hydbd., fols. 58a-59a.
6. *Kh.S.*, N.A.I., pp. 60-65; Ms. Aligh, fols. 26b-29a; *S.N.* Hydbd., fols. 59b-61b.
7. *Ibid.*
8. *Ibid.*
9. *S.N.* Hydbd., fol. 58a.
10. *S.N.* Hydbd., fol. 59a.
11. *Ibid.*

4. Local Administrative Structure Under Shahjahan And Aurangzeb

The reorganisation of the local administration under Shahjahan tremendously affected the position of the *Karori*. Of course, as before, he continued with the same territorial jurisdiction over a small circle of few *Parganas*.[1] In early Shahjahan's reign, apart from his function of collection of revenues in accordance with the past tradition, he also continued to exercise the *Faujdari* powers in his circle.[2] On this account, he enjoyed a superior status than the *Amin* of his circle and even commanded general superintendence over the latter.[3] But with the creation of *Chakla* circles under Sadaullah Khan's administration, his position was greatly undermined.

By and large, the *Karori* was shelved of his *Faujdari* powers. At the *Chakla* level or in a circle with numerous inter-*Sarkar Parganas*, the powers of the *Faujdar* and the *Amin* were combined in the same officer and the *Karories* of the division worked under his direction. Even in a smaller circle where the *Amin* had jurisdiction over a few specified *Parganas*, he invariably exercised the *Faujdari* powers. He commanded higher status than the *Karori* of he circle and exercised general superintendence over his work.

During Shahjahan's administration, his financial position also suffered. Rai Rajan Jaswant Rai, financial Superintendent and Assistant (*Peshkar*) of Islam Khan, ordered a thorough scrutiny of the village *Patwari* documents to see that the *Karories* should not be eligible to any other pecuniary advantage excepting their entitlement in the collection of the revenues.[4] Any other traceable customary pecuniary charge (*Rasum*) was to be reimbursed to the State treasury under the administration of Sadullah Khan, the rice master of the *Karori.* Hitherto, the remuneration received was Rs. 5/- against revenue collection of Rs. 100/- but henceforth he got Rs. 5/- against collection of Rs. 105/-.[5] It is evident from the *R.A.* that such an official status and financial position of the *Karori* continued till the end of Aurangzeb's reign.[6]

During Shahjahan's administration, with the organisation of '*Chakla*' circles in a *Subah*, the treasury regulations also underwent a change. At the *Pargana* level, the *Fotahdar* continued to be in-charge of the sub-treasury.[7] As under Akbar's administration, the *FotahKhana* was administered jointly by the *Shiqdar* and the *Fotahdar.* But the main treasury (*Khazana*) came to be located at the '*Chakla*' headquarters.[8] A few *Tahsil Khazanchis* were appointed at the 'Chakla *Khazanna'* and every *Tahsil Khazanchi* had some *Pargana* sub-treasuries (*FotahKhanas*) under his jurisdiction.[9] The *Tahsil Fotahdars* of the *Parganas* would despatch the revenue collections to the *Khazanchi* of their circle at the '*Chakla Khazana'* where full accounts were maintained for all the *Parganas*.[10] The *Khazanchi* was also responsible for the disbursement of the sanctioned amounts to the state '*mansabdars*'.[11]

It seems that under Shahjahan and Aurangzeb, no change was effected in the organisation of the local *Pargana* administration which continued to run on the pattern of Akbar's administration. Of course, for these reigns more intimate picture of the working of the *Pargana* administration is available from the Rajasthan Archives and correspondence and various *Dasturulamls*. In the *Khalsa Dr. Paibagi Parganas*, the Shiqdar discharged both the functions for the assessment and the collection of the revenues and was repectively responsible to the *Amin* and the *Karori* of his circle.[12] Usually, he combined the offices of the *Amin* and *Shiqdar*.[13] For the purposes of assessment, he virtually enjoyed the status of *Amin* of the *Pargana*. In the *Jagir Parganas* too, he commanded similar position. For the collection of the revenues, he was responsible for the *Amil* of the *Jagirdar*[14] and for assessment to the *Amin* of the *Parganas*.[15] In such of the *Jagir Parganas* in certain far territories, where the office of the *Amin* was not regularly established, he was also the *Amin* of the *Pargana*.[16] The other *Pargana* officials viz. the '*Karkun*',[17] the '*Fotahdar*', the Surveyor measurement staff, the *Chaudharies*, *Qanungos*, *Patwaries* and *Miuqaddams* continued to function as under Akbar's administration.[18]

References

1. R.A.J. Maharaja's letter's, regd. no. 943 dated 40th R.Y. A.H. 1107 shows Sheikh Mohammad Saiyyad as the *Karori* of the *Parganas* of Bhosawar and Udai. (*Subah* Agra), *Ibid.*, category no. 4 regd. no. 347 dated 8th Rabi 49th R.Y. A.H. 1117 records Mohammad Raza as the *Karori* of the Paibaqi *Parganas* of *Sarkar Kakrun* (*Subah*); F.K. Edinburgh, fols. 39b-40a in a Parwana of appointment of a *Karori* puts 4 *Parganas* under his jurisdiction. It is evident that where a single *Pargana* is associated with a *Karori*, the *Pargana* signifies a circle of *Mahals*. This is as good for the *Karori's* jurisdiction as for the *Faujdar* or the *Amin*. See chapter on *Faujdar* for discussion on the *Faujdar's* jurisdiction.
2. *Khs.S.*, N.A.I., p. 32; Ms. Aligh, fol. 16a.
3. *Ibid.*
4. *Ibid.*
5. Khwafi, I., pp. 737-38. Khwafi praises Sadaullah Khan's administration and considers this measure as an act of financial achievement which saved huge amount of revenues to the State. At the same time, he narrates on anecdote that Sadaullah later on used to say if his pen had not moved on the particular day when he reduced the remunerations of the *Karories*, the latter would not have suffered this financial set back. As against this version, *Kh.S.*, N.A.I., p. 32 mentions that Sadaullah Khan reduced the remunerations of the *Karori* from 10% to 5 %. Still at another place, *Ibid.*, p. 42, mentions *Karori's* charges at Rs. 5/- against collection of Rs. 117/-. In this connection, Khwafi's version seems to be more plausible.
6. R.A.J. 'Misc. Persian Letters' regd. no. 363, dated 20th Rajab 37th R.Y. A.H. 1104/1750 Samat/1693 A.D. confirms the fact that the *Karori* worked under the supervision of the *Amin* and was entitles to 5% on the revenue collections.
7. *S.N.* Hydbd., fols. 73a-74a; *Khs.S.*, N.A.I., pp. 42-48; Ms. Aligh, fols. 20a-22a.
8. *S.N.* Hydbd., fols. 73a-74a.
9. *Ibid.*, fols. 73a-75a.
10. *Ibid.*
11. *Ibid.*, fols. 75a-75b.
12. M.I., Berlin, fols. 5a, 6a-7a. *Murraqat-i Hasan*, p. 229; Riazudwidad, fol. 35b; *Baharistan-i Maani*, fols. 19a-b; Ms. Orient. Quart 258 Berlin, fols. 305a-306b; Ms. Quart 248 Berlin, fols. 9a-b.
13. R.A.J. *Akhbarat, Waqai Pargana Othal*, regd. no. 679, dated 15th Jamada I 49th R.Y. A.H. 117/12th August 1705 A.D. mentions Har Narian as *Shiqdar* and *Amin* of *Pargana* Othal (*Subah* Malwa); *Ibid.*, regd. no. 707, dated 15th Jamada II 49th R.Y. A.H. 117 mentions Ram Chand as *Amin* and *Shiqdar* of *Pargana* Othal. Also 'Misc. Persian Letters', regd. no. 241 dated A.H. 1146/ 17905/1733 A.D.; Baikus, fols. 8b-11a.
14. R.A.J., *Ibid.*, M.S., pp. 96, 109.
15. R.A.J., *Ibid.*
16. M.S., pp. 18, 180, 187-90. The author petitions to Shahjahan for the appointment of *Amin* in the territory of Sehwan and not to allow the *Shiqdars* and *Qanungos* etc. to finalise the assessment on the *Ryots*.

17. See f.n. 13. R.A.J. regd. no. 707 clearly mentions Ramchand as *Amin* and *Shiqdar* and Madan Singh as *Karkun*. A later Mughal information reveals that at times, the offices of the *Shiqdar* and *Karkun* could be combined (R.A.J. regd. no. 241 vide f.n. 13).
18. See under Chapter III.

II. *Sarkar* Administration

1. Diwan-i Sarkar in the Mughal Administration

In the present paper, I have attempted to analyse the position of the Diwan in the division of the *Sarkar*, a territorial administrative sub-division of a Mughal *Subah*. My examination is based mainly on two documents of the Mughal period, namely a *Roznamcha* (daily news-report) of early Aurangzeb's reign and a *Wajibularz* (schedule of regulations) of Shahjahan's reign narrating the appointment and the duties of *Diwan-i-Sarkar* respectively. The above cited *Roznamcha* duly stamped and despatched by Mohammad Daud Khalij, the *Waqainavis* of Baglana (*Subah* Khandesh) dated the 18th Rabiulsani, 4th regnal year (of Aurangzeb), A.H. 1072 (December 11th, 1661 A.D.) forms a part of an important collection of original *Roznamchas* available at the Central Records Office and the Asifiyah Library, Hyderabad.[1] These documents deal with the military and the revenue affairs of the Deccan. The *Roznamcha* under discussion refers to the appointment of Tirhakam Das as the *Diwan* of *Sarkar* Baglana, *Subah* Khandesh, *vide* appointment order (*Parwana*) dated 29th Rabiulwal, 4th regnal year (of Aurangzeb) A.H. 1072 (22nd November, 1661 A.D.) issued by Zainulabideen, *Diwan* of *Subah* Khandesh. The translation of the relevant portion of the *Roznamcha* runs as follows: "...... and Tirhakam Das, agent of Zainulabideen, *Diwan* of *Subah* Khandesh reached (here) for taking over the post of *Diwan-i Sarkar* of Baglana. The *Parwana* dated 29th of Rabiulwal of 4th regnal year (A.H. 1072/22 November, 1661 A.D.) duly stamped by Zainulabideen. *Diwan* of *Subah* Khandesh directs the *Desais*, *Qanungos* and *Muqaddams* of *Sarkar* Baglana, *Sarkar* Khandesh, to know that since the respected Khwaja Tirhakam Das has been appointed as the *Diwan* of the above *Sarkar*, they should all recognize the aforesaid person as the *Mutsaddi* for this job and should acknowledge his position for this post. The appointee should familiarise himself with the assessment '*Jama*' of the *Parganas* in the likewise manner of *Khwaja Lal Chand* the previous *Diwan,* and should despatch the documents based on the actual facts and after having been attested by the *Desais* and the *Qanungos* to the Exalted Court. He should not neglect to see that the personnel of the *Jagirdars* did not spread their hand of tyranny over the *ryots.* He would also endeavour that the *ryots* should reclaim the *banjar* land and cultivate orchards. They should all note the above......"[2] This evidence for the prevalence of the *Diwan's* office in the *Sarkar* division of a *Subah* is equally supported by the daily report of the *Waqainavis'* of other *Sarkars* of Deccan *Subahs* available at the Central Records Office, Hyderabad.[3] The second of the above mentioned sources is a *Wajibularz* forming a portion of an extremely rare manuscript of Shahjahan's reign comprising *Farmans, nishans* and *parwanas* issued in the reigns of Akbar, Jahangir and Shahjahan, and at present preserved in the *Bibliotheque Nationale.* Paris. This *Wajibularz* narrates the duties of the newly appointed *Diwan-i Sarkar,* Surat, *Subah* Gujrat.[4]

Hitherto the historians of the Mughal administration have held the view that the office of *Diwan* as the Finance-cum-Revenue Minister existed at the Central and the Provincial Headquarters. But the above two documents afford for the first time direct contemporary evidence proving the existence of the office of the *Diwan* as Finance-cum-Revenue Officer at the Headquarters of the *Sarkar* division. In Shahjahan's reign, with the regrouping of the *Parganas,* a new division of a *Chakla* was created in some of the Provinces.[5] There was a *Diwan* in every *Chakla* and invariably the offices of the *Diwan* and the *Faujdar* were combined in the same person.[6] At times when the *Faujdar's* division did not coincide with the territorial limits of the entire *Sarkar* but was a large circle comprising numerous *Parganas, a Diwan* was attached with the *Faujdar.*[7] The *Diwans* of the Centre and the Provinces were designated as *Diwaniayan-i Azaam* (high dignitary *Diwans)* and that of the *Sarkars* simply as *Diwaniayan.*[8] That this practice was not confined only to the Deccan *Subahs* and Gujrat and was a regular feature of the uniform pattern of the administration of the Mughal Empire is sufficiently confirmed by the references in the contemporary chronicles and *Insha* literature (correspondence and literary works) since Akbar's reign which find copious annotation in the foregoing description on the position of the *Diwan-i Sarkar.*

Diwan-i Sarkar:—The head of the revenue administration of the *Sarkar* division was known as *Diwan-i Sarkar.* Except for a single casual instance in the *Akbarnama* which puts Azizullah Khan as *Diwan-i Sarkar* of Malwa,[9] *Ain-i Akbari* and all other Persian sources of Akbar's reign say nothing about the designation of the revenue officer-in-charge of the *Sarkar* division. *Ain-i Akbari* describes in detail the duties of the *Amalguzar*[10] but is completely silent on the fact of his territorial jurisdiction. All the same, based on its authority, Dr. P. Saran concludes that the chief revenue officer of the *Sarkar* was the *Amilguzar* or *Amil.*[11] In fact, the latter was in-charge of merely one of the revenue circles in the *Sarkar* division. For the reign of Jahangir and more especially for the reigns of Shahjahan and Aurangzeb, there is ample contemporary evidence which supports the documents referred to earlier and puts the *Diwan* as the finance officer in-charge of the *Sarkar* division.[12]

As to his functions and duties, the *Diwan-i Sarkar* exercised general superintendence and control over the revenue administration of the *Parganas* in the *Sarkar*. He had to work for the prosperity of his territory and to look after the interests of the *ryots* and the tax-payers.[13] He had to equally safeguard the financial interests of the State, the frugality as the main prop of his policy.[14] He had to act in co-operation and consultation with the chief executive officer (*Faujdar* or *Hakim*) of the *Sarkar*.[15] The final documents of income and expenditure to be despatched to the Central Government had to be attested both by the *Diwan* and the *Faujdar.*[16] At times, he acted even as a check against any aggressive or arbitrary policy of the *Faujdar* of the *Sarkar.*[17] Apart from the general supervision of the revenue administration of the *Parganas* under him, he was especially responsible for scrutinising the assessment and the *'Jama'* documents submitted to him duly signed by his subordinate revenue staff of the *Parganas* and after careful examination, he had to forward these documents to the Central Government.[18] Moreover, the *Diwan* had the special responsibility for supervision over the administration of the *jagirs* of the *Sarkar.* He had to execute the royal orders for the assignment of *jagirs* and had essentially to safeguard the interests of the *ryots* against any undue oppression on the part of the agents of the assignees in his circle.[19] He was as well the watch and ward officer of the *Khalsa* administration in his territory.[20] He had to keep an eye on the activities of the *Karories* and the *Faujdars* under him. He would take care that the agents of the latter did not oppress the *ryots* and no unauthorised cesses were collected.[21] As a safeguard, he would check up the original ledgers *(Kaghaz-i Kham* of *Patwari*) of a few of the villages of every *Pargana* for every crop after having got them translated into Persian. In case the audit report showed misappropriation of any amount or levy of extra cesses, he would at once suspend the revenue officer concerned and appoint his substitute. After having taken security from the *Chaudharies* and the *Qanungos* for the ascertainment of facts and enquiry, if any misappropriation or charge of illegal cesses was proved, he would dismiss the suspended officer.[22] In case of transfer of any revenue officer, he would see that realisations were made within prescribed time-limit and charge of full accounts was taken.[23]

The *Diwan-i Sarkar* had to advance the agricultural development of his territory through the extension of cultivable areas more especially by bringing the cultivable waste land *(Banjar)* under crops and also by encouraging the cultivation of the high-grade crops and the orchards.[24] With this end in view, he had to adopt the policy of encouragement and moderation. He had to enforce the regulations regarding the cultivation of *Banjar* land both on the revenue officials and the tenants. He would issue instructions to the effect that the terms of understanding on which the *ryots* who got *Banjar* land were to be binding on the revenue officials who could not raise a demand except as already stipulated in the agreement. In case the *ryots* did not cultivate such a land, they were to be chastised. All such agreements with the *ryots* were to be enforced by the officials and the land had to be essentially entered in the revenue documents in the names of the cultivators. Such entries effected were unalterable.[25] The *Diwan-i Sarkar* had also to look into cases of defaulting migrant *ryots* with standing arrears against them, if any, from their home village to other places within the Imperial territory or to the land of the autonomous Rajas.[26] He had to issue instructions for the recall of all such migrants to their original home in the *Pargana* and to see that agricultural produce was augmented. In case such of the *ryots* chose to return to their original home and undertook the cultivation of their land, they were not to be harassed by the revenue officials.[27] He had also to call for all documents pertaining to assessment and remissions on account of natural calamities, if any, and to forward them to the Provincial *Diwan's* office for appropriate sanction and final submission to the Royal Court.[28] He had to especially grant remissions to the victims of natural calamities in consultation with the *Faujdar* of the *Sarkar.*[29] He had to enforce the regulations regarding the grant of *Taccavi* (agricultural loans), *Madad-i-Maash* assignments, stipends and grant for free kitchens (*langars*).[30] He would see that the *Taccavi* loans were essentially advanced to the cultivators in accordance with the past practice and that the realization on account of their recovery were remitted to the Royal treasury.[31] He had as well to enforce the State grant of *Jagirs* conceded by a Royal *Farman* or *Nishan* or on proposal made by the Sarkar or Provincial Officer.[32] He had also to sanction the monthly emoluments of the staff working for the collection of the land revenue *(Seh'bandi)* on the *Faujdar's* land, if any, and also to provide monthly salaries to the latter's staff as well as his personal staff in accordance with the regulations.[33] He had also to enforce the regulations for monthly cash salaries paid to the staff employees in the forts and the office of the *Mushrif* and the *Tahsildar.*[34] He would see that the assignees and the cash salaried staff employed in the forts and the offices discharged their obligations as stipulated in their respective appointment orders (*Sanads*) in accordance with the established custom.[35] As to his own emoluments, he was always awarded a *mansab* and salary in assignment or cash on that account.[36] Apart from it he was also usually awarded an *Inam* of cultivable land of good quality.[37]

References

1. Central Records Office (C.R.O.) Hyderabad; also its attested copy bearing an official stamp of Nizamul Mulk Asaf Jah (1720-48 A.D.) vide Collection No. 15 Asifiah Library, Hyderabad; also '*Selected Waqai of the Deccan (1660-1671 A.D.)*' published by C.R.O., Hyderabad Government, 1953, edited by Dr. Yusuf Hussain, Persian text, pp. 133-34. After the annexation of Baglana to the Mughal Empire in 1637 A.D. by Prince Aurangzeb (*Badshah Nama* II, Abdul Hamid Lahori. *Bib. Ind.*, pp. 106-09), the original territory of Baglana along with few other *Parganas* was formed as a regular *Sarkar* of *Subah* Khandesh. See *Delhi Bedehi Subahjat-i-Deccan*, no. 1184, C.R.O., Hyderabad, fols. 96a-119b; also '*Selected Waqai*', Pers. Text, p. 140, published in Proceedings of the *Indian Historical Records Commission*, 1962.
2. *Ibid.*
3. Two *Roznamchas* by Mir Mohammad Abdel Fateh, the *Waqainavis* of *Sarkar* Ramgir, dated 16th Ramzan Mubarik, A.H. 1071/6th May, 1661 A.D. and 20th Shawwal, A.H. 1071/9th June, 1661 A.D., vide '*Selected Waqai*', Pers. text, pp. 69-71; put Nasrulla as the *Diwan* of *Sarkar* Ramgir. Two other *Roznamchas* by Ibrahim Khalij dated 23rd Jamadi I, 1072 A.H./5th January, 1662 A.D. and 1st Rajab, 1072 A.H./10th February, 1662 A.D. Pers. text, pp. 72, 78, mention Lal Chand as the *Diwan* of *Sarkar* Ramgir and state some of his revenue functions.
4. Ms. 482, *Bibliotheque Nationale* (B.N.) Paris, fols. 181a-185a. The post of *Diwan* of *Sarkar* Surat and the important role played by him in the financial administration is well borne out by the English factory records. *The English factories in India*, 1634-36, 236; 1637-41, p. 109; also Introduction, p. XXVI.
5. *Khulasatus Siyaq*, National Archives of India, New Delhi, p. 32; M.U. Aligarh, No. 74, *Sulaiman Collection*, fol. 16a.
6. *Maktubat-a Khan Jahan Muzaffar Khan wa Gwalior Nama*, Br. M. Rieu, iii, 837, Add. 16, 859, fol. 52a.
7. Late in Aurangzeb's reign Bhupat Rai, the author of *Insha-i Roshun Kulam* (I.O. No. 417), claims himself to be the *Diwan* of Nawab Radundaz Khan, the *Faujdar* of Baiswara which had the territorial jurisdiction over all the *Sarkar* of Lucknow (*Subah* Oudh) except Lucknow proper and its neighbourhood. (Elliot, Charles Alfred, '*Chronicles of Oonao*', p. 107).
8. The designation of *Diwan* as the financial officer was a generic term. There were Central and Provincial *Diwans* as well as a *Diwan* for the *Sarkar*. The *Diwans* of the Centre and the Provinces were designated as *Diwaniyan-i Azaam* (High Dignitary *Diwans*) and that of the *Sarkars* simply *as Diwaniyan*. See Ms. Suppl. 482 B.N. Paris, fols. 181a; *Makatibat-a Allami*, Ms. N.A.I., pp. 94-95. *Akbar Nama* (A.N. Br. M. Add. 27. 247, fols. 332a-332b) in the 27th year revenue regulations while narrating the obligations of the *Amalguzar* and the *Jagirdar*, refers to *the Diwan's* office but does not specifically show him either as *Diwan-i Subah* or *Diwan-i Sarkar.* But in *Makatibat-i Abul Fazl* (N.A.I.) in a letter to Prince Murad, Abul Fazl complains of the corruption present amongst the *Diwan* and the *Diwaniyan.* This refers as much to the Central and the Provincial *Diwans* as to the subordinate *Diwans* of the *Sarkars.*

9. *A.N.* Pers. text, II p. 330. In the 13th year, Shahabuddin Ahmad Khan after having fought against Gujrat came to Ujjain for discharging the duties of Arnini (financial-*cum*-revenue) whereas Mirza Azizullah, *Diwan* of *Sarkar* Malwa was deputed to get the fort of Ujjain repaired in anticipation of trouble from the insurgents.
10. *Ain-i Akbari,* Br. M. Add. 7652, fols. 142a-143b.
11. Dr. P. Saran. *The Provincial Government of the Mughals*, pp. 285-87.
12. *Baharistan-i Ghaibi* (Ms. Suppl. Pers. 252, B.N., Paris, fols. 273a, 284b, 285a-286a) shows separate appointment of a *Diwan* for the newly conquered territory of Kutch though otherwise attached under the administration of the *Subah* of Bengal. For Shahjahan's reign, Ms. B.N., Paris. fols. 181a-186a, quotes a *Wajibularz* (mentioned in the main text) on the appointment of the *Diwan* of *Sarkar* Surat *(Subah* Gujarat). Also *Padshah Nama* of Abdul Hamid Lahori, Ms. Patna, fol. 126a, mentions the appointment of Diyanat Khan on the transfer of Rai Kali Dass as the *Diwan* and *Amin* of *Sarkar* Sirhind (*Subah* Delhi) on the 3rd of *Rabiulawwal*, 5th year of the reign. This appointment is confirmed by *Padshah Nama* of Qaznivi (Ms. Rampur, *Tarikh-i Farsi*, No. 280, p. 497) which states that on this year Hakirn Jamali Kashi, the *Diwan* of *Sarkar* Sirhind was bestowed the title of Diyanat Khan. Amil Salih *(Bib. Indica,* Vol. I, p. 330) quotes the appointment of Todar Mal Afzal Khani as the *Diwan, Amin* and *Fauzdar* of *Sarkar* Sirhind in the 3rd year. That the Sarkar of Sirhind was in the Khalsa jurisdiction is confirmed in the 5th year appointment, *Ibid*., p. 344. Similarly, Lahori quotes the appointment of *Diwans* in other *Sarkars* on fols. 150a and 250a. For Aurangzeb's reign, a news report from the *Waqainavis* of *Baglana.* i.e., *Roznamcha-i Waqai Baglana* (*Subah* Khandesh, Deccan) dated 18th of *Rabiulsani,* 4th regnal year, A.H. 1072 quoted in the main text. Also *Nigar Nama-i Munshi* (Ms. Pers. E.I. *Bod.* Oxford, fols. 78a-78b; Ms. N.A.I., fols. 61b-62a; Ms. M.U. Aligarh, fols. 121a-123b) quotes the appointment Sanad of *Diwan* of *Sarkar* of Sambhal (*Subah* Agra). Also *Mirat* I, pp. 284-85 states an order issued to Shamsuddin, the *Diwan* of *Sarkar* Sorath and Islam Nagar to the effect that he should assign some villages to the *Zamindar* of Nawa Nagar as Jagir. *Mirat* I, p. 234, also records the appointment of Roshan Zamir as the *Diwan* and *Amin* of Bandar Surat. An Aurangzeb's *Farman* quoted in *Mirat* I, p. 374, clearly refers to the *Diwans* and *Amins* of the *Khalsa Sharifa* and in its order to the *Diwan* of the *Subah* (Gujrat) requires him to instruct the former to follow a particular procedure mentioned therein for putting down their signatures in the letters addressed to the Royal Court. Abul Fazl Mamuri in his continuation of Mohammad Sadiq Khan's *Tawarikh-i Shahjahani* (Ms. *Tarikh-i Farsi,* No. 567, Rampur, p. 450) mentions the appointment of *Diwans* and *Karonis* at different places in Cooch-Behar. *Tarikh-i Sindh,* Ms. 599, K.B. Patna, fols. 139a, 142b, mentions the appointment of Mirza Qasim and Nawab Izzat Khan as the *Diwans* of the *Parganas* of (*Sarkar*) Bhakkar in the years AH. 1042 and 1072 (1632 and 1661 A.D.) respectively. Also see *Ahakam-i Alamgiri,* Ms. *Insha-i Adab Farsi,* No. 11, Rampur. p. 20. The above cited examples clearly show that the *Diwan-i Sarkar* was a regular feature of the Mughal administration and was uniformly applicable to the whole of the Empire.

13. Ms. Suppl. 482, *B.N.* Paris, fol. 181b. *Nigar Nama-I Munshi. Bodleian Library*, Oxford, fol. 78a, N.A.I., fol. 61b; also the original Sanad quoted by Elliot in '*Chronicles of Oonao*', p. 108.
14. Ms. Suppl. 482. B.N. Paris, fol. 181b, *Ibid.*
15. *Ibid.*, folo. 181a. It seems that in Aurangzeb's reign the Office of the Diwan was combined with those of the *Amin* and the *Fauzdar* of the *Sarkar* in the same person. Elliot in '*Chronicles of Oonao*', p. 108, while discussing the nature of *Fauzdar's* position in the 17th century, quotes a *Sanad* conferring an appointment on Syed Munawar, a member of Oonao family, as the *Fauzdar*, *Diwan* and *Amin* of *Sarkar* Kanauj (*Subah* Agra).
16. *Ibid.*
17. *The English Factories in India*, 1637-1641, Jan. 4, 1639 A.D., pp. 92, 109.
18. *Roznamcha-i Waqai Baglana*, dated 18 *Rabiulsani*, A.H. 1072, *op. cit. n.I.*; Also *Nigar Nama-i Munshi, Bod.* Oxford; fol. 78a; N.A.I., fol. 61a.
19. *Ibid.*
20. *Roznamcha* of the *Waqainavis* of *Sarkar* Ramgir dated 23rd Jamadi I, 1072 A.H./5th January, 1662 A.D. vide the '*Selected Waqai*', Pers. Text, pp. 72-73.
21. *Nigar Nama, Bod.* Oxford, fol. 78a; N.A.I., fol. 61b; Elliot, '*Chronicles of Oonao*', p. 108.
22. *Nigar Nama*, Bod. Oxford, fols. 78a-b; fols. 61b-62a, *Ibid.*
23. *Ibid.*
24. Ms. *B.N.* Paris, fol. 181b.
25. *Ibid.*
26. *Ibid.*, fols. 181b-182b. The *Wajibularz* especially enjoins the *Diwan* to look into all such cases of emigrants from the *Parganas* of Surat either to the territories of the autonomous Rajas or foreign territory of Europeans (*Farhangis*).
27. *Ibid.*, fol. 182.
28. *Ibid.*
29. Ms. *B.N.* paris, fol. 182.
30. *Ibid.*, fol. 184a.
31. *Ibid.*
32. *Ibid.*
33. *Ibid.*, fol. 183b.
34. *Ibid.*, fol. 184a.
35. *Ibid.*, fol. 184b.
36. *Ibid.* The *Wajibularz* mentions the increase of *mansab* of 50 *Zat* and 10 *Sawar* for the *Diwan* who finally held the *mansab* of 250 *Zat* and 60 *Sawar* Class I.
37. *Ibid.*, fols. 184b-185a. The *Diwan* of Surat was given an *Inam* of 50 *bigas* of cultivable land for an orchard in village *Kartar* Kam-*Qasba Chaurasi* (*Pargana* Chaurasi, *Sarkar* Champner, *Subah* Gujrat) on the highway to Ahmedabad.

2. Faujdar

Notwithstanding the fact that the administrative and the revenue circles were the same, it may well be conceded that such circles were not always rigidly aligned with the *Pargana* and the *Sarkar* divisions of the *Subah*. The latter, of course, served as the essential units for the maintenance of the revenue accounts and the framework for the executive and revenue administration. The *Ain* simply states that the *Faujdar* had a jurisdiction over several *Parganas*.[1] It is not correct to associate the latter essentially with a *Sarkar* division.[2] In fact, the appointment of a *Faujdar* was made for a number of specified *Parganas*. The evidence for the reigns of Akbar and Jahangir shows that at the lower level, a group of few named *Parganas* in a *Sarkar* division, would form the Circle for administration.[3] At the higher level, several *Parganas* in a Sarkar[4] or a *jure Sarkar*[5] or even a larger territory than a *Sarkar* comprising a full *Sarkar* division and a few *Parganas* from another *Sarkar*[6] or even two full *Sarkars*[7] could form a higher '*Faujdar's*' jurisdiction. Various factors governed the territorial jurisdiction of such a Circle in a *Subah*.

As the *Faujdar's* main function was to realize *Peshkash* from the *Zamindars* and land revenue from the recalcitrant territories and the amount of revenues of one region differed from another, the territorial extent of one administrative Circle would vary from another depending on the local geographical, strategical, political, and financial factors. Such circles usually become traditional in extent though they were always subject to both 'ad-hoc' and periodical reshufflings carried out from one reign to another.

Moreland's analysis of the high administrative charges with different territorial limits than the *Sarkar* divisions is not inaccurate. But where he has erred is that he has failed to realize that such divisions were identical both for the executive and the revenue administration. Sir Thomas Roe's list of highest administrative circles under Jahangir seems to be quite tenable and Dr. Saran's criticism of the authenticity of Roe's report is absolutely unjustified.[8] Saran, in his discussion has challenged the very authenticity of Roe's information due to serious omissions in his report wherein the country between Agra and Bihar, and the major part of Rajputana are not mentioned at all. Apart from it, Saran in support of his contention, has advanced various other arguments, (a) There is much discrepancy in Roe's list and Moreland's version of territorial divisions. (b) As according to Moreland's calculation, the area of a *Faujdar* would generally be larger than a *Sarkar*, many of the *Sarkars* would fall partly under the jurisdiction of one *Faujdar*, and partly that of another, and thus the *Amal Guzar* (whom Saran thinks to be a full-fledged *Sarkar* official) would be thrown at the mercy of more than one *Faujdar* in the execution of his duties. (c) Abul Fazl could not have ignored such an important fact of administrative organisation while he took care to describe the revenue, military and other contemporary source. (d) Qaziwini in *PadShahnama* mentions the appointment of *Faujdars* of *Sarkars* and refers to the term '*Faujdari-i-Sarkar*'. Neither Qaziwini nor any other contemporary writer does refer to any other kind of administrative divisions. The term '*Faujdar*' as an official name for any executive territorial jurisdiction is nowhere used. (e) The term '*Naheti*' used in the *Ain* as identified by Moreland with *Faujdar* charge denotes the formal designation of the officer appointed by the '*Farman-Sabti*' rather than an "administrative charge" under the *Faujdar*.[9]

A careful analysis of the above controversy shows that some of Saran's objections (Nos. b and d) are rather weak. As to point (b), Saran is not right in assigning *Amal Guzar* as the officer of the full division of *Sarkar*. As for point (d), quoted from Qaziwini, in the context of the general language used by the chroniclers, the term '*Faujdari-i-Sarkar*' may also imply the appointment of a *Faujdar* in a portion of *Sarkar's* division and not necessarily for the entire division of the *Sarkar*.

Dr. Saran's main contention that the administrative and revenue territorial units were identical in territory is quite correct but to say that in a *subah* no other administrative-cum-revenue circles than the *Sarkar* or the *Pargana* units existed is completely wrong. Unlike the *Ain*, Roe's report of the territories of the Mughal Empire does not run *Subah*-wise with details of *Sarkar* and *Parganas* of a *Subah*. On the contrary, it provides a list of the main centers of administration in the *Subahs* wherein administrative officers both for executive and revenue administration were appointed. The list by itself may be incomplete but it is suggestive of the manner in which circles known after the regions were carved out in a *Subah*. After the preparation of Roe's report with the extension and consolidation of the Mughal territories under Jahangir himself and his successors, the number of such circles was both reshuffled and increased. For example, for the *Subah* of Lahore, *Ain* quotes six divisions, five Doab *Sarkars* and few *Parganas* outside Doabs viz. *Bet* Jalandhar Doab, *Bari* Doab, Rechnau Doab, Chenhat Doab, Sindh Sagar Doab and Beyond the five rivers.[9] Roe's list gives 7 divisions, Panjab (i.e. Lahore), Attock, Jenba (Jammu), Peithan (Paithan), NakarKuti (Nagarkot), Syba (Siba), Jesual (Jaswan).[10] In fact, the *Subah* of Panjab was divided into various groups of the *Parganas* under the command of *Faujdar*. For the reigns of Shah Jahan and Aurangzeb, apart from the five main *Sarkars*, only two hill circles viz. Jammu and Nagarkot are on record.[11] Peithan, Nagarkot, Siba, Jaswan and various other hill *Parganas* were put under the command of one *Faujdar* of Kangra whereas Jammu formed a similar full circle comprising various *Parganas*. The *Parganas* of the *Subah* were formed into various *Chaklas*-each *Chakla* under the jurisdiction of a *Faujdar* and *Amin*.

The jurisdiction of a *Faujdar* can be well understood for the reigns of Shahjahan and Aurangzeb. So far, the main difficulty has arisen due to the fact that the chronicles and the official literature associate the appointment of a *Faujdar* or *Amin* with a particular *Sarkar* or a *Pargana* which would not essentially mean that the appointee's jurisdiction would be confined to either a *Sarkar* or a single *Pargana*. For such appointments, the general statements of the chronicles and the official orders are usually silent about the full jurisdiction of the Circle. The association of the appointment of a *Faujdar* in a particular *Sarkar* could have two meanings, i.e. with a jurisdiction over a full *Sarkar* division and secondly that his jurisdiction was much less than a full *Sarkar* but a jurisdiction within itself. When an appointment was made for a larger territory than a *Sarkar*, an appointment could specify a *Sarkar* and additional territory from another *Sarkar*.[12] But at times, an appointment was just associated with a region, whether named after the headquarters of a *Sarkar* or some other traditional geographical nomenclature.[13] A *Faujdar* and *Amin* was appointed for this division whose jurisdiction covered several named *Parganas* which could be inter-*Sarkar* in composition.

As already noted, a *Chakla* could comprise *Parganas* drawn from a few *Sarkars* which could be inter-*Subah* in character as well.[14] Of course, this was extremely rare. Such inter-*Sarkar* and inter-grouping of *Parganas* forming one administrative (considerations administrative) block could have similar regional and ethnic characteristics with the same administrative problems. Some contemporary evidence is available to support the above contention. Lahori states that in the 13th R.Y. of Shahjahan, Todar Mal Afzal Khani was appointed *Diwan*, *Amin* and *Faujdar* of *Sarkar* Sirhind[15] but in the 14th R.Y., his jurisdiction was extended as to cover both Sirhind and Lakhi jungle territories.[16] Mohd. Warris states that in the 29th R.Y. of Shahjahan, Mir Arab Khizri was appointed *Faujdar* and *Amin* of *Sarkar* Etawah and the *Khalsa Parganas* of *Sarkar* Kalpi and Shahpur.[17] Makterbat Khan Jahan records the appointment of a *Faujdar* and *Amin* with jurisdiction over *Chakla* Hissar, *Pargana* Thatta and Bhatinda.[18] Similarly, it also states the appointment of Sh. Ahmad Bin ShZain as the *Faujdar* of *Chakla* Gwalior and Madho Singh Wala.[19] For *Subah* Bengal and Orissa, *Murraqat-i Hasan* shows the appointment of a *Faujdar* of Talmal with jurisdiction over larger territory than *Chakla* Midnapur, Jalser and Hijli.[20] Similarly, it also quotes a *Parwana* issued by Mian Mohd. Jan (*Faujdar*) to the *Faujdars* and *Thanadars* in his jurisdiction extending from Bahdrak to *Subah* Malwa.[21] *Adab-i Alamgiri* also quotes the appointment of a *Faujdar* and *Diwan* in *Sarkar* Mahur, etc. showing the circle of jurisdiction greater than a *Sarkar*.[22] Sometimes high nobles were appointed as *Faujdars* for two *Sarkar* divisions or even larger territories than that. Jalal Taba Taba quotes the appointment of Turbat Khan as the *Faujdar* of the *Sarkars* of Sirhind and Hissar.[23] Apart from the fact, it is quite clear from the archival evidence Aurangzeb's reign that a strong *Faujdar* and *Amin* was appointed over numerous inter-*Sarkar Parganas* selected at random which could not be easily managed by the *Karoris* or the *Jagirdars* because of recalcitrance of the *ryots* or *Zamindars*.[24] At times, a homogenous recalcitrant region covering more than a *Chakla* would be put under one *Faujdar*. For Aurangzeb's reign, an original greater *Farman* of Aurangzeb, dated 22nd Shalian, 30th R.Y./8th April, 1694, quotes the appointment of Raja Bishan Singh (of Amber) as the *Faujdar* of Islamabad (alias *Chakla* Mathura) and Hindaun and Biana territories.[25] Another *Farman* dated 22nd Jamada I 37th R.Y./19th Dec. 1695 confirms the grant of *Faujdari* of Islamabad (*Chakla* Mathura) and Hindaun with an increase of 50 lacs of *dams* in *Inam* to the Maharaja.[26]

As the term *Faujdar* was quite generic, it could command jurisdiction as much over a lesser territory as over the entire *Subah* itself. The *Subahdar* himself commanded *Faujdari* powers. The Rajasthan Archives quote the appointment of Maharaja Jai Singh as *Subahdar* and *Faujdar* of Akharabad (*Subah*) in 1631 A.D. with an increase of 4,600 *sawars* and 5 *Krores* and 2 lacs of *dams* in *Inam*.[27] Similarly, Muqarram Khan was appointed *Subahdar* and *Faujdar* of *Subah* Lahore in 1693 A.D.[28] At times, a person was appointed as *Faujdar* with jurisdiction in two *Subahs*.[29]

It is rather significant that a *Faujdar* with jurisdiction wider than a *Chakla* or a *Sarkar* were made only to high *mansabdari* and in special circumstances. The Rajasthan Archives do not reveal any set Circles over and above a *Chakla* or *Sarkar*. The additional *Parganas* could be attached to a *Chakla* and detached from it varying with the personality and importance of an appointee and the political circumstances prevalent in the region of the appointee. The usual *Faujdari* circles were those of a full *Chakla*, or a group of few *Parganas* in a *Chakla*. As regards the smallest circle of a *Faujdar*, a *Chakla* or a *Sarkar* was usually divided into few Circles, each Circle comprising a few named *Mahals*. At times, the documents show the appointment of a *Faujdar* of one single *Pargana*. But this is quite deceptive for this should not necessarily mean that the *Faujdar* would have jurisdiction over a single *Pargana*. Ordinarily, a few more *Mahals* were attached to one named *Pargana* (with etc.) and in the appointment order, the jurisdiction over the other *Mahals* were taken in an implied manner.[30] Some original appointment orders, though apparently issued for a named *Pargana*, also show details of the other *Parganas* attached to this Circle at the end of the document. The Circle of *Parganas* or *Mahals* went after the name of one main *Pargana* and the attached area was always taken for granted. The number of the *Parganas* attached would vary from one Circle to another depending upon the revenues and the importance of the *Pargana*. Taking some of the documents literally, it is possible that a *Faujdar* would be appointed for a single *Pargana* as well which would form a full Circle by itself. But in the context, it seems rather improbable or extremely rare. This may still be left open till further evidence is available. Ordinarily, an appointment over a group of *Parganas* was made from within the same *Sarkar* division; there was no rigidity in this respect either, there are cases on record where a *Faujdar* would be granted *Parganas* from more than one *Sarkar* division. A *Faujdar* may have jurisdiction over a few *Parganas* and only some *Thanas* of another *Pargana*, all in the same *Sarkar*.[31] Similarly, he could command a few *Parganas* from one or two different *Sarkar*-division.[32] This would not, however, establish any permanent inter-*Pargana* or inter-*Sarkar Faujdari* circle. The frequency of the change of hands of the *Parganas* known from the Rajasthan Archives clearly shows that despite the existence of *Faujdari* circles within the same *Sarkar*, occasional addition of *Thanas* or *Parganas* from other *Sarkars* of the same *Subah*, and if warranted by geographical considerations, even from another *Subah* were also made. Any transfer of a *Faujdar* or removal of a *Pargana* or a part thereof from his jurisdiction on grounds of inefficiency demanded a fresh review of the situation.[33] Similarly, reshuffling of the territorial jurisdiction of the *Faujdars* was done for meeting any recalcitrant situation in any region and a competent *Mansabdar* was entrusted with such territories for administration and the realization of the revenues.[34] Similarly, with any enhancement in jurisdiction and extension of *tankhawah jagir*, the State would insist on the extension of the *Faujdari* jurisdiction too and may add to his jurisdiction at random.[35] On the contrary, a *Mansabdar* in lieu of any special services rendered to the State may himself ask for the additional grant of *Faujdari* of particular *Parganas* easily manageable by him.[36] At times, such a *Faujdari* appointment for realising revenues from the recalcitrant areas could have simultaneous jurisdiction from more than one *Sarkar* division.[37] Such assignments were, of course, given to high *Mansabdars* who could also have *Faujdars* of smaller circles under their control.[38] It is quite significant that a high *Mansabdar* having *Faujdari* rights of various *Parganas* situated at different places and even in different *Sarkars* appointed his own *Gumashtas* (representatives)[39] and was also assisted by a *Naib Faujdar* in his *Faujdari Parganas*.[40] All such factors led to a deviation from the rigid application of a set and coherent *Faujdari*-cum-revenue Circles within a *Chakla* or *Sarkar*.

It is quite significant that a *Faujdar's* territorial jurisdiction could be limited by the factor of demarcation between the *Khalsa* and the *jagir* lands in the *Subahs* of the Mughal territories. Though a *Faujdar* could be appointed in a territorial division comprising both the *Khalsa* and *jagir* in his jurisdiction, ordinarily a distinction was made in this respect as well. Many a *Jagirdar* were vested both with the assignment of revenues and *Faujdar* powers in *Thanas*. Similarly, appointment of the *Faujdars* was also made for the exclusive *Khalsa* or *Paibaqi Parganas*. This is true both for the higher and the smaller territorial circles of the *Faujdars*. Where a *Jagirdar* was not vested with *Faujdari* powers, a separate *Faujdar* would be appointed with jurisdiction exclusively over the *Jagir Parganas*. This was usually the practice in case of large assignments of the high *Mansabdars* wherein *Faujdars* would be appointed by the State. For all that, there is conclusive evidence available for the reigns of Shahjahan and Aurangzeb. For Shah Jahan's reign, Mohd. Warris quotes the appointment of the *Faujdars* exclusively for the *Khalsa Parganas*.[41] Similarly, for Aurangzeb's reign, the Rajasthan Archives are full of instances of *Faujdari* appointments, either exclusively in the *Khalsa* or *Paibaqi*[42] and *Jagir Parganas*.[43]

On the basis of Sir Thomas Roe's report entitled "The Kingdoms and Provinces Subject to the Great Mogoll" Moreland concludes that within the *Subah*, there were two separate and completely distinct territorial divisions – One, *Sarkar* purely for fiscal purposes and the second *Faujdari* for general administration under the charge of *Faujdar*. As against 105 fiscal territorial divisions of *Sarkars* noted in *Ain*, Moreland suggests that the Empire under Akbar was divided into 59 *Faujdari* charges and their number increased to sixty during the reigns of Jahangir and Shah Jahan. Thus calculated, a '*Faujdari* charge' would be much larger in territorial extent than a single *Sarkar* and that the surplus territory would be covered from the *Parganas* of other *Sarkars* or a *Sarkar* as needed for the territories constituting a single '*Faujdari* Charge'. On the contrary, Saran has categorically rejected Moreland's theory of separate *Faujdari* charges as distinct from the *Sarkars* within the same *Subah* and holds that the territorial division of *Sarkar* was as much for fiscal purposes as for general administration.

Very recently, Dr. Noman Siddiqi has upheld Moreland's contention of '*Faujdari*' constituting a separate and distinct administrative unit and quite independent of the fiscal divisions of *Sarkar* and *Parganas*. Though Siddiqi has correctly pointed out the existence of '*Faujdars*" Circles within the division of the *Sarkar*, he has missed the fact of the prevalence of similar revenue Circles within the territorial limits of the same *Sarkar* and it is difficult to prove that the above two Circles, namely for executive administration and revenue administration, were not mostly identical. Both Moreland and Siddiqi have misunderstood the nature of *Faujdari* and its jurisdiction. The term '*Faujdari*' does not stand for territorial division. It is rather an act of military and executive administration in contrast to *Amaldari* or *Man Amal* or *Diwani* or *Karori* for an act of revenue administration – all these terms being affixed to a territorial circle comprising numerous *Parganas* more than a *Sarkar*, a *Sarkar*, a few *Parganas* or a single *Pargana*. This is true for every reign from Akbar to Aurangzeb. As to his duties, apart from his police and military powers, a *Faujdar* was in-charge of overall administration inclusive of the revenue department. The *Shiqdar* of a *Pargana* and *Karori* of *Parganas* were as responsible to him for the realization of land revenue as to the *Diwan*. The available evidence that from the reign of Jahangir, the office of the *Faujdar* was at times combined with that of *Amin* or *Diwan* or *Karori* within the same territorial circle knocks out the theory of separate *Faujdari* Circles. How could the *Faujdari* and fiscal offices of two separate territorial Circles be combined in the same person? All this rules out the possibility of separate *Faujdari* Circles as district from their fiscal counterparts. It is evident from the entire range of Mughal literature that the designation of *Faujdar* is rather generic. It is equally applicable to the jurisdiction over a *Subah*, a few *Sarkars*, numerous inter-*Sarkar Parganas*, a *Sarkar*, a group of *Parganas* smaller than a *Sarkar* or a single *Pargana*. Thus whatever be the circle of a *Faujdar's* jurisdiction – the basic unit of administration was the *Pargana*, which, for purely administrative purposes was further divided into *Thanas* – each *Thana* with a jurisdiction over few villages in its Circle. The *Pargana* was a common unit both to the *Faujdari* jurisdiction and fiscal division. Only this can account for the powers of the *Faujdar* over the revenue administration and also the fact of combining the *Faujdar's* office with either *Amin* or *Karori*. Regardless of the jurisdiction of the largest administrative division, the *Faujdar* with any jurisdiction dealt with the same territorial units as earmarked for fiscal purposes, which is an ample proof of an integrated administration both for *Faujdari* and revenue purposes.

References

1. *Ain*, Br. M. Add. 7652, fols. 141a-142a; Ms. Hamilton Berlin, fols. 118b-119a.
2. Though Dr. Saran concedes the fact that the designation of *Faujdar* was generic and that there were *Faujdars* at the frontier outposts, he thinks that for internal organisation, the *Faujdar* was in-charge of a *Sarkar* division (*Provincial Government*, pp. 96-102).
3. *A.N.* III, p. 33. Sayyid Hamid Bokhari was entrusted with the administration of Dhaulqah and Danduqah (*Sarkar* Ahmadabad, *Subah* Gujrat); *Waqai-i Asad Beg*, Ms. Aligh, p. 8, while narrating the events leading to the murder of Abul Fazl, mentions Sheikh Mustaffa as the *Faujdar* of Kala Bagh. (*Subah* Malwa). Asad Beg also mentions (p. 3) that he had accompanied the deceased Sheikh Abul Fazl upto Sarouj but he was directed by the *Faujdar* of the *Parganas* of Tara (*Faujdar-i Parganat-i Tara*) of *Subah* Malwa to go back to the Royal Court. Baharistan mentions that on conquest the whole territory of Kuch Bihar was divided into 20 circles: Some of these were entrusted to the *Jagirdars* and the *Faujdars* were to help them in the realization of the land revenue (*B.G.* Ms. B.N. Paris, fol. 145b. Also tr. Borah, I, pp. 272-74).
4. *T.J.* Ms. Rampur, Jahangir mentions the appointment of Mir Mahmud with the title of 'Tayur Khan' as the *Faujdar* of some of the *Parganas* in *Subah* Multan (p. 458); Hashim Khusti as the *Faujdar* of some of the *Parganas* of Mewat (p. 695); Arab Khwafi as the *Faujdar* of Doab (*Faujdar-i Miana Doab*) with the title of 800Z 500S. (p. 729). Also *B.G.* tr. Borah, I, pp. 218, 328.
5. *A.N.* III, p. 198. Qawim Khan as the administrator of Narnaul (*Subah* Agra); Jahangir's *Farman* dated 25th Muharram A.H. 1016/22nd May 1607, (C.R.O. Hydbd. *Magribi Collection*) appoints Jan Beg as the *Faujdar* of *Sarkar* Baroda, *Subah* Gujrat. Also *T.J.* tr. Rodgers, p. 178 mentions Tarbiyat Khan as the *Faujdar* of *Sarkar* Alwar (5th R.Y.).
6. *A.N.* I, p. 33. Qutub Uddin Khan was given the administration of *Sarkar* Baroach and adjoining areas (*Subah* Gujrat) in A.H. 980/1572-73.
7. *Ibid.* II, p. 331 states that Shihabuddin Khan, the *Faujdar* of *Sarkar* Saraunj and Shah Budagh Khan (*Subah* Malwa) was also the administrator (*Hakim*) of *Sarkar* Sarangpur (*Ibid.*) in *A.H.* 975/1567-68; also *Tabqat*, II, p. 222., *T.J.* Ms. Rampur, p. 255 mentions that Daulat Khan, the *Faujdar* of Allahabad and *Sarkar* Jaunpur (*Subah* Allahabad) holding the previous *mausale* of 1000 was given additional mansab of 500.
8. Saran, '*Provincial Government*', pp. 88-109.
9. *Ain*, tr. J. II, pp. 320-28.
10. *The Journal of Sir Thomas Roe*, pp. 655-66; '*The Embassy of Sir Thomas Roe to India*', ed. Foster, p. 489. Roe gives a list of 37 divisions. The names are those of the Provinces as well as some of the regions. Roe claims that he obtained the names of the Provinces from a list in the Royal Library. De Laet, pp. 4-15 more or less copied Roe and gives the same number of the Provinces though he has dropped Roe on the border of Bengal and added Jeselmeere.
11. *Kh. S.* N.A.I., pp. 121-32, Ms. Aligh, fols. 30a-b.

12. See f. nos. 6, 7.
13. For example, Mewat was not a *Sarkar* in any *Subah* but the territories of Mewat covered a few *Parganas* from each of the Sarkars of Riwari (*Subah* Delhi), Narnol and Alwar, Tijarah (*Subah* Agra) vide Shahjahan's *Farman*, R.A.J. dated 2nd Shawwal 24th R.Y. A.H. 1060.
The above mentioned *Farman* quotes the appointment of Kirat Singh s/o Mirza Raja Jai Singh to all the *Parganas* of Mewat. The details of the *Parganas* are given in the *Farman*. Jahangir mentions the appointment of Hashim Khusti to some of the *Parganas* in Mewat. (*T.J.* Ms. Rampur, p. 695). Roe in his report, 'Account of the Kingdoms, and Provinces of the Great Mogoll' vide '*The Journal of Sir Thomas Roe*', pp. 655-66, and De Laet, pp. 4-15 mention Mewat with Chief City called Narnol. For Aurangzeb's reign, R.A.J. *Akhbarat* regd. No. 1521/2 dated 1st Jamada II 23rd R.Y. mentions Mohtasim Khan as the *Faujdar* of Mewat (Here a few *Parganas* of Mewat). Similarly, the *Parganas* of the territory of Doab constituted a division of a *Faujdar*. Vide *T.J.*, Ms. Rampur, p. 729; also *Akhbarat* dated 14th Zilhaj 10th R.Y. (Aurangzeb). Likewise, appointment of a *Faujdar* was made for the territory of Lakhi Jungle (*Subah* Delhi) which was often entrusted to the *Faujdar* of *Chakla* Hisar. Maktubat-o Khan Jahan, Br. M. Letters of Jalal Hisari, dated 8th and 9th R.Y. (Aurangzeb), fols. 55b-57b; Lahori, Ms. Patna, fol. 271a. For *Subah* Gujrat, the *Ain* (tr. J. II, pp. 248-49) mentions the territories of Machhukhanta, Jambuji, Chaubisi comprising a few *Parganas* each.
14. *Ibid.*
15. Lahori, Ms. Patna, fol. 265b.
16. *Ibid.*, fol. 271a.
17. Warris, Ms. Rampur, p. 295.
18. *Maktubat-i Khan Jahan*, Br. M. Letters of Jalal hisari, fol. 62a-b.
19. *Ibid.*, fols. 2a-b.
20. *Muraqat-i Hasan*, pp. 78, 280-81.
21. *Ibid.*, pp. 325-26. Similarly, Bahadur Khan is mentioned (p. 311) as the *Faujdar* of the *Mahals* of Ganges (*Faujdar-i Mahal-i Gang*) in 1023 A.H. It is difficult to determine whether these *Mahals* were within the same *Sarkar* of inter-*Sarkar* in jurisdiction.
22. *Adab*, Ms. Rampur, pp. 99-100.
23. *Jalal Taba Taba*, Padshah Nama, Ms. Patna, p. 33.
24. R.A.J. Category No. 3 regd. No. 520 (dated Aurangzeb's reign) quotes a petition from Shri Chand, *Sahukar* of Ajmer to Nawab-ul-Umra sending a list of 23 desolate *Parganas* (*Subah* Ajmer) due to maladministration of the previous *Jagirdars* and *Faujdars* with a request that these *Parganas* after Confiscation to the *Khalsa* may be given in *Faujdari* to Mirza Raja Jai Singh and that he may be entrusted with the charge of *Amin* and *Karorbandi*. The petitioner submits that he would undertake to furnish a reliable surety for regularly depositing the money in the Royal treasury on each harvest.
25. R.A.J. Serial No. 24, no. 33 Ph.
26. *Ibid.* O.H. Records, Serial No. 28, No. 36 Ph; another *Parwana* O.H.R. Serial No. 78, No. 64 Ph dated 10th Shawwal 5th R.Y. (Farukhsaiyer)/6th September

1717 grants Kanwar Sheo Singh the *Faujdari* of Hindaun, Bayana and Ruplas. Also *Akhbarat*, no. 1721, dated 3rd of Zilhaj, 24th R.Y. (Aurangzeb) appoints Saiyaid Massud as the Faujdar of Itawa (*Chakla*) and Chaturyar.

27. *Ibid*., O.H.R., Kapat Dawara Documents, Serial No. 6, No. 371 R.
28. R.A.J. *Akhbarat* dated 11th Rabi II/1st December 1693.
29. *Ibid*. Category no. 3, regd. No. 3.
30. R.A.J. *Vakil Report*, regd. no. 341/194 dated 21st *Ramzan* 33rd R.Y. A.H. 1100/1689 A.D. A letter from Kesho Rai (*Vakil*) to Maharaja (Bishen Singh of Amber) informs that he had already submitted to the Emperor for the grant of *Faujdari* of Kamah (*Sarkar* Sahar *Subah* Agra) comprising four *Mahals* to Jeet Singh and that he had offered Rs. 10000/- as *Peshkash* for it. Consequently, a *Parwana* for the *Faujdari* of Kamah was issued by Nawab Bakshi Mulk Ruh Ullah Khan in the name of Jeet Singh. It is quite significant to note that the *Parwana* mentions the grant of *Faujdari* of Kamah whereas the details of the jurisdiction of Kamah over four *Mahals* are only given in the letter. Similarly, a proposal (*Tajwiznamah*) made by Maharaja (Jai Singh, the *Subahdar* of Malwa), vide Category no. 4 regd. No. 750 dated 25th Shaban 5th R.Y. (Bahadur Shah) A.H. 1123/1711 A.D. to the Royal Court recommends that the *Faujdari* and *Qiladari* of Raisin and *Faujdari* of Ratanpur (*Subah* Malwa) may be granted to Mutiqad Khan, son of late Amir Khan. The details of proposal show *Faujdari* over five *Mahals*. Raisin is shown as one *Mahal* whereas the *Faujdari* of Ratanpur is shown with four named *Parganas*. Apart from Ratanpur, three other *Parganas* are mentioned which are associated with the *Faujdari* of Ratanpur. Also R.A.J. Akhbarat, quotes that the *Faujdar* of Shadipur Pilanai, who had been formerly divested of the *Faujdari* of two *Mahals* of *Parganas* Kora, was reinstated with the *Faujdari* of the latter. This clearly shows that Shadipur Pilanai and even the *Pargana* of Kora had more than one *Pargana* attached to its *Faujdari* circle. A *Hasbulhukam* (memorandum) vide Maharaja's Letters, case no. 686(4) dated 25th Safar 40th R.Y. A.H. 1107/1696 mentions *Pargana* Akbarabad (*Subah* Agra) with a total (of three *Mahals* in its jurisdiction). Also 'Maharaja's Letters' regd. No. 3195 dated 9th Zilqad 6th R.Y. (Farrakhi) 1717 A.D. mentions Guman Singh, the *Zamindar* of Hathras as the *Faujdar* of Jalesar etc. (*Sarkar* Agra) indicating a wider jurisdiction than a Single *Pargana* of Jalesar.
31. *Mirat* I, pp. 289-90.
32. *Ibid.*
33. R.A.J. *Akhbarat*, dated 20th Safar 10th R.Y. (Aurangzeb) quotes a representation from the *Vakil* of Abullah Khan, the previous *Faujdar* of Narwar that *Pargana* Bosai transferred from his *Jagir* should be restored to him. The Royal Court decided that the said *Pargana* should be restored to his *Jagir* but the *Faujdari* of only half of the *Pargana* should remain with him whereas half of the *Faujdari* should be entrusted to Jan Khan. For transfers and fresh appointments in *Parganas* for *Faujdari* purposes, also see 'Maharaja's Letters' regd. No. 1123, dated 11th Jamada II 49th R.Y. A.H. 1117/17 R.A.J. Category no. 4 regd. No. 2922 dated A.H. 1123/1711 A.D.
34. R.A.J. Aurangzeb's *Farman* issued to Maharaja Ram Singh (of Amber) O.H.R., Kapat Dawara Documents, Serial no. 20, No. 27 (Phc) dated 24th

Rabi I 31st R.Y./6th Jan, 1689, grants *Faujdari* of Islamabad (alias Mathura) for suppressing and punishing the recalcitrant Raja, the *Jat Zamindar*. The *Farman* bears the Emperor's own handwriting for the accomplishment of the above task; also Aurangzeb's *Farmans* vide Serial no. 24, No. 33 Ph dated 22nd Shaban, 36th R.Y./8th April, 1694 issued to Maharaja of Bishen Singh (of Amber) granting the *Faujdari* of Islamabad; another *Farman* no. 28, No. 36 Ph dated 22nd Jamada I 37th R.Y./19th December, 1695 granting the *Faujdari* of Islamabad and Hindaun; also *Vakil Report*, regd. No. 385/303 dated 34th R.Y. (Aurangzeb) A.H. 1102/1691 A.D. granting the *Faujdari* of Bianah, Hindaun and Bhosawar to the Maharaja (of Amber).

35. R.A.J. *Akhbarat*, 11th Jamada I 10th R.Y. (Aurangzeb) narrates the confirmation in the present *Jagirs* and enhancement of mausale of Fida Khan, the *Faujdar* of Allahabad on the condition of entrusting to him and his son the *Faujdari* of Sultanpur. Also *Vakil Report* regd. no. 136/147 dated 4th Zilqad 32nd R.Y. A.H. 1099 (Aurangzeb) confirms the enhancement of 20 lacs of *Dams* to the Maharaja of Amber on the condition of *Faujdari* charge of Kamah, etc. (*Sarkar* Sahar *Subah* Agra); *Ibid.*, regd. no. 369/239 dated 28th Shaban 34th R.Y. A.H. 1101/17th May 1690 A.D. confirms in grant of *Faujdari* of *Pargana* Kahori to Shahkar Ullah Khan with an additional *mansab* of 200S.
36. R.A.J. *Vakil Report* regd. no. 191/271 dated 23rd Shaban 34th R.Y. (Aurangzeb), A.H. 1102/12th May 1691 A.D. narrates a representation of the *Vakil* of Maharaja (of Amber) for the additional grant of 15 *lacs* of *dams* on the condition of *Faujdari* of Kahori and Toda Bhim. Also R.A.J. Category no. 2 regd. no. 796 dated 40th R.Y. A.H. 1107/1695 A.D. quotes a representation from Alam Chand for the appointment of a *Faujdar* of Hindaun (*Subah* Agra) for realising the revenues after the suppression of disturbance in the recalcitrant areas; also *Akhbarat*, regd. no. 1928/1-2 dated 5th Rajab 24th R.Y. (*Ibid.*).
37. R.A.J. Category no. 4 regd. no. 149 (Aurangzeb's reign). A copy of Rashid Khan's (the Central Diwan) order for entrusting the disturbed *Paibaqi Parganas* in the *Sarkars* of Kol and Islamabad in the *Faujdari* of Raja Bishen Singh for realising the revenues from the recalcitrant Jat areas. Also *Maktubat-i Khan Jahan*, Br. M. fols. 2a-b, 11a-b; *Ibid.* Letter of Jalal Hisari, for 25b, 47b-48a, 54b, 55b, 57a-b, 62a-b; *Murraqat-i Hasan*, Ms. Rampur, pp. 325-27 quotes a directive dated 11th Rabi I 2nd R.Y. (Aurangzeb) from Mian Mohammad Jan to the *Faujdars* and *Thanadars* of the territories of *Sarkars* from Bhadrak to Malod, the border of *Subah* Orissa.
38. R.A.J. *Vakil Report* regd. no. 191/271 dated 23rd Shabban 34th R.Y. (Aurangzeb) A.H. 1102/12th May 1691 A.D. narrates the Royal order granting the *Faujdari* of Kohari with an additional assignment of 15 *lacs dams* and at the same time confirming the appointment of Shakar Ullah Khan as the *Faujdar* and *Amin* of *Pargana* Kohari. Also *Murraqat-i Hasan, Ibid.*; *Maktubat-i Khan Jahan*, Br. M. and letters of Jalal Hisari. *Ibid.*
39. R.A.J. 'Maharaja's Letters', Case no. 686 (K) dated 2nd Ramzan 40th R.Y. (Aurangzeb) A.H. 1107/1703 A.D.; Category no. 4 regd. no. 149 (Aurangzeb's reign); *Ibid.*, regd. no. 2922 dated A.H. 1123/1711 A.D.

40. R.A.J. Category no. 2 regd. no. 1049 dated 50th R.Y. A.H. 1117/1705 A.D. quotes the appointment of Dharamjas, the *Amil* of *Pargana* F. Nariana (*Subah* Ajmer) as the Niab *Faujdar* of the foresaid *Pargana*, which was in the *Faujdari* of the Maharaja (of Amber). Also 'Maharaja's Letters' regd. no. 2088 dated 2nd Zilhaj 5th R.Y. (Farrakhi) A.H. 1128/1716 A.D. quotes a Hasbul hukam desiring the Maharaja (of Amber) to direct his *Niab Faujdar* of Islamabad (Mathura) not to charge custom duties on Corn and to allow its unrestricted movement for lowering its price. Also O.H.R., Serial no. 88, No. 90C quotes a *Parwana* dated 1st Moharram 6th R.Y. (Farrakhi)/24th December 1717 A.D. appointing Jagram as the *Niab Faujdar* of *Pargana* Malarana in the *Faujdari* of the Maharaja (Amber).
41. *Warris*, Ms. Rampur, pp. 18-19, mentions Rai Todar Mal Diwan, *Amin* and *Faujdar* of the *Khalsa* (*Parganas*) of Sirhind, etc.; Sheikh Gillani as the *Diwan*, *Amin* and *Faujdar* of the *Khalsa* (*Parganas*) in *Subah* Multan (*Ibid*., p. 19); the *Faujdar* of Iraj and the *Khalsa* (*Parganas*) of Gwalior. (*Ibid*., p. 20).
42. R.A.J. *Vakil Report*, regd. no. 191/271 dated 23rd Shaban 34th R.Y. 1102 A.H./ 12th May 1691 A.D.; *Ibid*., regd. no. 251/366 dated 10th Zilhaj A.H. 1103/ 1692 A.D.; 'Maharaja's Letters', Case No. 675 dated 29th Rabi II 38th R.Y. A.H. 1106/1694 A.D.; Category No. 3 regd. no. 520 (Aurangzeb's reign).
43. *Ibid*., regd. no. 373/276 dated 3rd Zilhaj A.H. 1101/28th August 1690 A.D.; 'Maharaja's Letters', regd. no. 627 35th R.Y. A.H. 1103/1691 A.D.; *Ibid*., regd. no. 829, 39th R.Y. A.H. 1106; *Ibid*., regd. no. 832 39th R.Y. A.H. 1106; *Ibid*., regd. no. 1123 49th R.Y. A.H. 1117; also *Nigar Nama*, Ms. Bod. Oxfd., fols. 75b-77a; Ms. N.A.I., fols. 60b-61b, 63a.

3. Faujdar–Functions And Duties

The institution of *Faujdari* was an indispensable and most important organ of the land revenue administration under the Mughals. A *Faujdar* was always a *Mansabdar* of the State and maintained troops in lieu of his *mansab*. He formed an important link between the military and the civil administration of the *Subah* set up. In a state where political disturbances on the part of the local *Zamindars* and recalcitrant tribes was a recurrent feature of the society, it is hard to imagine a civil administration completely divorced from the military establishment. Nevertheless, though backed by a military contingent, throughout the Mughal age from Akbar to Aurangzeb, the *Faujdar* appears to be an executive officer of a civil administration. As the head of the administrative division comprising numerous *Parganas*, whether inter-*Sarkar* or of a full *Sarkar* or a still lesser territorial jurisdiction, he represented the *Subahadar* and exercised multifarious powers viz. military, police, revenue and judicial. The role of the Mughal *Faujdar* in the revenue administration truly represents the medieval concept of a society wherein large sections of tribes settled on *Zamindari* principles lacked consciousness for the payment of State taxes unless coerced through armed action and as such, rendered a clear-cut demarcation between the military and civil departments of the State well nigh impossible. It is not within the scope of this work to explain the details of the functions of the *Faujdar* except those related with the land revenue administration.

The Mughal *Faujdar* was par excellence the Collector of revenue with exclusive jurisdiction over the recalcitrant (*mutmarid* or *Zur Talb*) peasants and *Zamindars*. He had also an exclusive charge to collect revenues and fixed tribute (*Peshkash* and *Nalbandi*) from the hereditary princely Chiefs (*Zamindars*) in his jurisdiction. For the reigns of Akbar and Jahangir, *Ain-i Akbari* and *Baharistan* are the only known sources which give a general but an intimate idea of the duties of a *Faujdar*. But for the reigns of Shahjahan and Aurangzeb, there are vast sources which throw flood of light on the revenue obligations of a *Faujdar*. Except for some differences as explained later, the responsibilities and duties of a *Faujdar* remained practically the same throughout the Mughal age.

As an administrator, the *Faujdar* was responsible for the maintenance of law and order and the enforcement of state regulations in his division. As such, he had on the part of a person who defied the authority and law of the State. The *Ain* clearly brings out the important revenue duties of a *Faujdar*.[1] He exercised control over both the *Khalsa* and the *Jagir* territories in his jurisdiction. His main function was to bring around either through conciliary method or armed action any peasant or the collector of

Khalsa revenues (*Amal Guzar-i Khalsa*) or a *jagirdar*, whosoever proved refractory. As a precaution against the misuse of the vast military powers against the recalcitrants, the principal revenue officials of the locality were required to attest in writing the fact of recalcitrance for non-payment of the revenues in the area. After the suppression of the recalcitrants, the first consideration of the *Faujdar* was to check up the balance of the land revenue due from a village. In *Akbar Nama*, the 27th Year's revenue regulations of Todar Mal enjoin the local revenue officials to prepare a detailed periodical list of both revenue paying (*raiyat-i khas*) and turbulent (*mutmarid*) villages in every *Pargana* and to forward the same to the Royal Court for appropriate appointment of collectors for realisation of land revenue.[2] It also empowers the *Faujdar* to afford full armed help to the *Karories* and the *Jagirdars* in crushing the rebellious persons living in the ravines and those having evaded payment of land revenue sought protection in the jungles or forts or ravines.[3] While the *Ain* and *Akbar Nama* put it briefly as general instructions, the later sources viz. Rajasthan Archives and *Siyaq Nama* explain the procedure of such assistance on the part of the *Faujdar* in greater details. In actual practice, there was a standing rule that the *Faujdar* could move to suppress the recalcitrants in the *Jagir* or *Khalsa* villages only after the *Jagirdar* or the *Karori* signed a bond (*muchalka*) to the effect that they had failed to realize revenues from particular villages which had been declared as recalcitrant (*Zur Talb*).[4] This equally served as a check against any delinquent attitude on the part of the *Karories* who just to save much of botheration on their own part would record the villages as recalcitrant and realize the revenues when provided with military support from the *Faujdar*.[5] Based on the revenue documents of the past few years, the *Karori* had to submit a detailed report of the revenue paying (*raiyati*) and recalcitrant (*Zur Talb*) villages in his territorial jurisdiction.[6] After having received a written request from the *Karori* or the *Jagirdar* for military assistance, the *Faujdar* would try to persuade a few of the *Muqaddams* of the recalcitrant villages for the payment of the revenues and, if successful at conciliation, would obtain written consent from the *Karori* or the *Amil* of the *Jagirdar* to that effect.[7] He would resort to armed action for pillaging the village and the punishment of the rebels only if the unruly *Muqaddams* refused submission.[8] At the same time, he had to safeguard that no harm was done to the ordinary *ryots* (*Riaya-i Raiza*) and that the booty acquired from the village would be handed over to the *Amil* after having got receipt for the same.[9]

Jahangir's Farman, dated 22nd May 1607 A.D. of the grant of *Faujdari* of *Sarkar* Baroda, *Subah* Gujrat, to Jan Beg directs the latter to take charge of the said territory, to administer it well, to root out disagreeable and seditious elements and to do his best in encouraging and promoting cultivation and habitation in his territorial jurisdiction.[10] *Baharistan-i Ghaibi* stresses the role of a *Faujdar* in the newly expanded territories in Bengal, Kuch Bihar and Assam. The *Faujdar* possessed full administrative powers over the *Karories* in his jurisdiction and was responsible for law and order and realisation of revenues from the recently subdued *Zamindars*.[11] He had also to present the latter at periodical intervals at the Governor's Court.[12] He was essentially responsible for the realisation of full revenues in his jurisdiction.

For ShahJahan's reign, the Royal *Farmans* of the *Faujdar's* appointment make only a brief general statement of the latter's duties. Shahjahan's *Farman* dated 1648 A.D. appointing Kirat Singh, son of Mirza Raja Jai Singh as the *Faujdar* of the *Parganas* of Mewat (*Chakla*) underlines the duties of suppression of refractoriness on the part of the recalcitrants and keeping the *ryots* happy and contented.[13] Apart from this, ShahJahan's *Farmans* are on record for the ad-hoc appointment of high *Mansabdars* for the performance of *Faujdari* duties in specific arrears for aiding the local *Karories* and *Jagirdars* in suppressing the recalcitrance and local disturbance.[14] More than these *Farmans*, the contemporary official correspondence about the revenue problems is quite revealing about the revenue functions of the *Faujdar*. The letters of Khan Jahan Saiyid Muzaffar Khan, Barha, the *Faujdar* and *Diwan* of *Chakla* Hissar addressed to the Royal Court deal with the *Faujdari* problems for the realisation of revenues from the recalcitrant *Zamindars* and tribes in *Chaklas* of Hissar, Gwalior, Mianawali and Islamabad.[15] The letters of Jalal Hissari and Balkrishan Brahman addressed to Khan-i Jahan Muzaffar Khan not only emphasise such problems[16] but also give details of the management of the revenue administration and the irrigation facilities to be extended by the *Faujdars* of the *Chaklas* of Hissar and Sirhind to the local *Zamindars* and the *ryots*.[17] The *Faujdar* had to inspect the irrigation canals regularly.[18] It is equally significant to note that from the reign of Shahjahan onwards, the *Faujdar* of a high division, whether a *Chakla* or a *Sarkar* or various enumerated *Parganas*, exercised the powers of the *Amin* as well.[19] At times, the *Faujdari* and *Diwani* functions were also vested in the same officer.[20] This practice of combining offices continued till the end of Aurangzeb's reign.[21] Such a combination of offices in the person of the *Faujdar* clearly illustrates that the possession of military authority on his part was not incompatible with his dominating civil position as the revenue administrator of the *Parganas*.

For Aurangzeb's reign, there is abundant of contemporary archival evidence which gives details of the revenue functions of the *Faujdar*. The Rajasthan Archives show that in case of any arrears of land revenue in the *Khalsa* lands due to either slackness on the part of the *Karories* or recalcitrance on the part of the *Zamindars* or the *ryots*, the entire responsibility rested with the *Faujdar* who was reprimanded by the Central Government for such inefficiency.[22] It was incumbent on the *Faujdar's* part to suppress the insurgents and realise revenues from recalcitrant *Zamindars* and the *ryots*.[23] He owned full responsibility for the deployment of the contingents and full equipment of the *Thanas* under his jurisdiction.[24] While exercising complete authority over the *Pargana* and the *Dehat Thanadars* under him, he would issue them detailed directives for the realisation of the revenues and suppression of the recalcitrants.[25] Like the Rajasthan Archives, *Siyaq Nama* not only exonerates the *Karori* from the responsibility of collecting revenues from the recalcitrant (*Zur Talb*) areas but narrates more elaborate procedure for this purpose.[26] A *Faujdar* could entrust the *Karori* with the realisation of the revenues from such areas but if the latter failed in the job, the entire responsibility would lie with the *Faujdar* himself. The *Faujdar* could, of course, entrust the job to any intermediary and the amount thus successfully realised from the recalcitrant areas shall have to be remitted to the treasury (*Fotahkhana*) and the commission of the *Karori* on this amount shall be paid from the treasury. A *Jagirdar* or a *Mustajir* (Revenue Farmer) could also appoint a *Faujdar* on his own behalf to collect revenues from the recalcitrant areas.[27]

The *Faujdar* had also to safeguard the interests of both the *tankhwah jagir* and *madad-i maash* assignees in his division. He had to see that the Royal assignment orders were properly executed by the revenue officials who were required to make correct demarcation and division (*Taqsim*) between the *Jagir* and *Khalsa* territorties.[28] In case of need, he had to extend armed assistance to the *tankhwah Jagir* assignees in the realisation of revenues from the recalcitrant areas and *Peshkash* (revenues) from the *Zamindars* assigned in *Jagir*.[29] Where the *Faujdar* was given his own *Jagir* within his *Faujdari* division, the task of revenue collection was greatly facilitated. As most of the high *Mansabdars* holding large assignments were absentee *Jagirdars* to their *Amils*, the onus of helping the latter in the realisation of the revenues from the recalcitrant areas fell on the *Faujdar* of the division.[30] At times, the *Faujdar* had to reprimand and issue orders to the local *Pargana* revenue officials to afford full co-operation to the *Amils* of the absentee *Jagirdars* in timely assessment and realisations of the revenues and maintenance of proper accounts.[31] He had also to assist the *madad-i maash* assignees in realising rent from their tenants or any other party which may have illegally usurped the rents. In such cases, he would issue directions to the *Thanadars* to realise the amount and deliver to the concerned assignees.[32]

The *Faujdar* essentially possessed the powers of '*Tehsildar-i Peshkash*' and the two offices were always combined in one and the same officer.[33] As the Collector of *Peshkash* (*Tehsildar-i Peshkash*), he was responsible for the realisation of the revenues (*Peshkash*) from such of the territories of the *Zamindars* (here hereditary chiefs) which did not form a part of the *Watan Jagir* of the latter.[34] Such revenues could be regularly assessed in the *Amli* territories or could be fixed as lump sum (*Peshkash-i muqarari*) in *Gair Amli* territories. In fact, the collection of *Peshkash* from such *Zamindars* was one of the most important functions of the *Faujdar*. Even though such *Zamindari* territories were usually given in *tankhwah Jagirs* to the *Mansabdars*, it remained the sole responsibility of the *Faujdar* to collect *Peshkash* from such *Zamindars* in his division. He maintained a full list of the *tankhwah Jagir* assignments made in such *Zamindari* territories and had also to maintain detailed accounts of the realisations and balance of the revenues (*Peshkash* due from the *Zamindars* and their territories).[35] If any of such *Zamindars* proved refractory and evaded payment of *Peshkash* to a *Jagirdar* or the *Khalsa* officer whatever the case may be, the responsibility for the suppression of the *Zamindar* and realisation of *Peshkash* lay entirely with the *Faujdar* of the division.[36] A *Zamindar* also owed *Peshkash* in lieu of ceremonial gifts to be paid to the State.[37]

The *Faujdar* had also to collect *Peshkash* (charges) from the Jagirdars[38] in lieu of the military service rendered to them, ceremonial presents that they owed to the State as *Mansabdars*[39] and also in lieu for the realisation of the revenues in their territories. It seems that the expenses of the *Faujdar's* contingent deployed by the *Jagirdar* for the revenue realisations were met by the latter and paid as *Peshkash* to the State.[40] In case of any dilapidated financial condition of a *Jagirdar*, the *Faujdar* could exempt the latter from the payment of *Peshkash* and intimate the fact to the Royal Court.[41]

On directions from *Diwan-i Subah*, the *Faujdar* had to recover any dues or arrears (*mutalba*) from the *Mansabdar-Jagirdars* in lieu of either loans taken from the State[42] or revenues collected from their own *Jagir* but to which they had no entitlement due to any appointment or transfer during the mid-crop seasons.[43]

For all his revenue duties and obligations, the *Faujdar* was responsible to the *Diwan-i Subah*. He had to render full accounts of the revenue realisations under him to the *Subah* authorities. He had to send an *Amin* and some of the *Qanungos* and *Chaudharies* to the *Subah* headquarters for the finalisation of the revenue accounts.[44] He was also responsible for the dispatch of the revenues of his *Parganas* to the *Subah* treasury. The office of the Provincial *Diwan* could direct any of the *Faujdar's* revenue officers to remit the revenues to the Royal treasury.[45] A *Faujdar* was required to clear his own dues to the State (*mutalba*) in annual installments and in case of failure of payment, the Royal Court could order the attachment of any specified amount from his *tankhwah Jagir* to the *Khalsa*.[46] If any *Faujdar* failed to discharge his revenue duties properly on a report against him by the *Diwan-i Subah*, he would be transferred by the Royal Court.[47]

Naib Faujdar

It is evident from some of the documents of Aurangzeb's reign and later Mughal period that at various places, a *Faujdar* was also assisted by a *Naib-Faujdar*. The *Naib Faujdar* was appointed directly by the Central Government.[48] He discharged the same duties as the *Faujdar* of the division and was responsible to the latter.[49] It is not clear if the practice of appointing *Naib Faujdar* existed throughout age since earlier times but it was getting quite widespread in the reign of Aurangzeb and later period.[50]

References

1. *Ain*, Br. M. Add. 7652, fols. 141a-142a; Ms. Hamilton, Berlin, fols. 118b-119a.
2. *A.N.*, Br. M. Add. 27, 247, fol. 332a (8th Clause).
3. *Ibid.*, fols. 331b-332a.
4. R.A.J. Category no. 4 regd. no. 1395 dated 14th Safar 37th R.Y. (Aurangzeb) A.H. 1105/1693 A.D. Letter from Megh Raj Vakil to Maharaja (of Amber as the *Faujdar* of *Parganas* in *Subah* Agra quotes the above rule and warns the latter not to suppress the insurgents (*mufasids*) in Hindaun without the execution of such bonds.
5. *Ibid.* The letter states that the *Amins* and the *Karories* are usually used to note down a territory with the turbulents (*mufasids*) but when the army approached, the latter came and flattered the *Karories* and were declared as revenue paying (*raiyati*).
6. *Ibid.*
7. *S.N.* Hydbd., fols. 52a-b.
8. *Ibid.*
9. *Ibid.*
10. C.R.O. Hydbd., Magribi Collection, Jahangir, 25th Muharram A.H. 1016/ 22nd May 1607.
11. B.G. tr. Borah I, pp. 218, 272-74; Ms. B. N. Paris, fol. 96a.
12. *Ibid.* p. 328.
13. R.A.J. Shahjahan's *Farman* dated 2nd Shawwal 24th R.Y./A.H. 1060/1648 A.D.
14. *Ibid.* Shahjahan's *Farman* dated 22nd Shabban 5th R.Y. addressed to Raja Jai Singh to suppress Kaiseri Singh and Kalyan Dass the turbulent *Zamindars* in the *Parganas* of Ruspur and Hariana, *Subah* Ajmer; another *Farman* dated 20th Muharram 10th R.Y. A.H. 1047/1635 A.D. addressed to Raja Jai Singh to suppress the recalcitrant *ryots* in the *Khalsa Mahals* of Hindaun (*Subah* Agra) and to help the *Karories* in the realisation of the revenues; a *Farman* dated 12th Rajab 24th R.Y. A.H. 1060/1648 A.D. addressed to Mirza Raja Jai Singh to suppress the insurgents in the hills of Kakka and Pahari and to settle the *ryots* and the *Jagirdars* peacefully.
15. *Maktubat-i Khan Jahan*, Br. M. fols. 2a-b, 41, 11a-b.
16. *Ibid.* Letters of Jalal Hijari and Balkrishan Brahman, fols. 25b, 47b-48a, 52a, 54b, 55b, 57a-b, 62a-b, 63a-b.
17. *Ibid.*, fols. 108a-b.
18. S.D.A.R., pp. 128, 132, Sayyid Mansur, *Faujdar* of Baglana (*Subah* Khandesh, Deccan) inspected the irrigation canals at the villages of Uljhapur and Jakhera.
19. *Kh.S.*, N.A.I., p. 32, Ms. Berlin, fols. 159a-b, letters of Jalal Hisari vide *Maktubat-i Khan Jahan*, Br. M. 59b, 62a-b; Lahori, Ms. Patna, fol. 126a; Amil Salih, I, p. 330.
20. *Ibid.* Also my Paper on *Diwan-i Sarkar* in the 'Mughal Administration', I.H.R.C. 1961-62.

21. R.A.J. *Akhbarat*, regd. no. 1521/2 dated 1st Jamada II 23rd R.Y. (Aurangzeb) quotes that it was customary to combine the offices of the *Faujdar* and the *Amin* at certain specified *Parganas*. Accordingly, on representation from Mutsim Khan, the *Faujdar* of Mewat, the *Faujdari* and *Amini* of the *Parganas* of Bariath and Singhana was also assigned to him; regd. no. 1837 dated 1st Rabi I 24th R.Y. (*Ibid.*) quotes the appointment of Mohammad Sujab vide transfer of Saadat Mand, as the *Faujdar* and *Amin* of Sambar (*Subah* Ajmer). *Ibid.* dated 19th Rabi II 9th R.Y. (*Ibid.*); also regd. no. 1514/2 dated 24th Jamada I 23rd R.Y. (*Ibid.*). *Nigar Nama*, N.A.I., fols. 23b, 53a-55a, 60b-61b; Ms. Bod. Oxfd., fols. 75b-77a.
22. R.A.J. *Vakil Report*, regd. no. 251/366 dated 37th R.Y. A.H. 1103/1692 A.D. A letter from Megh Raj, Vakil to Maharaja (of Amber) quotes instruction of Rashid Khan (the Central Minister) to the *Vakil* that in the *Khalsa Parganas* of *Subah* Agra (in the *Faujdari* of the Maharaja) only 1 *lac* and 70 thousand *Dams* out of the total 22 *lacs* had been realised whereto the arrears had accumulated due to the refractory attitude of *ryots* and the lackness of the *Karories*. The Emperor was informed for reprimanding the Maharaja for it.
23. *Ibid.* The letter quotes strict orders of the Central Diwan, Rashid Khan to that effect; also Insha-i Roshan Kalam, Br. M. fol. 1b. Sher Andaz Khan, the *Faujdar* in *Subah* Oudh narrates his own experiences and problems for suppressing the recalcitrant *Zamindars* both in the *Khalsa* and *Jagir* lands in his jurisdiction. R.A.J. Category no. 2 regd. no. 796 dated 40th R.Y. A.H. 1107. In a letter Alam Chand requests for the appointment of a *Faujdar* of Hindaun (*Subah* Agra).
24. R.A.J. 'Maharaja's Letters', regd. no. 835, dated 39th R.Y. A.H. 1106; *Ibid.* Category no. 2 regd. no. 796 dated 49th R.Y. A.H. 1107/1696 A.D.; 'Maharaja's Letters', case no. 749 dated 39th R.Y. A.H. 1106. Murqat-i Hasan, pp. 78-79, 260-61, 309. (R.A.J. Misc. Pers. Letters regd. no. 174 dated 11th Shawwal A.H. 1120/1708 A.D. quotes a bond (*muchalka*) by the *Faujdar* and *Amin* of *Pargana* Kotputli for the appointment of his own contingent in the Thanas of the *Pargana*. *Nigar Nama*, Bod. Oxfd., fols. 75b-77a; Mirat Suppl. pp. 193-94, 198, 208.
25. R.A.J. Category no. 4 regd. no. 405 dated 19th Jamada I 49th R.Y. A.H. 1117/ 1705 A.D.; *Ibid.* regd. no. 2856 dated 19th Rabi II A.H. 1124/1712 A.D.
26. *S.N.* Hydbd., fols. 52b-53a.
27. R.A.J. Misc. Pers. Letters regd. no. 72 dated 3rd Zilqad 38th R.Y. (Aurangzeb).
28. R.A.J. Category no. 2 regd. no. 393 dated 20th Rabi I 39th R.Y. A.H. 1106/ 1695 A.D.
29. R.A.J. 'Maharaja's Letters', case no. 789 dated 39th R.Y. (Aurangzeb) A.H. 1106; *Ibid.* Case no. 686 (P) dated 6th Shawwal 40th R.Y. A.H. 1107/1696 A.D.
30. *Ibid.* Case no. 624 dated 35th R.Y. A.H. 1103/1691 A.D.
31. *Ibid.*, regd. no. 832 dated 39th R.Y. A.H. 1106.
32. *Ibid.* Case no. 686 (P) dated 6th Shawwal 40th R.Y. A.H. 1107/1696 A.D.; case no. 749 dated 39th R.Y. A.H. 1106 respectively.
33. R.A.J. *Akhbarat*, regd. no. 1436, dated 5th Rabi I 23rd R.Y. (Aurangzeb); *Ibid.*, dated 15th Safar 36th R.Y. (*Ibid.*); Muraqat-i Hasan, pp. 78-79, 254-55, 267,

280-81, 309-13. In fact, the term Tehsildar though literally meaning a Collector was associated with the *Faujdar* who was competent to realize revenues from the recalcitrants. *Akbar Nama* in its 27th year's revenue regulations of Todar Mal states that in case of revenue paying *ryots* of the villages, it is the duty of the *Amils* (*Karories*) rather than that of the *Tehsildar* to realize the revenue and to deposit in the Treasury. (*A.N.* Br. M. Add. 27, 247, fol. 332b). The designation '*Tehsildar-i Peshkash*' meaning Collector of *Peshkash* from the *Zamindars* was invariably associated with the *Faujdar*. For Akbar's reign, Farishta, p. 510, mentions the appointment of Qazi Ali as the *Diwan* and Hassan Beg Badakshi as the *Tehsiladar* and Collector of Kharaj (*Peshkash*) in Kashmir. The designation of *Tehsildar-i Peshkash* was known throughout the Mughal age. See Mamuri, p. 626; *Mirat-i Alam*, fol. 111a; Khwafi, II. p. 461.

34. See f.n. 31.
35. R.A.J. Category no. 3 regd. nos. 339 and 969. (Aurangzeb's reign) give the details of the *Peshkash* realised from the *Zamindars* in *Subah* Malwa.
36. See f.n. 31.
37. MS. Orient. Quart 258, Berlin, fols. 160a-162a states that every *Amir*, *Mansabdar* and a *Zamindar* owed to the Royal Court ceremonial gifts at the time of Id viz. Nazar-i Halai, Idul fiter, Id ul Ziha; New Year (Nau Roz), and guestship (*Mehmani*). Such dues to the State were regularly assessed for every *Subah* and had to be paid by the *Jagirdars* and *Zamindars* as *Peshkash*.
38. R.A.J. Misc. Persian Letters, regd. no. 770 dated 17th Jamada I 49th R.Y. A.H. 1117/1705 A.D. A letter informs Chander Bhan that the *Peshkash* amount of Arjun Singh etc. *Jagirdars* of *Pargana* Bhorasa was fixed and that he should realise the amount from the *Jagirdars*; *Ibid.* regd. no. 780 directs Hari Ram to realise *Peshkash* from Sultan Singh, *Jagirdar* of *Pargana* Tauli and to deposit in the treasury; *Ibid.* Another letter regd. no. 602 dated Rabi II A.H. 1117/1705/1762 Samat informs that strict orders were issued from the Royal Court for the collection of *Peshkash* from *Pargana* Dhar and a *Pargana* was already sent to the *Jagirdar* of Dhar in this connection. It desires that the *Jagirdar* may be directed to send the *Peshkash* regularly.
39. See f.n. 31.
40. R.A.J. Waqai *Pargana* Bhorasah *Sarkar* Sarangpur (*Subah* Malwa) regd. no. 644 dated 7th Rajah 49th R.Y. (Aurangzeb); also regd. no. 630 dated 13th Jamada I 49th R.Y.
41. R.A.J. Category no. 2 regd. no. 1027 (Aurangzeb's reign).
42. R.A.J. 'Maharaja's Letters', regd. no. 686 (f) dated 5th Rajab 39th R.Y./A.H. 1107/1695 A.D.
43. *Ibid.*, dated 39th R.Y.
44. R.A.J. 'Maharaja's Letters', regd. no. 840 dated 39th R.Y. A.H. 1106/1696 A.D. The Provincial Diwan requires the A.D. Maharaja holding *Faujdari* in the *Parganas* of *Subah* Agra to send the *Amin* Sheikh Ahsanallah, a few of the *Choudharis* and *Qanungos* of the *Parganas* along with the original accounts to the Capital at Akbarabad; also case no. 675 dated 29th Rabi II 38th R.Y./1694 A.D. The Subah Diwan, Mohammad Ali, desires the Maharaja Bishan Singh (the *Faujdar* of the *Parganas* in *Subah* Agra) to send the *Qanungos* of

Toda and Bayana etc. (*Subah* Agra) to along with the copies of the Tumars (of revenues) to Akbarabad to settle the accounts. The letter gives details of how the revenue documents dispatched by the *Faujdar* were subjected to full scrutiny by the *Diwan's* Office at the *Subah* headquarters. Also *Ibid.* regd. no. 829 dated 39th R.Y. A.H. 1106; *Ibid.*, case no. 584 (a) dated 3rd Ramzan 35th R.Y. A.H. 1102; *Ibid.* regd. no. 955 dated 41st R.Y. A.H. 1108.

45. *Ibid.* regd. no. 822 dated 39th R.Y. A.H. 1106.
46. R.A.J. *Akhbarat*, dated 4th Rajab 10th R.Y. (Aurangzeb).
47. *Ibid.* dated 8th Safar 10th R.Y. (*Ibid.*); dated 13th Muharram 10th R.Y. (*Ibid.*).
48. R.A.J. Category no. 2 regd. no. 1049 dated 50th R.Y. (Aurangzeb) A.H. 1117/1705 A.D. appoints Dharanijas as *Niab Faujdar* in *Pargana* Malarana (*Subah* Ajmer); O.H.R. Serial no. 88 No. 90C dated 1st Moharram 6th R.Y. (Farrakhi) appoints Jagram as the *Niab Faujdar* of *Pargana* Malarna; also Akhbarat, 44th R.Y. (Aurangzeb) mentions the *Niab* of *Nusart* Jang, *Faujdar* of Karnatak (Deccan).
49. R.A.J. 'Maharaja's Letters', regd. no. 2088 dated 5th R.Y. (Farrakhi) A.H. 1128/1716 A.D.
50. See f.n. 45; also R.A.J., O.H.R., N.R. 100, a copy of Tumar of *Pargana* Nolahi dated 29th Safar 49th R.Y./1112 Fasli/1702 A.D.

4. Bitikchi

The *Bitikchi*[1] was the assessment officer attached with the *Karori* for the same revenue circle.[2] He acted as a subordinate official of the *Karori* and was responsible to him.[3] He was an expert revenue accountant. He also acted as the Superintendent of *Karori's* office and as such was indispensable to him.[4]

His primary function was to make an assessment of the State demand on the individual cultivators and the villages under his jurisdiction. He had to familiarise himself thoroughly with the customs, regulations, conditions of agriculture and the cultivators of his circle.[5] For the purposes of Survey and measurement, he was assisted by the *Pargana Munsif* and his subordinate staff or surveyors.[6] With their help he had to get prepared the village survey (*Zabt* or *Khasra*) records as already noted for their functions.[7] For the completion of the survey documents of a village he would also consult the last ten years assessment document (*Muwazina-i Deh Sala*) taken from the *Qanungo*, and determined the assessment of each cultivator and assessed the revenue demand (*Jama*) of the whole village compiled in the *Jamabandi*.[8] Similarly, a total *Jamabandi* embodying these of all the villages would be prepared for the whole *Pargana*. On the basis of this assessment, collections were to be made by the *Amil* and his staff.[9] Similarly, he would compile for every village and the entire *Pargana* another consolidated assessment document for both the crops, *Rabi* and *Kharif*, named *Sayah Tashkkish Jama*.[10] He had to despatch the village survey abstract (*Zabt* or *Khasra*) and the *Pargana* assessment documents (*Jamabandi* and *Mujmil*) to the Central Office at the end of every harvest and year respectively.[11] As superintendent of the *Karori's* office, assisted by the *Pargana* staff, he had to manage even the documents of realisations, balance and expenditure of the *Pargana*.[12] As such, he had to submit the documents of *Taujih* comprising the realisation (*Asal*) and balance (*Baqi*) of every village and for the entire *Pargana* to the *Amil*. If while preparing the *Taujih*, he could not get the documents of the previous years, he had to ascertain the cultivation of every cultivator from the *Patwari*. In the day ledger (*Roznamcha*), he had to enter the name of the collection official (*Tahsildar*) for every village. He would receive from the *Muqaddams* and the *Patwaris* the copies of the *Taujihs* of their respective villages along with the demand memorandums served to the cultivators. After having scrutinised them thoroughly, he would fine the official concerned for any falsification. He would submit daily the accounts of realisation and balance from every village to the collector. He had also to manage the treasury realisations. He had to see that the name of every husbandman depositing the rent was entered and that a receipt signed by the treasurer issued to him. At the end of every harvest, he had to record the collections and balances from each village and to compare them with the *Patwari.* Any cultivator desiring reference to his account was to be given full satisfaction. Every day, the receipts and disbursements under each name and heading had to be entered in the daily ledger (*Roznamcha*) and had to be verified by the Collector and the treasurer. The accounts of such daily ledgers had to be despatched to the Royal Court every month whereas the receipts and disbursements of the treasurer attested by latter had to be forwarded at the end of every harvest. At the year's end when the time of revenue collections closed, he would record balances due from every village and submit the records to the Collector along with a copy to be forwarded to the Royal Court. He had also to despatch daily the price-current of the *Mohurs*, rupees and other articles duly attested by the reliable persons. When relieved from office, he would submit detailed accounts of the balances and advances to the Collector as well to the Royal Court.[13]

References

1. Literally, *Bitikchi* means a writer or scribe. Enc. Isl.i, 734, Jarrett II. p. 50. Abul Fazl has used the term in two-fold sense, as an assessment officer (*Ain*, Br. M. 7652, fol. 144a, Hamilton, Berlin, fols. 121a-b) and also as an ordinary clerk (*Ain*, fols. 143a-b; fol. 120b). Here, *Bitikchi* stands for the Assessment Officer.
2. *Ain-i Khazana* (*Ain*, Hamilton, Berlin, fol. 6a) records, "Incorruptible *Bitikchis* were selected to assist them (*Karories*), and intelligent treasurers were appointed, one for each." (tr. Blochmann, I, p. 13). *Akbar Nama* (Br. M. O.R. Add. 26, 207, fol. 161b) in the 27th year's regulations of Todar Mal complains that the *Amils Guzar* of the *Khalsa* were maintaining a staff of two *Bitikchis* each, a *Karkun* and a *Khas Nawis*. As both of them were corrupt, being in collusion with the headmen of the villages, they oppressed the peasantry and that in future, in place of two, only one trustworthy officer be appointed as *Bitikchi*. As against this, *A.N.*, Br. M. Add. O.R. 27, 247, fol. 331b gives a different version. It states that the *Karori* or *Amal-i Khalsa* were maintaining two *Navindas* (writers), a *Karkun* and a *Khas Nawis*, who being in connivance with the *Chaudharies*, *Qanungos* and *Muqaddams* of the villages were responsible for heavy expenditure and consequent distress of the *ryots* and that in future only one trustworthy and honest person may be appointed. Hereafter, the practice of attaching only one *Bitikchi* with the *Amalguzar* was continued which is confirmed by *Ain-i Bitikchi*. *Tarikh-i Arif Qandhari* Ms. Rampur uses his designation in a non-technical sense as *Karkun* which is equally borne by the above statement of *Akbar Nama*. But in any case, the *Bitikchi* or *Karkun* attached with the *Karori* was a distinct official from that of a *Karkun* attached with the *Shiqdar* who acted under the authority of the former for the purposes of assessment. That the *Bitikchi* as an assessment officer had the territorial jurisdiction of a few *Parganas* under him is confirmed by *Akbar Nama;s* statement of the appointment of 14 *Bitikchi* in 38 *Parganas* of the *Sarkar* of Kashmir. (See ref. No. 16 under *Karori*). He had essentially identical territorial jurisdiction with the *Karori*.
3. The office of the *Bitikchi* (Assessment Officer) remained a part of the *Karori* administration till the reign of Shahjahan when he was replaced by the *Amin* and his office was completely separated from that of the *Karori*. Thereafter, he became exclusively an independent Assessment Officer and was divested of other executive functions narrated in *Ain*.
4. *Ain*, Br. M. Add., 7652, fol. 143b. Hamilton, Berlin, fol. 121b.
5. *Ibid.*
6. *Ibid.*, fols. 143b-144a; Hamilton, *Ibid.*
7. See *Munsif* and his staff under Survey and Measurement Party of the Pargana.
8. *Ibid.*
9. *Ibid.*, fol. 144a; *Ibid.*
10. *Farhang-i Kardani*, Ms. 83 Edinburgh, fol. 39b.
11. *Ain*, fol. 144a; *Ibid.*

12. The nature of these documents and his duties connected with them has been narrated in *Ain* (fol. 144a; fol. 121b) as explained in the above following passage.
13. *Ibid.*, fol. 144a; fol. 121b.

III. Pargana Administration

1. Pargana

The *Pargana* was an administrative and a fiscal territorial unit composed of few *Tappahs* and their respective *Mauzas* in its jurisdiction. The number of *Mauzas* in its jurisdiction varied from one *Pargana* to another. Its administrative headquarters were located at a big *qasba* after which the *Pargana* was named and was also the seat of official residence of the *Pargana* officials. The *Pargana* constituting the headquarters of the *Sarkar* division or the capital of a *Subah* was known as *Pargana Haveli.*[1] As inherited from the Afghan regime, the head of the *Pargana* administration was the *Shiqdar* who was both an administrator and a revenue officer. At times, though rarely, in a large *Pargana* inhabited especially by turbulent *ryots* or tribes, there were two *Shiqdars*, one each in-charge of a division of the *Pargana.*[2] The *Shiqdar* was assisted by various *Pargana* officials viz. (*Karkun*), (*Khazandar*) and *Munsif* and his staff of *Dabit*, *Jaribhash*, *Paimayandah*, *Thanadar* and *Tappahadars* who had all respective duties to perform under his supervision.[3] He himself was responsible to the *Amal Guzar* of *Khalsa* or to the *Jagirdar* if the *Pargana* was in an assignment.

Basing his interpretation on the *Ain-i-Amal Guzar* (Code of instructions to the *Amal Guzar*) in the *Ain-i Akbari*, Dr. Saran has reached the conclusion that the *Amal Guzar* was the revenue officer of the division of the *Sarkar* and that there was an *Amil* as the revenue official of the *Pargana.*[4] In the *Pargana* administration, the *Shiqdar* was the executive head of the general administration whereas the *Amil* was in-charge of the revenue department. The *Shiqdar* assisted the latter in the collection of the land revenue from recalcitrant cultivators. Dr. Qureshi has challenged Dr. Saran's thesis and concludes that the *Amal Guzar* was the head of the administration in the *Pargana* and that the offices of the *Amal Guzar*, the

Amil and the *Shiqdar* are the same.[5] Accordingly, the *Ain-i-Amal Guzar* relates the duties and functions of the *Shiqdar* as the head of the *Pargana* administration. Though Dr. Qureshi has rightly put the terms of the *Amal Guzar* and the *Amil* as synonymous, his identification of the latter with the *Shiqdar* is incorrect. He has based his analysis only on deductive inferences drawn from the *Ains* of *Amal Guzar*, *Bitikchi* and the *Khazanadar* of *Ain-i Akbari*.[6] But in view of the direct evidence available from the other sources of Akbar's reign and the documents of the Mughal age, neither of the opinions of Dr. Saran or that of Dr. Qureshi can be upheld.

Akbar Nama frequently uses the designations of *Amal Guzar* and *Amil* as interchangeable.[7] *Makatbat-i-Alami* of Abul Fazl in a *Dasturul aml* issued to the *Amils* and the *Mutsaddis* of the Empire, while explaining the obligations of the *Diwan* makes a clear reference to *Dasturulaml-i-Amil* which the context shows is evidently the same as *Ain-i Aml Guzar* of *Ain-i Akbari*.[8] At the same time, *Akbar Nama* for the implementation of its 27th year reforms of Todar Mal puts the *Amal Guzar* of *Khalsa* and the *Karori* as interchangeable officials in contrast to the *Jagirdar*.[9] The unit of *Pargana* could fall as much in the *Khalsa* administration as in the *Jagir* if given in assignment. If the *Amal Guzar* and the *Shiqdar* were to be the same official, how could the former be put in distinct contrast to the *Jagirdar* with separate spheres of administration? In the *Khalsa* administration, the *Shiqdar* represented the *Amal Guzar* who had usually much wider jurisdiction than a single unit of the *Pargana*. As further shown, the *Amal Guzar* of *Khalsa* was the same official as the *Karori*; as such the possibility of the *Amal Guzar* being the *Shiqdar* is completely ruled out. Even when, at times, the jurisdiction of the *Karori* came to be confined to a single *Pargana*, the office of the latter remained quite distinct from that of the *Shiqdar* who only assisted him in the revenue administration, while in case of an assignment of the entire *Pargana*, the *Shiqdar* acted on behalf of the *Jagirdar* who also possessed separate revenue staff under the charge as *Amil*. But undeniably, whether acting under the *Karori* of the *Khalsa* or *Jagirdar* and his *Amil*, the *Shiqdar* exercised the powers and the functions of an *Amil* in the *Pargana*[10] and was essentially a revenue officer. When his *Pargana* formed part of any *Jagir*, he was bound to safeguard the financial interests of the *Jagirdar* against any undue intrusion by any *Karori* of an adjacent *Khalsa* land.[11]

The *Ain-i Amal Guzar* is a comprehensive *Dasturulaml* for an act of revenue administration narrating the state policy and the principles guiding the *Amal Guzar* and the revenue officials in his jurisdiction. The functions narrated therein require on the part of the *Amal Guzar* and the revenue officers acting on his behalf an intimate contact with the cultivators and safeguarding their interests, extension of the agricultural land, the adoption of just procedure of survey and measurement, affording to the cultivators different methods of assessment, supervision over the staff for survey and measurement of land, the fixation of remunerations in accordance with the scales enumerated therein, getting the documents or 'record of rights' prepared by the village and the *Pargana* officials, the fixation of proper assessment on the cultivators, collection of the land revenue, management of the treasury, preservation of the records of various assignments along with their *Chaknamas*, enforcement of described code of conduct upon the officials under him, and to supply a full report on the condition of the people, assignees, matters relating to law and order and the market prices of the territories under his jurisdiction.[12]

Thus the *Ain-i-Amal Guzar* narrates not only the functions exclusive to the post of the *Amal Guzar* in person, but even those of the technical staff for survey and assessment and the revenue officials of the *Pargana* serving in his jurisdiction under his general supervision. The *Ain* equally serves as an instrument of instructions for all the revenue officials subordinate to the *Amal Guzar*, who were responsible for running the revenue administration with their specified respective duties and jurisdictions. As the *Shiqdar* was the revenue officer of the *Pargana* representing the *Amal Guzar*, many of the functions stated in the *Ain-i Amal Guzar* had to be performed by him. This accounts for the absence of a separate code of instructions for the *Shiqdar* in the *Ain-i-Akbari*. This equally accounts for the akinness of the various duties embodied in the *Ain-i Amal Guzar* with those required of the *Shiqdar* as narrated in *Ain-i Bitikchi* and *Ain-i Khazanadar*,[13] which has misled Dr. Qureshi to identify the *Shiqdar* with the office of the *Amal Guzar*.

References

1. *Mahzar-i Shahjahani*, p. 109 mentions two *Tappahs*, *Samjeh* and *Laka* in *Pargana* Lakut (*Sarkar* Sehwan, *Subah* Sindh) with *Shiqdar* each. Also on p. 163, two *Shiqdars* are mentioned for *Pargana* San (*Sehwan*). *Akbar Nama*, Br. M. Add. 26, 207, fol. 228b mentions Alla Bardi as the Shiqdar of Tappah Jajju (*Sarkar* Kashmir). Also *Swanih-i-Akbari*, fol. 85a uses the term '*Shiqdars* of the *Pargana*'. On the contrary, in a newly conquered territory, the *Shiqdar* as revenue administrator could as well be appointed with numerous *Parganas* under his jurisdiction. Though *Baharistan-i-Ghaibi* (N.B. Paris) ordinarily associates him with one *Pargana* only (fols. 5b, 96a, 290a), it also mentions (fol. 284a) Abdul Malik Seth as the *Shiqdar* of 14 *Parganas* stationed at Sunabazu (Dhaka, *Subah* Bengal) having presented a *Peshkash* of Rs. 1000 to Mirza Nathan's (author's) sister on his own behalf as well as that of the *Zamindars* of the *Parganas*. *Ain-i Akbari* and *Akbar Nama* do not show any specific jurisdiction with the *Shiqdar* but the later Persian chronicles. The English Factory records and the Jaipur Archives of the Mughal age clearly mention him with jurisdiction over one *Pargana* only (references quoted in the discussion on the duties of the *Shiqdar*).
2. As the *Shiqdar* was the revenue officer of the *Pargana* representing the *Amal Guzar*, all these officials described in the *Ain*, acted under his general supervision and control.
3. Saran, '*Provincial Government*', pp. 211-14.
4. Qureshi, 'The *Pargana* Officials under Akbar', *I.C.* January, 1942, pp. 87-93.
5. *Ibid.* pp. 89-93.
6. *Akbar Nama's* 30th year revenue reforms, Br. M. OR 26, 207, fols. 194a-b; Mr or quart 1822, Berlin, fols. 310b-312a. For its 27th year revenue reforms, Ms. Br. M. 26, 207 fols. 161b-163a; Ms. or. quart, 1822, Berlin, fols. 258b-260a. As against it, Ms. Br. M. Add. OR. 27, 247 for its 27th year reforms quite significantly throughout uses the term *Amali-Khalasa* in place *Amal Guzar-i Khalsa* as found in other versions.
7. *Makatabat-i Alami*, Ms. N.A. New Delhi, p. 95; *Insha-i Alami*, Ms. Orient. Oct. 1140, Berlin, fol. 42b. Another of such a general *Farman* of Akbar's reign dated 995 A.H. quoted in *Mirat-i-Ahemdi* vol. 1, p. 71 addressed to the *Mutsaddis*, Princes of the Royal blood, *Amirs*, *Mansabdars*, *Amils*, and *Kotwals*, also obliges the *Amils* to consult a separate *Dasturulaml* which in the context is presumably the same *Ain-i Amal Guzar* of *Ain-i Akbari*.
8. *A.N.*, Br. M. Add. 27, 247, fols. 331b-332b.
9. See discussion on Amal Guzar.
10. *Ain*, Br. M. Add. 7652 fols. 142a-143a; Ms. Hamilton I, Berlin, fols. 120a-121a.
11. *Ibid.*, fols. 143b-144b; and fols. 121b-122a respectively.
12. *The English Factories in India* (1618-21), p. 205.
13. *Ibid.*, pp. 204-05, 273, 294, 307.

2. Shiqdar

Both as an administrative and revenue officer of the *Pargana*, the *Shiqdar* had to perform multifarious duties. As such, his position remained the same throughout the Mughal age. In Jahangir's reign, the English Factory records mention him as the Governor of the *Pargana* with wide executive and fiscal powers.[1] He is portrayed with complete control over the market, the commercial transactions of the foreign traders, local artisans, weavers, traders and brokers.[2] Apart from this, he had police powers for the maintenance of law and order.[3] He executed the State policy and the day-to-day administration in the *Pargana.*[4] He was the custodian of the welfare and the prosperity of the *Pargana.*

As to his specific revenue duties, he had to look after the welfare of the *ryots* and the tenants and to fully safeguard their interests.[5] He had to encourage the extension of the agricultural land and to see that no tract of arable land undertaken by the *ryots* for cultivation remained uncultivated.[6] He was to encourage the cultivation of '*Jins-i Kamil*'[7] and also to see that through such measures, the revenues of the *Pargana* were augmented.[8] He was specially responsible for the administration of the *Madad-i-Maash* assignments.[9] *Mahzar-i Shahjahani* in the petition submitted to Shahjahan for the introduction of land revenue reforms in the *Parganas* of *Sarkar* Bhakkar (*Subah* Sindh) holds the *Shiqdar* entirely responsible for the realisation of the land revenue in the *Pargana.*[10] It even suggests that after the assessment has been made, the *Shiqdar* should get the *Jamabandi* (assessment) documents prepared *'Asamiwise'* (cultivator-wise) in his own presence so that the *Pargana* officials and dignitaries like the *Arbabs*, *Rais* and the *Qanungos* may not show their own dues in *Taujih* (Dues Ledger) in the name of the poor *ryots.*[11] *Makhzan ul Ihetsab* ascribes an important role to the *Shiqdar* in connection with the assessment, collection of the land revenue and the management of the treasury in the *Pargana.*[12] Though the *Amin* was responsible for the fixation of the survey and assessment, the *Shiqdar* had to accompany him on tour from village to village for the purposes of the inspection of the cultivated and un-cultivated areas of the villages. In consultation with the *Amin*, he had to devise ways and means for the extension of the agricultural land furthering the interests of both the State and the *ryots.* He had also to accompany him at the time of assessment of *Jamma* on the cultivators and had to recommend such of the *ryots* deserving moderate assessment and the *Taqavi* loans. He had to sign and stamp the final document assessment of *Siyaha Tashkhish* of the *Pargana*. The documents of *Pargana Taujih* were finally prepared by him and the *Karkun* at the *Chaabutra*, i.e. *Pargana* headquarters in the presence of the

Chaudharies, *Qanungos* and the *Muqaddams*. He could not transact such official business at his residence.

The *Shiqdar* was fully responsible for collection of the entire land revenue both for the *Kharif* and the *Rabi* crops. He would appoint certain honest and reliable persons as *Chakladars* and *Sitadar* (ad hoc circle collectors on commission basis) for the collection of the land revenue with the help of the *Tappahadars*, *Chaudharies* and the *Muqaddams* on the basis of the verified assessment documents. He had to make arrangements for *Sehbandi* i.e. detailing soldiers on cash or kind payment for assisting the *Chakladar* and the *Tappahadar* in the collection of the land revenue. The latter were to execute a bond to the effect that they would not employ any other soldiers for this purpose than those officially detailed. The 'ad hoc' circle collectors were to make collection from the *ryots* in fixed instalments without allowing a penny in arrears.

The *Shiqdar*, assisted by the *Karkun*, had full custody of the sub-treasury (*Fotahkhana*) management. The sub-treasury had to be essentially located at the residential premises of the *Shiqdar* or in a strong room with knowledge of the latter[13] as he bore full responsibility for its safety.[14] (The gate of the sub-treasury had two locks, the lower one of the *Karkun* and the upper one that of the *Shiqdar*). Both the *Shiqdar* and the *Karkun* had to be present in the sub-treasury throughout the period of realisation and (*Kharita*) had to be signed by each of them before they were deposited by the *Fotahdar* in the safe box under his personal lock. The *Shiqdar's* staff of the *Karkun* and the *Muharars* (clerks) had to prepare the daily accounts (*Roznamcha*) of the treasury in accordance with the regulations of the *Mustafi's* office. The daily receipt accounts had to be prepared month-wise. The *Shiqdar* had to despatch every week the amount of realisations duly escorted by the soldiers to the main treasury. The documents of realisation despatched had to be duly stamped by him and the *Karkun* along with the signature of the *Fotahdar*. For normal disbursement from the treasury, the prior sanction of the *Diwan* was necessary but he could incur an emergency expenditure on the recommendation of the *Fotahdar* and the *Karkun*. Such a case had to be intimated to the Government for confirmation.

References

1. *Mahzar-i Shahjahani*, pp. 38, 96. For such functions, he was responsible to the *Faujdar* or *Jagirdar* of his area.
2. *Akbar Nama*, Ms. Br. M. Add. 26, 207 fol. 147a mentions that in the 25th year census operations were carried out by the *Jagirdars*, *Shiqdars* and the *Daroghas*.
3. *Makatabat-i Alami* of Abul Fazl, N.A. New Delhi, p. 189 quotes a letter addressed to Mir Qawamud Din *Shiqdar*; Ms. no. Suppl. 482. N.B. Paris, fols. 158b-159a quotes a *Parwana* dated 1040 H appointing Khwaja Mukand Dass as *Shiqdar* of *Pargana* Batlai (*Sarkar* Surat); author *Parwana* of appointment fols. 169a-b. Also Durululm OR Walker 104 Bod. Oxford, fol. 137a quotes a Parwana dated 1096 Fasli (1686 A.D.) of appointment of Khwaja Sukha Nand vide transfer of Bhagwant Rai.
4. *Makhzanul Ihetsab*, Berlin, fol. 5b; Ms. Suppl. 482 N.B. Paris, fols. 30a, 161a; Durululm, Bod. Oxford fol. 137a.
5. *Makatabat-i-Alami.*
6. *Ibid.*; Ms. Suppl. 482 N.B. Paris, fols. 30a, 161a; Durululm Bod. Oxford, fol. 137a.
7. *Insha i Abdul Latif*, fols. 1b-3a.
8. *Mahzar-I-Shahjahani*, p. 22.
9. *Ibid.*, p. 18.
10. *Makhzanul Ihetsab*, Berlin, fols. 4b-7a gives a very comprehensive picture of the *Pargana* administration.
11. *Ain's* statement (Br. M. Add. 7652, fol. 144b. Ms. Hamilton I, Berlin, fol. 122a) for the prior approval and knowledge of the *Shiqdar* for the location of the sub-treasury is too general as according to the practice described above, it had essentially to be located in his guarded residential premises.
12. *Makhzanul Ihetsab*, Berlin, 6a.
13. *Ain*, Br. M. Add. 7652, fol. 144b; Ms. Hamilton I, Berlin, fol. 122a.
14. *Ibid.*

3. Zillah

During the Mughal rule in the 17th century, unlike the Chakla, a *Zillah* never acquired the character of a regular administrative unit of the *Subah* administration. The term '*Zillah*' connoted a direction of a territory[1] or a particular territorial block of a geographical or administrative region regardless of the latter's extent and size.[2] Usually, it meant a territorial circle comprising a few villages or a few *Parganas*.[3] But in general description, at times, a '*Zillah*' was considered coincidental in territorial extent with a *Chakla*[4] or a *Sarkar*[5] or even a still larger territory. Of course, it is evident from the working of the contemporary revenue administration that in some of the *Subahs*, a *Zillah* had become a regular fiscal region comprising inter-*Sarkar Parganas*.[6] The *Khalsa* or *Paibaqi Parganas* of the adjoining *Sarkars* could form one administrative circle (*Zillah*) under the charge of a revenue administrator for the purposes of assessment and collection of land revenue. It seems that the territorial jurisdiction of such an administrative circle (*Zillah*) was by no means fixed as it would vary either with the periodical transfer of the *Khalsa* vs. *Jagir Parganas* or even with the position of the revenue administrator entrusted with the administration of the *Khalsa* or *Paibaqi Parganas*. Quite distinct from such a wide jurisdiction of the *Zillah*, in some *Subahs*, a *Zillah* appears to be a fiscal territorial unit of a *Sarkar* division.[7] It was in the latter half of the 18th century that a *Zillah* underwent a further change in concept as to acquire a uniform administrative status. With the territorial reshuffling in the province of Bengal, a *Zillah* comprising a few *Parganas* became a regular territorial administrative unit in the *Sarkar* and the *Chakla* divisions.[8] It is only with the gradual spread of the British rule in North India in the 19th century that with further administrative changes, it became the basis of the district (*Zillah*) revenue administration.

References

1. Mohd. Warris, p. 69; Lahore I, p. 252 Mulakhas, fol. 259a; *Jahangir Nama* of Abdul Hassan, p. 140.
2. *A.N.* II, p. 281; *T.J.*, p. 109 *Chahar Chaman*, fol. 38b, Mohd. Sadiq 70, 150; Haft Anjman, Letter of Rustam Khan to Shahjahan; *Hadiq-ul aqalim*, fol. 59a; R.A.J. *Akhbarat* issued in the 44th R.Y. (Aurangzeb); Lubbut-*Tawrikh-i Hind*, fol. 84b; M.U. II., p. 319.
3. Ms. Br. M. Add. 6603, fol. 71b. This definition falls in line with even 17th century sources Mohd. Sadiq, p. 309 puts *Zillah Kola (Gola)* as a part of Bans Bareli (*Chakla* of *Subah* Agra). Isar Das, fol. 94a uses it for a *Qasba* in *Pargana* Atawa Dadr Cheh in Bundel Khand division. Also *Chahar Chaman*, fol. 38b; *Dasturul Insha* of Bigai Singh, fol. 344a.
4. *Amal Salih*, II, p. 345 associates it with Chakla Sirhind. Isar Das, fol. 139a puts *Zillah* Mathura which was in fact a *Chakla* division. R.A.J. Category 4 reg. no. 895 dated A.H. 1130/1718 puts '*Zillah Chakla Narnol*' as if identical in territory. *Guldasta-i Sukhan*, Ms. 876 Patna, fol. 169b puts *Zillah Kasbalk* (*Subah* Lahore) whereas *Ahkham*, p. 423 states it as a *Chakla*.
5. It also notes that the *Zillahs* were formed out of the erstwhile *Ghairamli* southern (*Uttari*) Parganas. *Kh.S.* N.A.I., p. 121 and other *Dasturulamls* count only 4 Sarkars with several Mahals in *Subah* Multan. *Kh.S.* Ms. Aligh., fols. 32a-b. shows the revenues of *Subah* Multan consisting of five *Sarkars* with further sub-divisions into 98 *Mahals* and 26 *Zillahs*. For four *Sarkars*, their *Mahal* divisions and the total revenues are given but for the fifth *Sarkar* viz. *Sarkar* Muazabad alias *Dera* 26 *Zillahs* and their total revenue is noted. Also Ms. '*Haqiqat Dami Wa Hasalat-i Mumalik-i Mahrusa*', dated A.H. 1130/1718 A.D., pp. 35, 38. Khwafi II, p. 281 associates *Zillah* with *Sarkar* Baklana (Deccan). Mamuri, p. 437 associates it with the whole division of Cooch Bihar consisting of 5 *Chaklas* with 89 *Parganas*. Also Khwafi II, pp. 137-38; *Mirat Suppl.*, p. 14 puts it for the territory of Sorath which was a *Sarkar* of *Subah* Gujrat.
6. R.A.J. Category no. 3 regd. no. 664 (Aurangzeb's reign). A memorandum (*Yaddasht*) gives details of the *Paibaqi Parganas* in *Zillah* Alamgirpur under the charge of Ahssan Ullah, the *Amin*. Alamgirpur was also one of the *Sarkars* in *Subah* Malwa. But the *Zillah* of Alamgirpur, though named after the *Sarkar*, comprises numerous inter-*Sarkar Paibaqi Parganas* drawn from four *Sarkars* viz. Alamgirpur, Chanderi, Sarangpur and Bijagarh (*Subah* Malwa). This shows that such a practice could have been prevalent in other *Subahs* as well.
7. Ms. Or. quart 258, fol. 144b; *Tarikh-i Bikermajit*, Ms. 2612 Patna, pp. 236-39; *Khulasatut Tawarikh* of Kalyan Singh, Ms. 594, Patna, fols. 65a-b.
8. *Dasturulaml Mustamil bar Dastur-i Badshahan*, Ms. 2489 Patna, fol. 19b.

4. Survey and Measurement Staff

Though the assessment of the *Pargana* was done by the *Bitikchi* (Assessment Officer) with jurisdiction over two to four *Parganas* under him,[1] he had survey and measurement staff posted in every *Pargana*. The *Munsif* or *Amin* was the official in-charge of the survey party in the *Pargana*. *Ain* mentions him with parallel jurisdiction along with the *Shiqdar* and the *Karkun*[2] and as such, he was a full *Pargana* Officer. *Ain-i Bitikchi* designates him as *Munsif* and holds him responsible to the *Bitikchi*.[3] *Ain-i Amal Guzar* states the perquisites of the *Munsif* which entirely tally with the perquisites of the *Amin* as in-charge of the survey party stated in *Akbar Nama*.[4] Later on while discussing the classification of the land, *Ain* itself makes an incidental reference to the *Amin* and states a new scale of payment for his measuring agents which entirely agree with the scale mentioned for the latter in *Akbar Nama*.[5] Evidently, Abul Fazl uses the terms of *Munsif* and *Amin* as synonymous. The *Amin* assisted by his subordinate survey staff was responsible for the measurement of both the cultivated and uncultivated arable fields, the preparation of the *Zabt* (Survey) records village wise incorporation in the details of the area for the matured as well as the failed crops.[6] Along with other officials, he had to attest for every village the survey documents of *Zabt* and *Muntkhib* prepared under his supervision.[7] Though the Survey documents prepared by him formed the basis of assessment and he had to assist the *Bitikchi* in the assessment work of the *Pargana*, the *Amin* in Akbar's reign was not the Assessment Officer. As such, the nature of his office differed from that of his predecessor under the Sur regime.[8] He had an establishment of Surveying staff consisting of a clerk (*Bitikchi*) a Land-Surveyor (*Jaribkash*) and four assessors named *Paimandan* or *Thanadars*.[9] The clerk (*Bitikchi* or *Navisinda* or *Zabit*)[10] prepared the drafts and the records of the villages surveyed. The Land-Surveyor (*Jaribkash*) was responsible for the actual conduct of operations with the help of the Surveyors. He had also to attest the *Zabt* (Survey) documents of the village.[11] The *Jaribkash* had a staff of four assessors (*Paimaindan* or *Thanadars*)[12] who conducted the actual survey and measurement operations. The *Amin* and his entire staff had to execute a bond to the effect that they would survey at least 250 *bighas* a day during the Rabi crop season when the days are long and 200 *bighas* a day during the *Kharif* crop season when the days are short.[13] As to their emoluments, Akbar enforced a regulation that the entire staff of *Commissairs* of the *Shiqdar*, *Karkun* and the *Amin* responsible for the Survey operations should be entitled to one *dam* per *bigha* surveyed.[14] Out of this budget, the *Amin* and his staff would get emoluments both in cash and kind on daily basis besides a monthly ration fixed for each member. According to the *Ain*, for every working day, the *Amin* and his staff would get 16 *dams* in cash and 31 *seers* (of wheat flour, oil and Grain) in kind.[15] Besides this, the entire staff would get a fixed monthly ration as per schedule.[16] *Amin*: 5 seers of wheat flour, ½ seer oil (ghee), 7 seers grain (for animals), 4 dams in cash for vegetables; *Bitikchi*: 4 seers of wheat flour, ½ seer oil, 4 seers grain, 4 dams for vegetables; *Jaribkash* and four *Thanadars* each: 8 seers of wheat flour, 1 seer oil, 5 seers grain and 5 *dams* for vegetables. Apart from the above establishment of the *Amin*, the *Commissairs* of the *Shiqdar* and the *Karkun* were expected to help the former in the survey and the measurement operations.[17]

References

1. See discussion on Bitikchi in this volume.
2. *Ain*, Br. M. Add. 7652, fol. 150b; Hamilton I Berlin, fol. 127a states the new scale of perquisites for the Commissaries of the *Shiqdar*, *Karkun* and *Amin* naturally equates them in their respective jurisdictional authority.
3. *Ain-i Akbari*, (*Ibid*., fol. 144a; fol. 121b) puts the *Munsif* as the head of the Surveying party whereas *Akbar Nama* (Br. M.O.R. 26, 207, fol. 163a) mentions the *Amin* as the head of the measurement party.
4. *Ibid*., fols. 143a-b; fol. 120b respectively. A.N.
5. *Ibid*., fol. 150b, fol. 127a; A.N. *Ibid*., fol. 163a.
6. *Ibid*., fol. 144a, fol. 121b; also *Khulasatus Siyaq*, Aligarh, fol. 12b.
7. *Khulasatus Siyaq*, Alighar fol. 12b quotes *Zabt* (Survey) draft of a village under the signatures of *Munsif*, *Karkun*, *Qanungo* and *Jaribkash*.
8. Under Shershah, the *Munsif* was an assessment officer of the entire *Pargana*. Under Akbar, the powers of assessment were vested with the Bitikchi. Dr. *Qureshi* has rightly identified the *Amin* with the *Munsif* (The *Pargana* Officials under Akbar, p. 93) but his assertion that the latter was also a *Pargana* assessment officer is incorrect.
9. *Ain*, fols. 143a-b, 144a; Hamilton, fol. 120b, 121b. As against the above statement of *Ain*, *Akbar Nama* (Br. M.O.R. 26, 207, fol. 163a) that the *Amin* had a staff of a writer (*Navisinda*) and three other persons. It seems that later on the number was increased and the version of *Ain* which was compiled later on has to be accepted as final.
10. Here *Bitikchi* in the *Ain* (fols. 143a-b, Hamilton 120b) stands for an ordinary clerk. In the latter sense, *Akbar Nama* (Br. M.O.R. 26, 207, fol. 163a) calls him as *Navisinda*. As in the present context, as a writer, he recorded the survey operations; he is also designated in *Ain-i Bitikchi* (fol. 144a, fol. 121b) as *Zabit*. Hence, in this context, *Abul Fazl* uses *Bitikchi*, *Navisinda* and *Zabit* as synonymous words. Dr. Qureshi's identification of *Zabit* with the *Munsif* as an assessment officer of the *Pargana* (*Pargana* Officials under Akbar, p. 93) is wrong as the *Ain* (fol. 144a, fol. 121a-b) within the same line of the passage requires the *Bitikchi* to note down the names of the *Munsif*, *Zabit*, *Jaribkash* and the *Thanadar*, thereby obviating any chance of these two officials holding the same office. Moreover, some of the original documents of *Madad-i Maash* assignments and sale deeds of the 17th century (M.U. Aligarh) bear the measured areas attested by the Surveying staff of the *Munsif*, the *Zabit*, the *Jaribkash*, the *Daroga* and the *Patwari*.
11. *Khulasatu-s Siyaq*, Aligarh, fol. 12b.
12. *Ain* in *Ain-i Bitikchi* (fol. 144a; fol. 121b) mentions *Thanadars* along with the *Jaribkash* whereas in *Ain-i Amalguzar* (fols. 143a-b; fol. 121b) associates *Paimainda* (i.e. a surveyor in the literal sense) with the *Jaribkash*. Here, the designation *Thanadar* is not used as a Police Official in-charge of a *Thana* acting under the *Faujdar* but as synonymous with *Paimainda*.
13. *Ibid*., fol. 150; fol. 127a; also A.N. Br. M.Ċ.R. 26, 207, fol. 163a.
14. *Ibid*; *Ibid*. Also see reference no. 17.
15. *Ibid*., fols. 143a-b; fol. 121b.

16. *Ibid.* As distinct from *Ain's* schedule of emoluments, *Akbar Nama* (Br. M.O.R. 26, 207, fol. 163a; Ms. or. quart 1822, Berlin, fol. 260a) gives a slightly different schedule. It mentions that instead of old charges, one *dam* per *bigha* of cultivation was fixed and out of this 24 *dams* were allowed to the measurement party. Their allowances were:- 15 *seers* flour at the price of 7 *dams*, 1¾ *seers* of butter (Roghan Zard i.e. Ghee) 5 *dams*, 2½ *seers* grain (for animals) 4 *dams*, cash 8 *dams*. Total 24 *dams*. Of this, the *Amin* would get 5 *seers* of wheat flour, ½ *seer* butter, 7 *seers* grain, 4 *dams* in cash. The writer (*Navsinda*), 4 *seers* wheat flour, ½ *seer* butter, 5½ *seers* grain, 2 *dams* cash; three servants (*Nafar*). In place of this word, A.N. Br. M.O.R. 27, 247, fol. 332b uses the term *Tanabkashan*). 6 *seers* of wheat flour, 3¼ *seers* butter, 3 *dams* in cash. It seems that the rates for the ration and the number of the assessors along with the *Jaribkash* were revised after the 27th year of Akbar's reign. *Ain* being compiled later on, its schedule may be accepted as final for Akbar's reign.
17. *Ain*, fol. 150b; fol. 127a.

5. Amal Guzar or Karori

Ain i Akbari describes in detail the duties of the *Amalguzar*. A minute study of '*Ain*' and *Akbar Nama* shows that the official designations of *Amal Guzar* and *Amil* are synonymous.[1] At the same time, *Akbar Nama* clearly distinguishes between the *AmalGuzar* of *Khalsa* and the *Jagirdar* with respective jurisdictions in different territories.[2] Apart from the assistance of the village and the *Pargana* officials, the *Jagirdar* had also his own staff for the land revenue collection under the charge of an *Amil*. But in due course of time, the designation of *Amil* came to be exclusively associated with the administration of the *Jagir* land whereas the *Amil* of the *Khalsa* land was known as *Karori*,[3] a term which remained in vogue throughout the Mughal period.

Origin of the Karori and the Karori Experimentation

The designation of the *Amil* (Collector) owes its inception to the 19th year of Akbar's reign.[4] The further need for the fixation of the *Jamma* based on *Hal-i-Hasil* for the purposes of assignments, the desire to eradicate corrupt practices of the assignees and discontentment amongst them,[5] the betterment of the condition of the *ryots* and the '*Madad i Maash*' assignees, and above all the extension of the cultivable area and the augmentation of the finances of the Royal treasury led to an extremely important experiment in the evolution of the land revenue administration.[6] The entire Imperial territories in Northern India excepting Bengal, Behar and Gujrat were declared as *Khalsa* lands.[7] In these territories, 182 expert *Amils* were appointed, each *Amil* being responsible for the administration of a territorial circle of *Parganas* and villages yielding an average one crore of *Tankas* of revenue – a fact which gave the *Amil* of the *Khalsa* land the popular name of a *Karori*.[8] A staff of two officials, a *Karkun* and a *Fotahdar* were attached with him.[9] The *Karori* was entrusted to get surveyed all the cultivated and uncultivated land of the villages, towns and *Parganas* under him, to get their boundaries demarcated and areas recorded, to get recorded the areas of all the cultivable land and see that all such land was brought under cultivation within a period of three years.[10] He was to make genuine efforts for the extension of agriculture. For the realisation of land revenue, he had to get the assessment done for both the *Rabi* and *Kharif* crops based on the principle of justice and righteousness while giving a special margin for the failed crops. He had to prepare a full list of the areas with the rent-free assignees and the other *ryots*. He had to make a full report on the condition of the *ryots* in his *Parganas* and to see that the stronger of the *ryots* should not oppress the poor ones. He would deposit the collections of the land revenue of his circle in the Royal Treasury.[11] Thus based on the reports of the *Karories*, a consolidated estimate of the total cultivable assessed areas and the *Jamma* was to be prepared. Despite the royal proclamation for strict enforcement of these regulations, the experiment proved to be a failure. Badauni points out the complete breakdown of this measure resulting in the tyranny of the *Karories* over the *ryots* and the ultimate chatisement of the *Karories* themselves at the hands of Todar Mal.[12]

Even though the plan of a *Karori* as colonising officer cum revenue collector with a territorial jurisdiction of one *Karor* of *Tankas* was surrendered, his office continued to be in existence. He finds a very frequent mention in *Akbar Nama's* 27th year's and 30th year's respective revenue regulations of Todar Mal and Fatah Ullah Shirazi as well as in the revenue literature of the 17th century.[13] But the extent of his jurisdiction and the nature of his obligations changed. Henceforth, the *Amal Guzar* of the *Khalsa* land was designated as *Karori* responsible not essentially for the collection of one *Karor* of *Tankas* but as the collector of the revenues of a few *Parganas* or even a single *Pargana*. The *Karori's* office has so far baffled the writers on the Mughal administration. Though Dr. Saran recognises the survival of his office as the revenue collector after the failure of the 19th year experiment of Akbar's reign, he has made no attempt to analyse his jurisdiction and functions and has failed to recognise his synonymity with the *Amal Guzar* of *Khalsa*. He wrongly takes the latter to be the revenue officer of the full division of the *Sarkar*.[14] Dr. Qureshi, on the other hand, is equally mistaken in identifying the *Amal Guzar* with the *Shiqdar* of the *Pargana*.[15] The main difficulty with both of these writers has been that they have rigidly tried to fit in the territorial jurisdictional authority of the officers stated in the *Ain* either with a *Pargana* or full division of the *Sarkar* and have omitted to analyse *Ain-i-Akbari* in connection with *Akbar Nama*, other contemporary sources of Akbar's reign and the revenue literature of the early 17th century. *Ain* is silent on the fact of the territorial jurisdiction of the *Amal Guzar*. At the same time, it stresses an intimate contact of the latter with the cultivators and the revenue administration of the villages.

Ordinarily for the purposes of land revenue assessment and collection, the numerous *Parganas* of the division of the *Sarkar* were divided into well-defined revenue circles, some of the latter reserved in the *Khalsa* administration, others given in assignment to the *Jagirdars*.[16] Though a few of the *Parganas* may be kept exclusively in the *Khalsa* administration, invariably in others, even within one *Pargana*, a few villages would be given in assignment. Thus for the purposes of the revenue collection, the *Parganas* or *mauzas* when assigned, were entrusted to the *Jagirdar* and his personal revenue staff whereas the exclusive *Khalsa Parganas* or the non-assigned villages of a *Pargana* were left under the administration of *Karories*. A *Karori* would have the territorial jurisdiction over a circle comprising usually of two to four *Parganas* and even sometimes on a single exclusive[17] *Khalsa Pargana* with large revenues. The territorial jurisdiction of every *Karori* was by no means uniform as it would essentially depend upon the approximate amount of the land revenue of the area in one circle and as well on the administrative convenience necessitated by the geographical features of the revenue circles. Such *Khalsa* revenue circles under *Karories* once parcelled out within the *Sarkar* division were usually continued though transfers from the *Jagir* to the *Khalsa* and vice versa resulted both in the 'ad hoc' and permanent reshuffling of the same.[18] All the same, in a circle whether with a few *Parganas* mixed with assignments or a single exclusively *Khalsa Pargana*, it was always possible for the *Karori* to keep in direct touch with the cultivators, the village and the *Pargana* officials for the revenue administration of his circle.[19]

As to his functions, the *Amal Guzar* of *Khalsa* or the *Karori* was the Chief revenue officer of a revenue circle of a few *Parganas* or a single large *Pargana*. He was responsible for the general superintendence of the land revenue administration of his circle. As such, the *Shiqdars* and the other *Pargana* and village officials in his circle worked under his directions and were responsible to him. If his circle covered only one large *Pargana*, he was the ex-officio head of the *Pargana* administration while the *Shiqdar* and other *Pargana* officials acted as his subordinates. For his circle, *Ain i Amal Guzar* quotes various duties and responsibilities for the *Karori* in the reign of Akbar. The *Ain i Amal Guzar* is a comprehensive *Dasturulaml* for an act of revenue administration narrating the State policy and the principles guiding the *Amal Guzar* and the revenue officials in his jurisdiction.[20] The functions narrated therein require on the part of the *Amal Guzar* and the revenue officials acting on his behalf an intimate contact with the cultivators and safeguarding of their interests, extension of agricultural land, the adoption of just procedure of survey and assessment, affording the cultivators different methods of assessment supervision over the staff for survey and measurement of land, the fixation of the latter's remunerations in accordance with the scales enumerated therein, getting the documents of the record of rights prepared by the villages and the *Pargana* officials, the fixation of proper assessment on the cultivators, collection of the land revenue, management of the treasury, preservation of the records of various assignments along with their *chaknamahs* (boundary demarcations), enforcement of prescribed code of conduct upon the officials under him, to supply a full report on the condition of the *ryots*, assignees, matters relating to law and order and the market prices of the territories under his jurisdiction.

At his headquarters, the *Karori* was always assisted by a *Bitikchi* (Assessment officer and Revenue Accountant) and a *Fotahdar* (Treasurer).[21] The *Bitikchi* was the assessment officer of the circle, subordinate and responsible to the *Karori*. Although the two officials enjoyed distinct offices, the *Karori* had the general powers of superintendence and control over the survey and assessment work of the *Bitikchi*. This accounts for the duplicate enumeration of such duties both in the *Ain i Amal Guzar* and the *Ain i Bitikchi*.[22] Both the officers are entrusted with the supervision and management of survey and assessment, the entry of assessment abstract in the village accounts, despatch of the assessment statements and then reports to the Imperial Court. Apart from it, the *Karori* was responsible for the collection of the land revenue on the basis of the assessment documents (*Tumar Jama Bandi*) prepared by the *Bitikchi* and his staff. As such, the entire machinery of collection of the villages and the *Pargana* explained hitherto, viz. the *Muqaddams*, *Chaudharies*, *Tappahdars* and the *Shiqdars* in his circle assisted him in the collection of the land revenue. All the revenues collected in his circle were to be essentially deposited in the treasury,[23] (*Fotah Khana*) for which he was always held personally responsible and had to execute a bond to that effect on his appointment. He had also to supervise and keep a vigil with utmost care over the working of the treasury stationed at his headquarters under the charge of the *Fotahdar*. He had to vigorously enforce the treasury regulations both on the husbandman and the treasury officials. The husbandman had to make payment in full weight but he had to be issued a receipt for whatever denomination of money he might bring. The collections were made by the revenue officials; they had to be deposited by them in the treasury and the receipts for the same had to be issued in favour of the *ryots*.[24] The sale-proceeds of the land revenue collected in kind and entered in the village and the *Pargana Tanjih* (realisation and balance ledger) were also to be deposited in the treasury and the receipts had to be issued in favour of the *ryots*. In case of any lapse for the issue of receipts, if any of the *ryots* claimed to have made the payment, the onus of the amount involved would entirely rest on the *Karori* and his officials.[25] For the purposes of receipt of revenues from the *ryots*, the *Karori* and the *Fotahdar* had to abide by the schedule of coinage of different denominations, old and new, and the ratio of their respective weights as enforced by the officers of the Royal mint and the Royal treasury.[26] After the collection of two lacs of *dams* in the treasury, the amount had to be despatched in the hands of the trusted agents to the royal treasury.[27] He was responsible for the monthly despatch of the account of the daily receipts and expenditure to the Imperial office.[28] During the period of assessment, the *Bitikchi's* office working under him, had to despatch weekly reports on the abstracts of the village assessments duly attested by the village *Patwari* and the *Pargana Karkun.*[29] At the end of every season, he had to send the details of revenue demand (*Jama*), realisations and arrears of each village in his jurisdiction. Moreover, a yearly abstract statement of the total income and expenditure was sent by him to the Imperial Office.[30] After the collections were over, he settled the accounts of the *Muqaddams, Chaudharies* and *Tappahdars* and paid their remunerations on the collections made.[31]

Above all, the *Karori* had to protect the interests of the *ryots* and had to show them utmost consideration.[32] He had to carefully watch the minutest details of the assessment and collection of the revenues at every harvest.[33] He had to see that the assessment on them was done with extreme caution and moderation in accordance with the regulations.[34] He was enjoined to make revenue collections strictly in accordance with the *Dasturul aml* and not to allow realisation of any illegal cesses or customary dues from anybody.[35] If any of his underlings realised more money than agreed upon in the assessment abstract, the excess amount was to be reckoned as a regular revenue and had to be reimbursed in the accounts of the concerned cultivator whereas the realising official was to be punished.[36] Any over-realisation through omission was also to be carried to the account of the next year and no second demand was to be made for it.[37] Any amount collected by the revenue officials from the *ryots* on account of joint village expenses (*Malba*) was to be deducted from the revenue demand.[38] In case any of the villages fell victim to a natural calamity, the *Karori* had to make a personal inspection and assessment of the loss in every field and to forward the abstract of remissions on the damaged land along with the code of regulations to the Imperial Office for appropriate sanction.[39] In case of excessive rains too, he had to give remission in accordance with the regulations.[40] The *Karori* was always especially enjoined to put in the best of efforts for improving the agricultural condition of the cultivators, to extend the culturable areas, to bring all existing cultivable land under cultivation and thereby to augment the State revenues of the villages and the *qasbas* from year to year.[41] As a safeguard against the diminishing of the cultivable areas, every year a consolidated statement of the total cultivable land of every *Pargana* and in possession with every cultivator was to be prepared. If comparison with the previous statement showed any decline in agriculture in any of the villages, the *Karori* had to conduct a full enquiry on the spot in the affected village. He would get every kind of land of the village, yielding one crop or two crops a year, surveyed afresh and would analyse the reasons for decline. If the cultivators had deserted the land due to his own oppression or any of his *Chaudharies* or *Muqaddams*, he was to be held accountable for it whereas the deserting *ryots* had to be exempted from the payment of the revenues. The report of his enquiry along with his recommendations had to be forwarded to the Imperial office.[42] The *Karori* and his staff had to tour every village and having taken note of the condition of the cultivators would depute agents to see that the fields were sown according to the understanding and that the cultivators should not leave any *Bigha* and *biswa* of cultivable land uncultivated.[43] He would appoint *Tappahdar* in every *Tappah* to look after the agricultural development of every village.[44] Full efforts were to be made for the extension of the cultivation of the high grade crops (*Jinsi Kamil*) and the needy cultivators who were either without seeds or oxen (for cultivation) were to be given agricultural loans[45] which were to be recovered by the *Muqaddams* in instalments at the time of the *Kharif* and the *Rabi* crops.[46] The *Karori* was forbidden to interfere in the Jagir administration of any of the assignments adjacent to his territory. He had to maintain in his office the record of the revenue documents pertaining to Abstract of Income (*Roznamcha-i-Tahsil*), additional income as compared to the past (*Roz Afzun Tahsil*); half yearly and full yearly village and Pargana assessment and balance of realisations (*Jama Wasil Baqi or Hisab*), regulations of the treasury with the signature of the *Qanungos* (*Dasturul aml Fotah Khanna*), individual village ledger (*Awrija Dahi Badehi*), total income and expenditure (*Mujmil* or *Goshwarai Awrija*), income and expenditure of the Treasurer (*Jama-Kharch i Tahvil Fotahdar*), copy of the abstract of the assessment of the villages (*Naqal i Sihaya i Tashkish wa Jamabandi i Dehat*), the village-wise security bonds of the *Muqaddams* (*Tamaskat-i-Zamni i Muqaddam Dehi Badehi*), and copy of the income, expenditure and arrears on account of the revenue administration of the previous *Karori*.[47]

Apart from the revenue administration, the *Karori* also exercised authority over the law and order situation in the villages. He had to deal with such of the turbulent persons living in the ravines who refused to pay their land revenue and sought protection on the jungles or forts or channels. He had even to protect the *ryots* of the neighbouring territories from such miscreants. He would first administer warning to such persons and demand the compensation for the damages. If despite this, they persisted in resistance, he would seek help from the *Faujdar* and devastate their hide-outs as well as their agricultural fields. Intimation for such an action had to be sent to the Auditors (*Mustaffis*) for not making a demand of revenue on this account. Even such of the persons who gave protection to the thieves and miscreants were to be punished.[48] The *Karori* had full authority over the *Muqaddams* even for the protection of the *ryots* or the foreigners against thefts and crimes. He could call the *Muqaddams* at his headquarters and take them to task for any negligence or connivance with such crimes.[49] For the reign of Jahangir, there is evidence to show that at times, his office was combined with that of the *Faujdar*.[50]

As to his remunerations, the *Karori* was entitled to 10% of the collections made in his circle, half of which could be paid in the shape of an assignment.[51] His emoluments were to be paid in four instalments and the last (fourth) instalment was to be withheld by the Auditors in case of arrears in the collections under his charge. This position of the salary was to be released only when the authorities were satisfied that arrears were not due to lack of efforts on his part but either because of the desertion of the *ryots* or because of his untimely removal from the charge.[52] He could debit the cost of the despatch of the accounts of the former Collector and of his subordinates on his expenditure side. He was to be paid his salary for the period spent in the *Pargana* for collection of the arrears even after his removal from the charge. He was entitled to pay any travelling allowances for the period he spent at the Court after his transfer or removal from office.[53] All such persons appointed on *'ad hoc'* basis for helping the *Karori* for the realisations were to be paid for the period they worked.[54] His footmen agents (*Paida*) for collection were to be paid equal in number to the troopers or to the half thereof.[55]

The position and obligations of the *Karori* required of him through the official instructions show that under Akbar, he was 'the Mughal-Maid' of all revenue work and much of the working of the land revenue machinery at the local level rested on his vigilance and integrity. In the initial stages after the creation of his office, the *Karori* administration was not free from corruption and malpractices. However, Badauni's scathing criticism of the administration of the *Karories* characterised by excessive demand, fraudulent practices in revenue collection, the oppression on the *ryots* and the sale of their wives and children for the recovery of land revenues[56] is a plain rhetoric exaggeration and cannot be substantiated by any other contemporary evidence. All the same, the substance of his charges of dishonest and malpractices on the part of the *Karories* cannot be brushed aside. Even after the surrender of the 19th year *Karori* experiment, his office as the Chief revenue officer and the Collector is not free from blemishment. Though the 27th year Revenue Regulations of Todar Mal deal with the inherent shortcomings in the working of the local revenue administration, they clearly point towards the former malpractice of over-realisation from the *ryots* by the revenue staff of the *Amal Guzar*.[57] They equally note that the diminishing in agriculture could as well be due to the oppression of the *ryots* on the part of the *Karori* or *Chaudhari* or *Muqaddam* leading to the desertion of the land and abscondance of the cultivators.[58] The repeated insistence for the issue of the receipts to the *ryots* for the revenues deposited in the treasury, failing which the responsibility of the amount involved to be owned by the revenue officials[59] casts doubt on the previous cases of misappropriation of the revenues and duplicate charges from the *ryots*. The new regulations issue comprehensive instructions to the *Karori* relating to matters of survey and assessment, collection of the land revenue, treasury management, coinage regulations, staff organisation of the *Karori* and law and order in the *Parganas*. Though all these have already been noted in the functions of the *Karori*, taken as a whole, they provide procedural safeguards for the protection of the interests of the *ryots* and aim at the betterment of the administration both under the *Karories* and the *Jagirdars*. Despite these regulations, the position and the administration of *Karori* was by no means perfectly stable. Moreover, old cases of revenue administration still in arrears since the time of Muzaffar Khan (presumably since 22nd year) required immediate settlement.[60] So after a short span of three years, i.e. in the 30th year, another report was prepared by Amir Fath Ullah Shirazi who was specially deputed as the Imperial Commissioner (*Aminal Mulk*) for this purpose.[61] This report corrects some of the flaws and omissions of the previous one. It introduces further changes in the Audit and Accounts procedure, safeguards the interests of the *ryots* through moderation of the procedure of assessment and clarification of the dues to be paid by them. At the same time, it improves the financial status of the *Karori* and facilitates the smooth working of his administration. It strictly directs the revenue clerks to be extremely careful in making correct entries of the arrears of the land revenue from the *ryots* as in the past ever since the 19th year, excessive entries of the arrears based on guess work were made and ultimately 1/6th or 1/5th of the balance had to be settled for payment.[62] It also states that the past rule of the rendering of the accounts by the revenue clerks based on the list of receipts issued to the *ryots* by the receiving revenue official had been violated and has led to misappropriation of the amounts by the *Amal Guzar* of *Khalsa* from the realisations made from the cultivators. It directs that in future, the receipt ledger be prepared in duplicate, one by the *Karori* and another by the Clerk independently.[63] It also states that hitherto the accounts of the *Karories* had been prepared on the basis of complete revenue year (*Sal i Kamil*) or on the basis of the *Karori* documents (*Nuskha i Karor Bandi*) written by hasty and inconsiderate persons which had led to the imprisonment of various officials. It directs that in future, the documents should be prepared on the basis of the current year (*Sali Paiwasta*).[64] It also complains that due to the negligence of the *Amil Ghuzars*, their agents have through oppression realised unwarranted amounts from the cultivators. It directs that in future, all realisations made by them should be compared with the authentic original ledger of the *Patwari* (*Kaghazi Kham i Patwari*) and that they should account for the collections made from the *Qanungos* and the *Muqaddams*.[65] It also directs that for the purposes of checking, one *Qanungo* from each *Pargana* should be deputed for the Central Government, that the accounts of the arrears shown by the former collector should be scrutinised thoroughly and that at the Central Government, a special news-writer (*Waqia Navis*) was to be deputed for correspondence with the agents of the Collectors.[66] The report also deals with the important aspects of the extension of the cultivation, relief in assessment on the *ryots*, the better conditions of pay and allowances for the Collector and more conciliatory attitude towards him,[67] which have all been stated in the functions and remunerations of the *Karori*.

In essence, all this period from the 19th year to the 30th year of Akbar's reign is a formative one with various trials, errors and reshufflings for the organisation of the local administration under the *Karori*. The official sources of *Akbar Nama* and *Ain-i-Akbari* themselves admit the omissions and shortcomings during this period. But after the 30th year, with the rigid enforcement of the improved revenue regulations, the local administration under the *Karories* acquired stability and ran smoothly. *Ain* gives a consolidated and sound picture of the administration. Neither *Akbar Nama* nor any other contemporary chronicle narrates any more innovatory administrative measure or complaint about the revenue administration of the local government. All later sources, even the officials documents, bestow praise on the successful operation of Akbar's administration and look back upon it as an ideal one for emulation.[68] All the same, the administrative machinery always needed some tightening up of any laxity on the part of the revenue officers. Jahangir, in one of his regulations issued on his accession to the throne, promulgated that the *Karories* and the *Jagirdars* should not forcibly dispossess the *ryots* of their land and should not convert it as their own for the purposes of cultivation.[69] In Jahangir's reign, the English Factory Records bear testimony to the smooth and stable running of the administration under *Karories*.[70]

References

1. *Ain*, Br. M. Add. 7652, *Ain-i-Amal Guzar, Ain-i-Bitikchi, Ain-i-Khazanadar*, fols. 142a-144b; Ms. Hamilton I, Berlin, fols. 120a-122a. *Akbar Nama's* 30th year revenue regulations, Br. B.O.R. 26, 207, fols. 194a-195a, Ms. Or. Quart 1822 Berlin, fols. 310b-312a. For 27th year revenue regulations, see fols. 161b-163a and fols. 258b-260a respectively. Ms. Br. M.O.R. 27, 247 for its 27th year reforms quite significantly throughout uses the term *Amal-i-Khalsa* instead of *Amal Guzar-i-Khalsa* as found in other versions.
2. *A.N., Ibid.*
3. In *Tuzuk-i-Jahangiri*, Ms. Orient. Oct. 101, Berlin, fol. 24b, Jahangir comments, "The *Amil* of *Sarkar Khalsa* is known as *Karori*. As my father in his earlier years (of administration) entrusted the revenues of a territory yielding one *Karor* of *dams* to one person (for realisation), on that account, the latter was called *Karori* and accordingly by way of custom, even now he is called *Karori*."
4. *A.N.*: Br. M. Add. 27, 247, fols. 270b-271a.
5. *Ibid.*
6. *Tarikh-i-Arif Qandhari*, Ms. *Tarikh-i-Farsi*, no. 415(K) pp. 178-79. *Tabaqat-i-Akbari* (Br. M. Or. 2274 fol. 203 in collation with Br. M. Add. 6543, fol. 238 states, "since much of the land of Hindustan was uncultivated and fallow, and was capable of being cultivated in the first year, to the advantage and profit alike of the peasants and the State, the Emperor after careful consideration ordered that the arrears of the *Parganas* of the Empire should be examined, and that the extent of land which, after cultivation, would yield one *Karor* of *tankas* should be separated off, and entrusted to an official. That official was to be designated *Karori*, and sent to the *Pargana* with a clerk and treasurer, so that by his efforts and exertions the uncultivated land should be brought under cultivation, and the correct demand realised." (Moreland's tr. 'Agrarian System', p. 102, with certain adaptations).

   Moreland in his discussion on the motives for the appointment of the *Karories* (Agrarian System, pp. 100-09) ascribes two versions–official and non-official. According to him, *Akbar Nama* affords view point and that the object was to remove the causes of dissatisfaction which was ruining the morale of the Imperial Service'. The second unofficial and creditable version is given by *Badauni* as well as Nizamud Din's *Tabqat-i-Akbari* which emphasise the object of the extension of cultivation, benefiting the peasants and increasing the revenue. He takes these two versions conflicting with each other and is inclined to believe only official view-point which he calls less creditable version, in the sense that the direct cause of the change was, in fact, Akbar's determination to put the remuneration of the Imperial Service on a more satisfactory basis'. Moreland also suggests that Akbar and the Revenue Ministry were divided in their opinions. Whereas Akbar's mind is represented by *Akbar Nama*, the Revenue Ministry in order to credit itself, introduced another motive which is well represented by unofficial sources. Later on, *Akbar Nama* omitted to mention the above controversy as it had passed into a dead point of history but, however, the view of the Ministry found expression in unofficial sources.

All this discussion on Moreland's part of the so-called official and unofficial viewpoints is irrelevant and lacks proper understanding of the nature of the reforms. There is no denying that *Akbar Nama* in the 18th year brings out some difference of opinion on the proposed Branding System between Akbar and Muzaffar Khan, the Vakil. Abul Fazl accuses the latter for his ingratitude and arrogance but does not state the exact points involved in controversy on the issue. (A.N. Beveridge). At the same time, he states that Akbar was fully supported by Todar Mal, the Finance Minister. Rai Ram Dass was appointed as *Naib Diwan* to Todar Mal. The reforms were actually carried out in the 19th year and Abul Fazl in his introduction to these reforms brings out both the motives, the regulation for the Army along with the welfare of the peasantry and the prosperity of the country. On the first point of the reorganisation of the services and the grades, he points out the unfair practice of the assignments based on undependable revenues of the areas which consequently led to corrupt practice on the part of some and discontentment among the losers. Consequently, the entire lands were declared *Khalsa* and the State servants were put on monthly cash salaries. After this, secondly though briefly, Abul Fazl takes up the points of the appointment of the *Karories* in the *Khalsa* lands for the land revenue collection, the regulation of the measurement for the increase of cultivation and the introduction of iron-ruged Bamboo Tarile. Apparently, though Abul Fazl gives priority to the question of the Imperial Services, he distinctly mentions the *Karori* experiment and the measurement reform. All the same, the crux of the problem remains that the maladjustment in the '*Hal-i-Hasil*' and the areas assigned had been at the bottom for trouble which led to the Karori experiment and the revenue reforms. Though it was a purely agrarian problem, it was essentially linked up with the assignment of the State servants and the troops to be maintained by them. In its chapter on '*Ain-i-Khazana*', *Ain-i-Akbari*, (Blochmann), Abul Fazl takes up only the financial and administrative aspects unconcerned with any problem of the Services personnel, i.e., the betterment of the condition of the *ryots*, the need for increase of the Royal revenues, the segregation of the *Jagir* and the *Khalsa* which demanded the appointment of the *Karories*. Here, he associates the idea with Ihetmad Khan – a fact not mentioned in *Akbar Nama*. However, by no means, Abul Fazl ignores the importance of the *Karori* experiment as a distinct agrarian reform though in *Akbar Nama*, he has been quite brief and general on this aspect. Moreover, though Mutamid Khan – an official historian of Jahangir – for his historical portion on Akbar's reign has mostly followed the pattern of *Akbar Nama*, is much more explicit on this point and puts the title of the reforms as, "Regulation of the Branding, (*Dagh*), the reorganisation of the '*Jamma*' of the Empire, and the appointment of the *Khalsa Amils* known as *Karories*." In his introduction of the reforms, emphasising the motives of the betterment of the condition of the *ryots* and the solution of the long-standing problem of the '*Jamma*' and '*Hal-i-Hasil*', he describes the introduction of the *Jarib* reform, the conversion of the land into *Khalsa*, the appointment of the *Karories* for the collection of the revenues, and lastly mentions the measures for the payment of the soldiers and the branding system. '*Tarikh-i-Arif Qandhari*' – a contemporary account of

Akbar's reign in its comprehensive description of these revenue reforms takes up the *Karori* experiment as a purely agrarian measure aimed at the betterment of the condition of the ryots and the *Madad-i-Maash* assignees. He mentions the problem of the branding of the horses as an independent one. Arif Qandhari's viewpoint, supported by Badauni and Nizamud Din, cannot be brushed aside as a secondary one. Hence, Moreland's discrimination between the official and the non-official versions is completely imaginary and false.

7. *A.N.*, Br. M. Add. 27, 247, fol. 271a. It states that in Northern India, the provinces of Bengal, Bihar and Gujrat were not included in this measure out of foresight whereas the territories of Kabul, Qandhar, Ghazni, Kashmir, Tatta, the tracts of Bajaur and Tira, Bangash, Sorath and Orissa had not been conquered so far. Mutamid Khan in *Iqbal Nama*, Ms. Rampure, Vol. II, p. 463 with a little different version, comments that the territories of Gujrat, Sorath, Behar, Bengal and Orissa were exempted from this measure as they were border states. *Tarikh-i-Arif Qandhari*, p. 179, names only the *Khalsa* declared territories stating that, "from the borders of Jaunpur and Benaras to the Indus river, Multan and Lahore, all were declared *Khalsa* and the *Jagir* was entirely abolished."
8. *Ibid.*
9. *Tarikh-i-Arif Qandhari*, p. 178.
10. *Ibid.*
11. *Ibid.* All the functions of the *Karori* described in the above passage have been noted from the same source.
12. *Muntkhab-ut-Tawarikh*, Ms. Elliot 248, Bod. Oxford, fols. 257b-258a; tr. Lowe, pp. 192-93.
13. *A.N.* Br. M.O.R. Add. 27, 247, Br. M.O.R. 26, 207, fols. 161b-163a; 194a-b and Ms. Or. quart. 1822, Berlin, fol. 310b-312a. For 17th cent. *Tuzuk-i-Jahangiri*, Ms. Orient. Oct. 101 Berlin, fol. 24b; The English Factories in India (1622-23), pp. 250-54. Also see *Karori* under Shah Jahan's administration.
14. Saran: '*Provincial Government*', pp. 284-87, 296-97.
15. Qureshi, 'The Pargana Officials under Akbar', pp. 87-93.
16. For Jahangir's reign, *Baharistan-i-Ghaibi* (Ms. Suppl. Pers. 252, B.N. Paris, fol. 145b) gives a direct evidence for such a plan for revenue collection. It states that after the conquest of Kuch, Abdu's-Salam was appointed there as the Commander of the Army with Mirza Hasan Mashhadi as his Diwan and Bakshi. The latter was ordered to arrange for the collection of revenues in the *Parganas*. The aforesaid Mirza, due to his great experience, divided the *Parganas* of Kuch territory into twenty well-defined circles. Some of the lands were given to *Mustajirs* (Revenue Farmers) by taking deed of acceptance from them for those *Parganas*." (tr. Borah, pp. 272-73). At another place, fol. 53a, it refers to the divisions of a conquered territory amongst the *Karories*, *Jagirdars* and *Zimmidars*. For Akbar's reign, not many references for *Mustajirs* (Revenue Farmers) can be traced but assignments were too common. *Akbar Nama* 9Br. M. Add. 26, 207, fol. 303a) also gives a clear

reference to the practice of the division of the *Parganas* of the *Sarkar* into regular and well-defined revenue circles for the purposes of survey and assessment which were presumably the circles for the revenue collection as well. As a relief against the oppression of the assignees in Kashmir, a new revenue regulation was enforced in the 42nd year of Akbar's reign. The entire territories of the Sarkar of Kashmir (*Subah* Kabul) were divided into 14 divisions and in every division, two *Bitikchis*, an Irarnian (Persian knowing) and an Indian (Hindi knowing) were appointed to prepare survey records of cultivated and uncultivated lands from the original village documents (*Kaghaz-i-Kham*) and to make assessment of the areas in accordance with the procedure stated therein. *Ain* (Br. M. Add. 7652 fol. 279b, Jarrett II, p. 367) gives 38 *Parganas* for the *Sarkar* of Kashmir though in his revenue return, Qazi Ali had reckoned at 41 *Parganas* (*Ain*, fol. 279b). Evidently with 14 divisions, each division would have two to three *Parganas* under its jurisdiction. *Akbar Nama* does not state further the arrangements made for the revenue collection. But it is known from *Akbar Nama* itself (Br. M.O.R. 26, 207, fol. 161b; Ms. Or. quart. 1822, fol. 258b) at another place that the two officials *Bitikchi* for survey and assessment and the *Amal Guzar* for land revenue collection were always appointed in the same revenue circle. This is equally supported by *Ain's* chapters on *Ain-i-Amal Guzar* and *Ain-i-Bitikchi*. Later on, Mutamid Khan (*Iqbal nama*, Ms. Aligarh 97, fol. 135a) explains this point more explicitly that for this revenue regulation in Kashmir, Abul Fazl was deputed to make appointment of the experienced *Bitikchis*. Clearly, this measure brought the Sarkar of Kashmir in line with the pattern of revenue administration of the other Provinces.

17. This practice was continued till the end of Aurangzeb's reign as *Khulastu-s-Siyaq* (Ms. N.A. New Delhi, pp. 31-34; Ms. Aligarh fols. 15b-16b), which traces the evolution of the *Karori's* office since Akbar's age while mentioning the changes in his functions effected in the reign of Shah Jahan does not refer to any change in his territorial jurisdiction. *Farhang-i-Kardani* (Ms. 83, Edinburgh, fol. 39b) quotes a *Parwana* of an appointment of a *Karori* and at end associates four *Parganas* detailed with the revenues of each with the administration of the same *Karori*. In this respect, Aligarh Ms. fols. 29a-b is defective. The *Parwana* appoints in the main text usually associate a *Karori* with one named *Pargana* which is quite misleading to take him as the officer of the same *Pargana* only. As a matter of practice, the appointment went with the largest of the *Parganas* of his revenue circle and all the named *Parganas* along with their revenues were specified at the end of the *Parwana*. Similarly, any reference to a *Karori* with a named *Pargana* in any of the chronicles would not essentially denote him as the officer of only the same *Pargana* for he was named after the largest of the *Parganas* in his circle. But some Mss. put him clearly in a non-conventional sense as the Karori of the Parganas. Ms. Suppl. 482, B.N. Paris, fol. 145b quotes a *Parwana* of 11th year of Shahjahan's reign concerning Khwaja Mohammad Qasim, the *Karori* of the *Parganas* of a *Sarkar*. An original document in the R.A. Jaipur (Letters addressed to Maharaja', Reg. no. 943 dated A.H. 1107) quotes the

appointment of Sheikh Mohammad Syed as the *Karori* of the *Parganas* of Baswar and Udai (Sarkar Agra, Subah Agra. Jarrett II, p. 193 states them as Bhosawar and Udai). Some documents quote the appointment even for one large *Pargana*. An original Bond, (category no. 4, Regd. no. 99 dated A.H. 1099) executed by Arshad Ulla puts him *Karori* of *Pargana* Malarana (Sarkar Rantambhor, Subah Ajmer). *Ain* (Jarrett II, p. 280) shows this *Pargana* as a large one with an area of 172,693 Bighas and 3,299,241 dams of revenue and even without any Suyurghal (*Madad-i-Maash* assignment) in it. *Mirat I*, p. 329 quotes the transfer of Abdur Rahman, the *Karori* of Patan Dev (Pattan Deo or Somnath, *Sarkar* Sorath, *Subah* Gujrat) was transferred as the *ryots* complained against him. *Ain* (Jarrett II, p. 263) shows the *Pargana* of Pattan Deo with 4,453,912 *dams* of revenue and without any Suyurghal assignment.

18. Such a practice continued throughout the Mughal age. In R.A. Jaipur, an original document, category no. 4, regd. no. 99 dated A.H. 1099 (1688 A.D.) quotes the transfer of *Pargana* Malarana (Sarkar Rantambhor) from the *Jagir* of late Raja Ram Singh on the latter's death and transferred to *Khalsa* under the charge of Karori Arshadullah.
19. As the *Amal Guzar* or *Karori* was not the officer of the full division of the *Sarkar* but of a revenue circle of the *Sarkar*, he could discharge the duties required of him in *Ain-i-Amal Guzar*.
20. *Ain*, Br. M. Add. 7652, fols. 142a-143b; Ms. Hamilton I, Berlin, fols. 120a-121a.
21. *A.N.*, Br. M. Add. 26, 207, fols. 161b-162b; Ms. Or. quart. 1822, Berlin, fols. 258b-260a. Also Tarikh-i-Arif Qandhari, p. 178.
22. *Ain*, Br. M. Add. 7652, fols. 142a-143b and fols. 143b-144a respectively; Ms. Hamilton I, Berlin, fols. 120a-121a and fol. 121b.
23. *Ibid*; also an original document, R.A. Jaipur, category 4, regd. no. 99 dated 2nd of Shawal A.H. 1099 (1688 A.D.) quotes a Bond (*Muchalka*) executed by Arshadullah, the *Karori* of *Pargana* Malarana that he would administer the aforesaid *Pargana* and from the beginning of the *Kharif* crop would deposit all the revenues realised in the Royal treasury without any hesitation. Also see *Insha-i-Harkarn*, Ms. Rampur, *Farhang-i-Kardani*, Ms. 83, Edinburgh, fol. 39b; Ms. Aligarh, fol. 29b.
24. *Ibid*. All these duties have been noted from *Ain-i-Amal Guzar*. Abul stresses this point in *Ain-i-Khazana* (*Ain*, Hamilton I, Berlin, fol. 6a) and comments, "And from kindness and care for the agricultural classes, it was commanded that the collectors should not insist upon the husbandman paying coin in full weight, but to give him a receipt for whatever money he might bring. This laudable regulation removed the rust of uncertainty from the minds of the Collectors, and relieved the subjects from a variety of oppressions, whilst the income became larger, and the State flourished." (tr. Blochmann I, pp. 13-14).
25. *A.N.*, Br. M. Add. 27,247, fol. 332a.
26. *Ibid.*, fol. 332b.
27. *Ain*, Br. M. Add. 7652, *Ain-i-Amal Guzar*, fol. 143b; Hamilton I, Berlin, fol. 121a. Also, *Ain-I-Khazana*, Hamilton, Berlin, fol. 6a.

28. *Ibid.*, fol. 143b, Hamilton, fol. 121a. Also, *Farhang-i-Kardani*, Ms. 83, Edinburgh, fol. 40a.
29. *Ibid.*, 143a, *Ibid.*, fol. 120b.
30. *Ibid., Ain-i-Bitikchi*, fol. 144a; Hamilton, fol. 121b. Also *Farhang-I-Kardani*, Edinburgh, fol. 40a.
31. *Farhang-i-Kardani*, Ms. Aligarh, fol. 29b. The Edinburgh Ms. is silent on this point.
32. *Ain* (fol. 142a, Hamilton, fol. 120a) enjoins the *Amal Guzar* to be 'a friend of the agriculturist'. Regarding collection it comments (fol. 143a, 120b) that he should collect the revenue in an amicable manner and should not make any unwarranted demand.
33. *A.N.*, Br. M. Add. 26, 207, fol. 161b; Ms. Or. quart. 1822, Berlin, fol. 258b. Clause I of 27th year's revenue regulations.
34. *Ibid.*
35. *Makatbat-i-Alami* or *Insha-i-Alami* of Abul Fazl quotes a Royal *Dasturul Aml* addressed to the *Amils* etc. of the Empire. Ms. N.A. Delhi, p. 95; Ms. Orient. Oct. 1140, Berlin, fol. 42b.
36. *A.N.*, Br. M. Add. 26, 207, fol. 161b; Add. OR 27, 247, fol. 331b, clause I of 27th year regulations.
37. *Ibid.*, fol. 194b, 5th clause 30th year regulations.
38. *Ibid.* 5th clause. *Ibid.*
39. *Ibid.*, Br. M. Add. 27, 247, fol. 332a, 5th clause 27th year regulations.
40. *Ibid.* 4th clause. *Ibid.*
41. *Makatabat-i-Alami*, *Dasturul Aml*, Ms. N.A. New Delhi, p. 95, Ms. Oreint. Oxt. 1140, Berlin, fol. 42a; also *Khullasatus Siyaq*, Ms. N.A. N. Delhi, p. 32, Ms. Aligarh, fol. 16a.
42. *A.N.*, Br. M. Add. 27, 247, fols. 331b-332a. Clauses 3rd and 4th, 27th year regulations.
43. *Khullasatus Siyaq*, N.A. N. Delhi, pp. 32-33; Ms. Aligarh, fol. 16a.
44. *Ibid.*, p. 33. Ms. Aligarh, fol. 16a is wrong in putting the word *Pattadar* for *Tappahdar*. Also see the duties of the *Tappahdar* in the *Pargana* administration.
45. *Ibid.*, p. 33. Ms. Aligarh, fol. 16b. Also, *Makatabat-i-Alami*, N.A. N. Delhi, Dasturulaml, p. 95; Ms. Orient. Oct. 1140, Berlin, fols. 42a-b.
46. *A.N..*, Br. M. Add. 27, 247, fol. 331b. 3rd clause 27th year regulations.
47. *Khullasatus Siyaq*, N.A. N. Delhi, p. 33. Ms. Aligarh, fol. 16b.
48. *A.N.*, Br. M. Add. 27, 247, fols. 331b-332a. 6th clause of 27th year regulations.
49. *The English Factories in India* (1622-23), pp. 250-51, 253-54 Nide John Willoughby's letters at Nosari (*Pargana* of *Sarkar* Surat J. II, p. 262) to Surat Factory, dated July 30, August 5 and 19, 1623 A.D. (Jahangir's reign) relate the theft of the masts of the ships with the connivance of a *Muqaddam* of Otta (village) named 'Coulla' having received the stolen goods. The authorities at Nosari got a *Parwana* from the Governor of Surat addressed to the *Karori* of Nosari and got full support from the latter in calling and threatening the suspected *Muqaddam* for making further thorough enquiries in the matter.

50. *Baharistan-i-Ghaibi*, tr. Borah, Vol. I, p. 271 mentions the appointment of Mirza Giw alias Mirza Babu as the *Karori* as well as the *Faujdar* of *Pargana* Kuntaghat in the newly conquered territory of Kuch. *Khullasatus Siyaq*, N.A. N. Delhi, p. 32, Ms. Aligarh fol. 16a, states that the practice of the combined office of *Faujdar* and *Karori* did exist before Shah Jahan's reign. In Akbar's reign, though *Akbar Nama* (Br. M. Add. 27, 247 fol. 332a) in the 27th year's regulations makes a distinct reference to the existence of the two offices, the possibility of sometimes combining the office cannot be ruled out in view of an evidence from '*Waqai Asad Beg*' (Ms. 40/270 A.S.C., Aligarh, p. 8).
51. *Khulasatus Siyaq*, Ms. N.A. N. Delhi, p. 32, Ms. Aligarh, fol. 16a.
52. *A.N.*, Br. M. Add. O.R. 26, 207, fol. 194b. 7th clause of 30th year regulations. This clause is more lenient and explicit than a similar clause of 27th year regulations of Todar Mal (7th clause, *A.N.*, Br. M. Add. 27, 247, fol. 332a) which simply states that the *Karori* could claim the 4th instalment of his remunerations only after he had cleared the collection of the revenue arrears from the *ryots*.
53. *Ibid.*, fol. 194b. Clauses 9, 10 and 11 of 30th year regulations.
54. *Ibid.*, 8th clause, *Ibid.*
55. *Ibid.*, fol. 195a. 14th clause. *Ibid.*
56. *Muntkhab-ut-Tawarikh*, Ms. Elliot 248, Bod. Oxford, fols. 257b-258a; tr. Lowe, pp. 192-93.
57. *A.N.*, Br. B.O.R. Add. 27, 247 fols. 331b. Clause 1.
58. *Ibid.*, fol. 332a. Clause 4.
59. *Ibid.*, fols. 332a-b, clauses 7th, 8th and 9th.
60. *Ibid.*, Br. M.O.R. 26, 207, fol. 194a.
61. *Ibid.*
62. *Ibid.* Clause I.
63. *Ibid.*, fol. 194b. Clause 2.
64. *Ibid.* Clause 3rd.
65. *Ibid.*, clause 4. Moreland's Summary of clauses 2-4 of this report (Agrarian System, p. 107) is not reliable. He takes clause 4 as 'obscure' and his version is completely defective. I have relied for translation after collating four Mss. of *Akbar Nama*, viz. Br. M.O.R. Add. 26, 207; Br. M. Add. 27, 247; Ms. Or. quart. 1822, Berlin and Printed text of R.A.S. Bengal.
66. *Ibid.*, fol. 195a. Clauses 15th and 13th.
67. *Ibid.*, fols. 194b-195a. Clauses 5-14. Moreland's criticism of Todar Mal's 27th year's revenue regulations ('*Agrarian System*', pp. 106-08) is highly uncharitable. He maintains that the regulations were too severe and aimed at the 'revival of the old, ferocious, process of audit called *Muhasaba*' which was in operation in the 14th century. He further contends that the methods of audit enforced by Todar Mal rendered the honest Collector's position intolerable and that the Collectors were held liable for more than was really due from them. He accuses Todar Mal of obstinacy and vindictiveness in dealing with the staff employed by his bitter enemy (i.e. Shah Mansur) which according to him is borne by Badauni's account. Moreland's criticism

of Todar Mal is mostly due to his failure to understand the technical nature and substance of the 30th year's regulations enforced by Fatah Ullah Shirazi which seem to him to be 'exceedingly obscure'. As already explained in the main text, the latter report undoubtedly improves pecuniary allowances of the Collector and gives him a little relief from the rigidity of the audit procedure with regard to his emoluments. All the same, it equally notes the cases of embazzlement and over-realisation of revenues from the *ryots* and prescribes still more precautionary procedure of checks and counter-checks against the malpractices of the Collector and his staff. Abul Fazl passes no stricture on Todar Mal's reforms and since the operation of the latter reforms showed the further need for fully meeting the agrarian and administrative instability, new regulations were enforced after three years when Todar Mal himself was the Revenue Minister and was advised to act under the counsel of Fatehullah Shirazi. Actually Badauni's statement, on which Moreland has built his theory, praises Todar Mal for punishing the guilty Collectors responsible for oppression on the *ryots* nd does not at all refer to any audit formailities enforced by him in his revenue regulations.

68. Mohammad Sadiq Khan in *Tawarikh-i-Shahjahani*, (Ms. Br. M.O.R. 174, fol. 185b, Ms. Rampur, p. 313) while describing Murshid Quli Khan's revenue reforms in Deccan *Subahs* comments that the latter built up the revenue and administrative structure of the *Parganas* on the lines of Todar Mal. Later on, *Aurangzeb's Farman* to Rasik Dass (Ms. Or. Oct. 113, Berlin, fols., also quoted in *Nigar Nama-i-Munshi*, Bod. Oxford, Ms. Pers. e. I, fols. 127a-128b) issues directions to the revenue officials for the improvements of the agrarian condition and at the same time enjoins the officials to work out the details of the land revenue administration and realisation in comparison with those of Raja Todar Mal's revenue administration in Akbar's age.
69. *Tuzuk-i-Jahangiri*, Ms. Rampur, p. 10; Ms. Orient Oct. 101, fol. 30a.
70. *The English Factories in India* (1622-23), pp. 253-54. See footnote reference no. 50. In a letter dated August 5, 1623, John Willoughby stationed at (*Pargana*) Nosari addressed to the Surat authorities clearly brings out the anxiety of the *Karori* for land revenue collection. Even though the *Karori* gave the English officials full support by calling and threatening the *Muqaddam* of Otta for full investigation in the recovery of the stolen masts of the English ship, the former fearing lest he should lose the old balance and fresh realisation of land revenue collection during the current harvest period, did not mistreat the *Muqaddam* and detained the latter for two to three days for settling the accounts of '*hassell*'. (revenue realisations).

6. Qanungo

The *Qanungo* held a very key position in the *Pargana* revenue administration and upon him rested not only most of its burden for record keeping, but the very nature and the spirit of the land administration in operation.[1] His office, as known to Shershah's administration, was further replenished and widened in competence and powers under Islam Shah, the Sur.[2] Thus inherited, it found wide patronage at the hands of Todar Mal, who not only reorganised it[3] but made it a uniform feature of the administration throughout the newly extended Empire.[4]

Every *Pargana* had a chief *Qanungo* stationed at the *Pargana* headquarters known as the '*Qanungo-i-Pargana*'. He had under him a few other field *Qanungos*, each being in-charge of a division in the *Pargana*. Moreland[5] and Saran[6] think that there was only one *Qanungo* in the *Pargana* but their view is based on the misunderstanding of *Ain's* reference to the *Qanungo's* office.[7] Moreover, *Akbar Namah*, in the 27th regnal year reforms introduced by Todar Mal refers to numerous *Qanungos* as working under *Amil-i-Khalsa* (of *Pargana*).[8] It further stipulates in one of the reforms carried out by Fatahullah Shirazi in the 30th regnal year, that "(the number of the *Qanungos* be increased inordinately and that if, one (of them) from every *Pargana*, were to remain (represent) at the Royal Court, that would add to the needed crystal-clear information on every subject (concerning the *Pargana* revenues)".[9] If there were only one *Qanungo* in the *Pargana*, how could he be spared for being attached with the Central Government? Above all, in the face of these reforms having been implemented earlier, how could *Ain*, when complied later (in the 42nd regnal year), vouch for one *Qanungo* for every *Pargana*?

The number of *Qanungos* fixed for each *Pargana* and the divisional jurisdiction of one *Qanungo* within the *Pargana* must have varied in accordance with its particular revenue needs even though recorded evidence for the reign of Aurangzeb puts the number at two.[10]

Unlike the *Muqaddam*, the *Patwari* and the *Choudhri*, the *Qanungo* was regarded as a full-fledged Government servant. He was appointed for life, though his tenure had to be consistent with efficiency and proper discharge of duties.[11] Technically, his office was not hereditary, though it would pass on to the male succession on petition from the candidate, subject to approval by the monarch.[12] The reign of Aurangzeb records some fresh appointments after the removal of the previous incumbents. Any sudden or temporary vacancy in the *Pargana* could be refilled by the *Subah* authorities.[13]

The *Qanungo* was the officer-in-charge of all the *Patwaris* in his jurisdiction. He had multifarious revenue duties connected with land revenue, customs and market affairs.[14] He had various duties in common with that of the *Choudhri* and there is evidence to show that in the reign of Shah Jahan, the office of the *Pargana Qanungo* was sometimes combined with that of the *Choudhri.*[15] He always had vast professional training and was essentially a technical expert in revenue matters. With his permanent tenure as against the frequently transferable *Pargana* officials and the assignees, he always furnished them with required information and relevant revenue documents. He was expected to show full co-operation to them. He equally served as a check on them against any financial or procedural irregularity[16] and more especially as a Government counterweight against the *Jagirdars* and the *Zamindars.*[17] He always stood for the interests of the *ryots*, and *Ain* designates him as the refuge of the husbandman.[18] In case of any oppression on the latter and over-exactions by the *Gumashtas* due to negligence of the *Amil*, he would with the help of the *Muqaddams*[19] and his agents, and after verification from the original records of the *Patwari*, make the offenders answerable for accounts and take them to task.[20]

He had to deal with the land revenue administration in all its comprehensive aspects, right from the survey to the assessment and collection of the revenue, preparation and the preservation of their respective documents in his office. He had always to equally safeguard the *ryots* against any oppression by the *Amil* or the agents of the assignees.[21] Like other officials, he too, was always enjoined by his appointment order to look after the prosperity of the *Pargana*, welfare of the *ryots* and to make special efforts for the increment of the agriculture.[22] On the arrival of the Assessing Officer in his circle, he had to produce the documents of *Taqsim*, *Dasturulaml* and other relevant survey and realisation documents pertaining to the previous years.[23]

As explained for the *Choudhury*, he was also to get advance notice for the assessment in his circle[24] and he had similar obligations for assisting the *Amin* in the accomplishment of the assessment work and the final assessment on the *ryots* could be made only with his approval.[25] But more than the *Choudhry*, he had also to attest the survey and assessment documents of *Khasra*, *Muntkhib*, *Jamabandi*, *Bayaha*, *Pashkhish Jamma* for the villages in his circle. Similarly, the *Pargana Qanungo* had to verify and maintain the assessment statistical registers of *Saya Tashkhish Jamma* and *Goshwara* for the entire *Pargana*. He had to accomplish this job, both for the *Khalsa* and the *Jagir* lands.

Along with the *Choudhry*, had had a kind duties for the realisation of the land revenues from the *Khalsa* lands, dues from *Jagirdars* and *Peshkash* from the *Zimidars* in his jurisdiction.[26] He had to attest and maintain all documents concerning reliations, viz. *Taujih*, *Awirija* and *Roznamcha* for the villages in his circle. Apart from the above documents also filed in the office of the *Pargana Qanungo*, the latter had to maintain the statistical registers relating to the realisation in the whole *Pargana* viz; *Saya Wasilbaqi; Jama-Kharch, Jama Hasilbaqi* and the *Tumar Jama.*

He had also to verify any differences involved in the original amount assessed and realised due to the incapacity of the *ryots* to pay as well check all remissions on account of drought and other calamities. Being informed of all types of assignments, he had to attest their *Chaknamahs* with the help of the *Patwari, Choudhri* and the *Muqaddam.* He had to help the assignees in the realisation of the land revenue,[30] which, had to be attested by him.[31] For any mortgage or sale transaction, his evidence and attestation in the Court of the *Qazi* was essential.[32]

The *Pargana Qanungo* was responsible for the custody of all lands records filed in his office, viz; the list of the villages, *Tappas* and their revenues alongwith the names of the *Choudhris* responsible for collection; list of the jurisdictions and revenues under the various *Zimidars* alongwith the security bonds of the latter executed by the *Choudhris*, the document of *Muwazna Deh Sala* and *Taqsim* of every village; the *Tumar* documents of the previous realisations, arrears and *Jamma Wasilbaqi* stamped by the *Amil.*[33] All these documents had to be produced by the *Qanungo* before the Assessing officer.[34] Besides this, he had to despatch regularly to the Central Government the documents of the *Taqsim* and the *Muwazan Deh Sala* showing also the maximum realisation-year (*San-i-Kamil*) and areas of every village, alongwith the *Dasturulaml* pertaining to the land realisations and customs, the regulations of the treasury, and the actual realisations of the previous years concerning both the *Khalsa* or the *Jagir* lands in the *Pargana.*[35] Any new territorial annexation was immediately followed by land survey operations and revenue estimates done by the *Amin* with the help of the *Qnungos* who were responsible for the preparation of Survey, assessment and *Taqsim* documents with details of the land under *Jagir* and *Khalsa.*[36]

Previously, the *Qanungo* was paid on the basis of I% of the collection made under him.[37] But in Akbar's reign, in keeping with the importance of his office, he was raised to the status of monthly salaried official. His office was divided into three grades with Rs. 50, 30 and 20 per month to be paid in the shape of assignment.[38] But later on, this practice seems to have been discontinued and there is sufficient evidence to show that from the reign of Shah Jahan onwards, the *Qanungo* like that of the *Choudhri*, was entitled to his *'Dastur'*, i.e. emoluments in accordance with the practice in the *Pargana* paid either in cash or through grant of rent-free land being equivalent to some percentage of the collections made under him.[39] He was equally entitled to some cash incidental charges.[40]

The *Qanungo's* office of the Mughal age has left a rich heritage to the functioning of the land administration to the later Mughal and the modern times. It continued in the 18th century with more or less the same status, duties and obligations.[41] Though in Bengal, like various other offices, it deteriorated in functioning,[42] its basic utility was never denied by the majority of the early British authorities.[43] In many of the other Province, its functioning won tribute even from the British revenue officers.[44] Its continued role and place in the present day district administration, even though with certain adaptations, is a wonderful testimony to its predecessor of the 16th and the 17th centuries.

References

1. Apart from the *Qanungo* for land revenue administration, another district office of the *Qanungo* for grain-market existed. N.B. Paris forl 149a quotes a *Parvana* dated A.H. 1048, 12th regnal year of Shahjahan's reign making an appointment of a *Qanungo* for the grain-market of Sarkar Surat (*Subah* Gujrat).
2. *Khulasut-ul-Tawarikh*, Berlin, fol 149a. Sujjan Rai Bhaudari credits Islam Shah with the reshuffling and adding to the duties of the *Pargana Qanungo*. He states his duties in general terms , viz. maintenance of the records pertaining to the condition of the *ryots*, planning for the prosperity and enhancement of agriculture, and acting as consultant on matters of land assessment, realisation of the revenue and welfare of the *ryots*.
3. *Mutakhab-al-Lubab* vol. I pp. 156-57, also describes Todar Mal's reforms in the 27th regnal year of Akbar in the Revenue Department regarding the reorganisation of the Persian translation department and the appointment of the revenue accountants from the communities of Muslim Khawajas and Hindu Kaisths, who, in course of time, became by profession a class of expert revenue officlals. A *Dasturulaml* No. 79, Hyderabad fol 16a, of later Mughal age points out that in the north, the office of the *Qanungo* was monopolised by the *Kaisth* Hindu community whereas in the Deccan states by the Brahmin.
4. Though *Akbar Namah*, Br. M. Add OR 27, 247 fol 331b, 332b in the 27th regnal year reforms by Todar Mal simply refers to the well established office of the *Qanungo* throughout the Empire and some of the obligations to be discharged by him, the later Mughal local sources viz. Ms. or Fol. 270, Berlin, fols 41b-43a, and Mirat Vol. I credit especially Todar Mal for the inception of this institution in Bengal and Gujrat respectively.
5. 'The Pargana Head Man' J.R.A.S. 1938, p. 134.
6. *Provincial Government*, p. 72.
7. *Ain*, Hamilton I Berlin, fols 126b-127a; Jaret tr. P. 89.
   Having finished with the analysis of classification of land with State demand under *Chachar* and *Paravti* lands, Abul Fazl passed on to pay tribute to the ameleorative measures of Akbar. He states the reduction of the duty on the manufacturers from 10% to 5% and refers to the past practice of division of 2% (of the revenue collections) between the *Patwari* and *Qanungo*. Then he briefly explains the nature of the *Patwari's* office, talks about the *Qanungo* as the refuge of the '*Husbandsman*' in the present tense and then about his past position, one *Qanungo* serving in one *Pargana*. He again switches over to the reformed nature of the fixation of his emoluments under Akbar, i.e. the abolition of the previous practice of his share (half of 2% shared with the *Patwari*) and the fixation of salary in three grades with Rs. 50, 30 and 20 per month respectively. Evidently, under the *Surs*, there was one *Qanungo* in a *Pargana* with the emoluments paid at the rate of 1% of the collections made under him. But Akbar did away with this practice and reinstituted the office with new pay scales for different grades of the *Qanungos.* Thus the number of the *Qanunogs* in every *Pargana* was increased and was filled within the

prescribed grades, though, no approximate number for appointment in a *Pargana* is specifically mentioned. If there were only one *Qanungo* in a *Pargana*, he could not be filled in three grades simultaneously nor could the position of one *Pargana Qanungo* differ so much from that of another *Pargana Qanungo* so as to be put in different grades. Jarett's translation of the sentence marked (A) '*wa dar har Pargana Yakay Bud*' as 'There is one in every district' is grammatically wrong unless *'Bud'* were read as *'Bawad'* which is not warranted by the context of the text quoted and explained above. Here, *'Bud'* definitely means '*Was*' and refers to the past rather than reading as '*Bawad*' standing for the present.

8. *A.N.* Br. M. OR 27, 247 fol 331b; this is later confirmed by Mukhzan ul Ihetsab, Berlin, fols 4b-6b; Also see reference No: 13 p.
9. *Ibid.*,. OR 26, 207, fol 195; Ms. Or. Quart; 1822 Berlin fol 311b. "Sixteenthly, great profit occurs to the *Qanungos.* If a man (Qanungo) from each *Pargana* remains at court, assuredly, there will be more enlightenment on this subject." (Beveridge p. 692 interprets the first sentence inaccurately.)
10. *Durul-ulum* or Walker 104b Bodl. Oxford fol 65b.
11. N.B. Paris, fols 91a-01b. A copy of *Farman* of Shah Jahan's reign directed to Sher Khan and Khawja Jahan while enumerating the documents to be despatched by the *Pargana Qanungo* through his clerk to the Central Government directs that a *Qanungo*, of any of the *Parganas*, failing to comply with this order, may be removed and a substitute be appointed in his place.
12. The office of the *Qanungo* was for life dependent on his good behaviour. But owing to its technical nature and professional training imparted by the father to the son and also because of the former's service rendered to the State, it came to acquire more or less hereditary character.
    In the 18th century Bengal, it became definitely hereditary. After lot of controversy under Warren Hastings, a detailed enquiry conducted by the British officers into family descent of the *Qanungos* of the *Parganas* confirmed its hereditary trait. (Ms. OR. quart 258, fols 175b, 183b, 185a.)
13. *N.B.* Paris fol 148a quotes a *Parwana*, dated 9th regnal year of Shahjahan's reign issued by Nawab Masi ul Zaman appointing a *Qanungo* in *Pargana Chaurasi, Sarkar Surat, Subah* Gujrat.
14. *Ibid.* The above *Parwana* and another *Farman* fol 91a-91b of Shah Jahan's reign are the only documents in the Mughal revenue literature which state the detailed duties of the *Pargana Qanungo* directly.
15. Jaipur, O.R.O. Case No. 7, dated A.H. 1071 (1661 A.D.) a sale deed records the evidence of Mukand Dass, the *Qanungo* and the *Choudhry* and also attested by *Qanungo* and *Choudhry* Mohan Dass of *Pargana* Shahjahbad. Also. Reg. 1721, Case No. 9, dated A.H. 1074 (1664 A.D.) attested by Balhider, the *Choudhri* and *Qanungo*, *Pargana* Shahjahanabad Sarker and Subah Shahjahanabad.
16. *Waqia i Sarkar Ranthambore,* p. 38, News dated the 3rd month i.e. Shahban, record an enquiry conducted by the Waqia Nawis into the embazzlement charges against the *Amin* and the *Karori* of the *Khalsa Parganas*. The

Qanungos of *Pargana* Binai (*Sarkar* Ajmer, *Subah* Ajmer) submitted a written complaint (*muchalka*) to the effect that Abul Qasim, the *Amin* and Islam Mohammad, the *Karori* had forcibly got their (*Qanungos'*) attestation on the superior documents of *Jamabandi*. Iftikhar Khan, the enquiry officer deputed by the Waqia Nawis, also confirmed it and the same was reported by the latter to the Royal Court. Also, Ms. or quart 258 Berlin fol 184a noted the advantage of fixed tenure and establishement of *Qanungo* against the transferable Governors, *Faujdars* and other revenue officers and serving as connecting link in the revenue administration as emphasised in Akbar's reign.

17. Ms. or quart 258 Berlin, fols 183a-185b, 186b. Also Ms. or Fol. 270, fol 43a mentions the independent establishment and office of the *Qanungo* urged by Todar Mal as a check against the *Zimindars*.
18. *Ain*, Hamilton I Fol 126a.
19. *Kaqaz-i-Kham-i-Patwari.*
20. *A.N.* Nr. M. or 26, 207, fol 194b; Ms. or quart 1822 Berlin, fol 310b. The translation of Beveridge p. 690 showing balance against the *Qanungos, Muqaddams* and *Sarkars* and demanding accounts from them is incorrect.
21. *Waqai*-Sarkar *Ranthambore,* p. 386; C.R.O. Jaipur. Misc. Persian letters, Reg. 1165, dated A.H., 1104; *Ibid.* letters to Majaraja's Reg. 2188, dated A.H. 1129.
22. *NIB*, Paris, fol 148a; in a *Parwana* of Shah Jahan's reign pertaining to the appointment of a *Pargana Qanungo* enumerates his duties.
23. *Makhzan ul Ihetsab;* Berlin 5a.
24. *Ibid.*
25. *Baharistan-i-Ghaibi*, N.B. Paris, fols 6ub, 311b; *Makhzan ul Ihetesab,* Berlin 4b-5b, *Murraqat-i-Hasan* Patna p. 328; *Farhauqi-i-Kardani,* Aligarh fol 29a; *Khullas-ul Sayaq,* Aligarh fol 10a.
26. *Makhzan ul Ihetsab,* Berlin fol 6a; Also *Intkhab i Dasutulaml* Br. M. Add 6599 fol 40b.
27. *Sayaq Nama* No: 858 Hyderabad, fol. 201a.
28. A *Farman* Br. M. Or 1757 fols 39a; 50b; Also *Dasturulaml* No: 748 Hyderabad, pp. 7, 13, 19, also Jaipur O.R.O. Misc. Pers. Letters' Reg. 623 dated A.H. 1117.
29. An original *Chaknamah* of *Madad-i-Maash*, Ajmer, dated A.H. 1075; Also *Dasturulaml* 748 Hyderabad p. 19.
30. Jaipur O.R.O. Misc. Pers. Letters', Reg. 142, dated A.H. 1099; Also category No: 3, Reg. 407.
31. *Ibid.* Original Tumar Documents (uncatalogued) dated the year 1098 Fasli (1683 A.D.: also Misc. Pers. Letters' Reg. 137a, dated the year *Fasli* 1090 (1683 A.D.).
32. *Ibid.* Bainamah, Case No. 7, dated A.H. 1071.
33. *Makhzan ul Ihetsab,* Berlin, fols 24a-28a.
34. *Ibid.* fol. 24a.
35. *N.B.* Paris fol 91a, a copy of Shahjahan's reign directed to Khwaja Jahan explains in details the duties of a *Pargana Qanungo*. This is the only *Farman* of its type traceable in the entire Mughal revenue literature.

36. *Waqai i Sarkar Ranthambore*, pp. 163, 170, brings out the important role played by the *Qanunogs* immediately after the annexation of Jodhpur in *Subah* Ajmer (Aurangzeb's reign) and the relevant documents prepared by them; Also *Baharistan-i-Ghaibi*, *N.B.* Paris.
37. *Ain* Hamilton I, Berlin, fols 126b. 2% of the collections made were shared by the *Patwari* and the *Qanungo* equally.
38. *Ibid.*, fols 126b-127a.
39. *Intkhab i Dasturulaml*, Bṛ. M. Add 6599, fol. 53a, 42b; Also *Makhzan ul Ihetsab*, Berlin fol. 74b; Also *Farhauqi Kardani,* Aligarh fol; This is further confirmed by the 18th century sources which quote in details the traditional position and emoluments of the *Qanungos*. Ms. or. quart 258 fols 178b, 184a, for Bengal and Behar, it mentions the *Qanungo's* office hereditary since generations with emoluments fixed at ½% of the amount of renveues realised. For some districts fol 183b, it mentions the emoluments in the shape of '*Rasum and Paotagi*' i.e. cash percentage of the amount realised along with negligible share from the produce of the cultivators. Also Ms. or fol 270, fol 42a, puts the emoluments at ½% in cash of the collections made.
40. *Intkhab-i-Dasturulaml, Ibid.*, 46a.
41. The functions of the *Qanungos* remains practically the same in the 18th and 19th centuries before the changes brought in by the British Government though their emoluments came to differ, varying with every Province. For the early 18th century, Wilson (*Glossary* p. 260) wrote about the *Qanungo*, "An expounder of the laws, but applied in Hindustan especially to village and district revenue officers, who under former Governments, recorded all circumstances within their sphere which concerned landed property and the realisation of the revenue, keeping registers of the value, tenure, extent and transfers of the lands, assisting in the measurement and survey of lands, reporting deaths and succession of revenue-payers, and explaining, when required, local practices and public regulations. They were paid by rent-free lands and various allowances and perquisities". This is equally confirmed in still more details for Bengal and Behar in Ms. or quart 258 Berlin, fols 175a-188a; Ms. or fol 270 Berlin, fols 41b-43a; Amini Report, as reproduced by Ramsbotham, for Banaras, selections from the *Duncan Records* p. 41 and Appendix XXIX. For the 19th century for Oudh, *Chronicles of Qonao* chapter V, for Ceded and Conquered Provinces, Selections from the Revenue Records of North Western Provinces, 1818-1820 and 1822-1833, for Ajmer, *Cavendish Enquiries* for Binai p. 3, for Delhi, *Records of Delhi Residency and Agency* p. 85, Records for Punjab Trevaskis, the *Land of Five Rivers,* pp. 26-27, for Deccan states, for *Qanungo* and *Deshpande*, *Dasturulaml* 676 Hyderabad fols 7a-10a, *Dasturulaml* 79 Hyderabad fols 15b-19b.
    As to the emoluments in the 18 and 19th centuries, for Bengal and Behar, see reference 45, which puts it at ½% of the amount realised, for Ajmer, Cavendish Enquiries, for Binai p.3 note the joint share of *Qanungo* and *Chaudries* from 2-1/2% of the amount collected alongwith 1/40th share of the produce of the cultivators to 2-1/2% along with some rent-free grant, for Delhi, Records of Delhi Residency and Agency p. 85 mention 2% to 20% on the collections, or a ready money allowance of from 100 to 200 rupees per annum.

42. Ms. or Quart 258 Berlin, fol 185b complains of the recent changes in the attitude of the *Qanungos*, having deviated from their original position by serving the ends of the *Zimindars* against the interests of the Government. Also R. Adair Collector of Baghalpore passed strictures about the *Mukaddams, Patwaries* and the *Qanungos*.....instead of performing the services which might be expected and which ought to be exacted from them; they are often themselves the instruments of the negligencies, frauds and oppressions which it was the original intention of their offices to prevent; and I could produce many instances that have come within my own knowledge to prove the reflections here cast upon them to be founded not on speculations but on facts. The same report also notes with regret the growing tendency of the *Qanungos* "to hold *Zimindaries*, *Talooks* or *Naunccuur* Villages, that those who are already in possession of them should be compelled either relinquish their offices, or dispose of their lands; the Union of two occupations of landholders and *Qanungos* being wholly repugnant to the objects intended in the institution of the latter; the opportunities offerd in which, there is room to suspect have occasioned many illegal appropriations to the former." (*Boglepore Records*, Patna Records Office, letter No: 51 dated 9th of September, 1787, addressed to John Shore, Esq. President and Members of the Board of Revenue).
43. *Ibid.* fol 185a-185b; *Ibid.* Mr. R Agdi, the collector of Bhagalpore in the same report suggests remedies by disassociating the office of *Qanungo* from the *Zimindari* and thereby bringing it back to its original position.
44. *Records of the Delhi Residency and Agency*,. p. 85, T. Fortescne Esqr. Civil Commissioner Delhi in his report dated 28th April, 1820, comments about the *Qanungos*, "They are intelligent, industrious and absolutely requisite."

7. The Amin

The term '*Amin*' was employed very widely for various officers with varying functions. Literally, it meant trustee, or an impartial administrator or a specially appointed officer commissioned for any assigned job. An administrative officer entitled, *Amin* could be deputed to perform duties for a particular contingency.[1] Thus quite distinct from an *Amin* as a revenue officer, there were *Amins* of the Provincial *Baitulmal*[2] the town *Baitulmal*,[3] the loans department of the Treasury (*Amin-i-Khazana-i-Masadat*),[4] Octroi (*Rahadari*) and markets[5] customs and duties (*Mahal-i-Sari*),[6] branding department (*Dag-otiashih)*,[7] *gold* and precious mines, personal Royal treasury and lands (*Sarf-i-Khas*),[8] gardens,[9] a Fort,[10] for construction of monuments,[11] Police *Kotwali* (*Choubutra Kotwali*),[12] Police posts (*Chaukis*).[13] Under Aurangzeb, after the imposition or *Jizya*, *Amins* were appointed for the administration of *Jizya* department.[14] At the provincial level, the offices of the *Amin* and the *Sadr* were invariably continued for judicial administration.[15]

An *Amin-i Subah* was appointed for the administration of justice or *Baitulmel* (treasury or branding department or revenue department).[16] The offices of the *Amin-i Subha* and the *Waqai Nawis* could be combined for the administration of *Baitulmal*[17] and revenue administration. At the *Pargana* level, the judicial offices of the *Amin* and the *Qazi* were combined in the same person.[18]

For purely revenue administration under Akbar, the *Amin's* office existed at the two-fold level the Provincial and the *Pargana*. The *Amin's Subah* was in charge of the assessment returns of the entire *Subah*[19] and worked in coordination with the *Diwan-i-Subah*. At the *Pargana* level, the *Amin* or *Munsif* was in-charge of the survey and the two level party.[20] As a matter of fact, under Akbar and Jahangir, the office of the *Amin* as the local Assessment Officer of the *Pargana* did not exist. In case of any natural calamity, the assessment powers were exercised by the *Bitikchi* and the *Karori*, who accomplished the job with the help of the *Pargana* officials. The *Karori* was in-charge of both the assessment and the collection of the revenues. At times, in the *Jagir Parganas*, the assessment work was done by specially deputed revenue officers with the help of the local *Pargana* officials and submitted the assessment report to the *Diwan-i Sarkar* and *Diwani Subah*. Apart from it, in case of any natural calamity, an *Amin* may be specially commissioned by the *Subah* administration to visit the affected areas and to afford compensation to the cultivators in consultation with the *Karori* of the Circle, the local *Pargana* officials and the *ryots*.

During Shahjahan's reign, the local revenue administration was reorganised. For the purposes of assessment of land revenue, Islam Khan, the *Diwan* Ala instituted the *Amin's* office in the local administration on permanent basis. An *Amin* was appointed for a revenue circle (*Mahal*) comprising a group of *Parganas*.[22] The assessment powers hitherto exercised by the *Karori* and the *Bitikchi* were vested with the *Amin*. The two officers, the *Amin* as assessment officer and the *Karori* as the Collector became completely different from each other. This became a permanent feature of the Mughal Administration. Under Sadaullah Khan's administration, with the creation of the Chaklas as large revenue circles in a *Subah*, the *Faujdari* and *Amini* powers were combined in the same officer who acted as the administrator of the *Chakla*.[23] He exercised full authority over the *Amins* and the *Karories* of the smaller circles of a few *Parganas* each.[24] It has already been discussed that for the higher circle, the jurisdiction of a *Faujdar* and *Amin* was not always alinged with a *Chakla* and could have various inter *Sarkar Khalsa* or *Paibaqi Parganas*.[25] In any case, it was the *Amin* of a small circle of a few *Pargana* who was the real assessment officer in the local administration. The jurisdiction of small revenue circles was ordinarily defined on more or less permanent basis.[26] It seems that in the *Khalsa Parganas*, the jurisdictions of an *Amin* and a *Karori* would run concurrently.[27] As a matter of general practice, separate officials were appointed as *Amin* and *Karori*.[28] It was very rarely that the powers for assessment (*Amini*) and collection (*Karori*) of revenues were vested with the same officer.[29] The *Amin* was also entitled as *Munsif*.[30]

As regards the duties of the *Amin*, he was the assessment officer of the *Parganas* in his circle. The details of the assessment work in the villages and the *Parganas* connected with the offices of the *Bitikchi* and the *Karori* have already been explained under Akbar's administration.[31] All these duties were henceforth entrusted to the *Amin*-who commanded full control over the Survey and the assessment staff of the *Parganas*. For Aurangzeb's reign, there is ample source material which gives a comprehensive view of the working of the *Amin's* office in the *Parganas*. The Rajasthan Archives quotes an original *Parwana* of an *Amin's* appointment in the *Paibaqi* and *Khalsa* Parganas stating therein his main obligations and duties.[32] He was enjoined to make assessment in accordance with the regulations and to see that any area or *Mahal* not subjected to regular assessment hitherto was assessed properly. He had to direct the *Karori* to collect the land revenue and the *Taqavi* loans on the basis of the assessment done by him. He had also to direct him to deposit all the collection in the State treasury and not to keep unto himself any *dam* without the appropriate sanction of the *Diwan*. He also instructed him not to allow the State revenues to fall in arrears. He would attest all the documents of the arrears of land revenue and the *Taqavi* loan, if any, and the commission deducted by the *Karori* and the local revenue officials for the collection of land revenue. He had to forward all the documents for the zonal records. He had to look after the enhancement of the agricultural produce and the welfare of the *ryots* and to see that no illegal cesses were collected. (R.A.J. 'Misc. Persian letters to State officials and Mughal centre officials' Regd No. 116 dated 8th Rajab 48th R.Y. A.H. 1116/9th *Katal Samat* 1761/1704 A.D) also Regd. No. 363 dated 2nd Rajab 37th R.Y. A.H. 1104/1750 Samat/1693 A.D). Thus it is evident that an *Amin* of higher circle could depute his own representative as *Amin* in the *Parganas* for the execution of the *Amini* obligations.[33] From the period of Sadaullah Khan's administrative organisation, the *Amin* of the *Parganas* enjoyed a higher status than that of a *Karori* and exercised general supervision even on the latter's work.[34] The offices and power of the *Faujdar* and *Amin* were invariably combined in the same person.[35] An *Amin* could also be appointed both exclusive jurisdiction over the *Jagir Parganas*. Ordinarily, in the *Jagir Parganas*, the offices of the *Amin, Shiqdar* and the *Karkun* of the *Parganas* were combined in the same official who was responsible to the *Amin* of the higher circle.[36] (MS-Persian Letters-Regd No. 241 dated A.H. 1146/1790S/1733 A.D) The *Makhzan-i-Ihetsab Maarub Dasturualm* (M.I) emphasises the importance of the role of the *Amin* as a man of ripe experience and intergrity and enjoins all other revenues officials to abide by his advice[37] (M.I. 5b- also Aurangzeb's verdict that the job of *Amini* is difficult where *Diwani* is easier-) It explains in details the procedure and the assessment work done by the *Amin* of the *Parganas*.[38] The sources to look like *Murraqat-i-Hasan* and *Farhang-i-Kardan* or *Kar-amozi*[40] have given relevant statistics serially and in a chronological order. The *Amin* was entrusted with the preparation of the comparative account of the 10 years (*Juma-i Dehsala*), the average (of the rent) of last year, and the year before. The *Amin* had to prepare a statement of assessment and explain it to *ryots*. The assessment was to be made keeping in view the condition of the villages or the cultivators under assessment. He had to give the terms of the agreement (*Patta*) for the *ryots* and to get a receipt for it. He had to correct the assessment document from time to time and in case of any natural calamity, he had to afford compensation to the *ryots* in the *Jama* documents. Keeping in view the prosperity and welfare of the *royts*, he would offer them any method of assessment, *Zabti, Ghallabakshi, Kankut* or any other method, whichever suited their interests. At the year's end, he would finalise the *Dhol Jamabandi* (assessment) and other *Juman Jama* documents and forward to the Royal Court after his own attestation and those of the *Karori, Qanungos* and the *Chaudharies*. He had also to issued order for the preparation of the *Chakabandi* (Boundary demarcations) documents and attest the same.[41] At the time of the boundary demarcation of the agrarian land for the *Madad-i-maash* assignees, he was represented by his *Gumashta* and *Munsif* (survey officer) of the *Pargana*.[42] (The revenue documents remained in his official custody, especially the original *Chaknama*.[43]

Apart from the office of the *Amin* as Assessment officer, there was another revenue official named *Amin-i-Roznamchar* who was in fact *Amin* of the *Pargana* responsible for making entries of the daily realisations and expenditure in a ledger named *Roznamcha*.[44] The detailed entries of the *Mal-O Jihat* and *Sair-O Jihat* were made in the *Roznamcha*. Such record was prepared village wise and *Tappah* wise for the entire *Pargana* and was verified by the *Fotahadar* and duly stamped by the *Karori's* office.

References

1. Having got dissatisfied with the administration of Khizr Khan in Bengal, Sher Shah appointed *Qazi* Fazilat as *Amin-i Bangala* as the agent of the Central Government to supervise the administration in Bengal. (Abbas, Ms. I. O, fol 108b; *Waqiat-i Mushtaqi*, Ms. Aligh (Br. M. copy) p. 216.) In his 30th R.Y. Akbar appointed Fath Ullah Shirazi as *Amin-al-Mulk* (*Amin* of the Empire) for the improvement of financial and revenue affairs of the Empire (A.N. Br. M. Add. 26, 207, fol 194a; tr. Ber. III, p. 687).
2. Mirat. Suppl. p. 26
3. R.A.J. *Akhbarat*, *Waqai Pargana* Othal; Also regd No. 1636, dated 16th Ramzan A.H. 1123/17th Oct. 1711 A.D.
4. R.A.J. *Akhbarat* regd No. 1487/2 dated 26th Rabi II 23rd R.Y. (Aurangzeb).
5. R.A.J. 'Misc. Pers. Letters', regd. No 355 dated 25th R.Y. A.H. 1093/1681 A.D; Also *Kh.* S, N.A.I., p. 56.
6. R.A.J *Akhbarat* regd No. 1502/I dated 12th *Jamada* I, 23rd R.Y. (Aurangzeb) ; Kh.S. *Ibid.*
7. *Ibid.* dated 22nd Shabban 44 R.Y. ;Mirat.
8. *Ibid.* dated 3rd Muharram 10th R.Y. (Aurangzeb) records a report from the *Amin* of *Parganas* and gold mines in *Subah* Patna (Bihar). It seems that the functions etc. were combined in the same person.
9. *Ibid.* regd. No. 1595 dated 16th Shabban 23rd R.Y. (Aurangzeb).
10. *Ibid.* dated 27th Rajab 36th R.Y. /28th October, 1692 A.D.
11. *Ibid.* regd No. 1504/2 dated 14th *Jamada* I 23rd R.y. (Aurangzeb).
12. *Ibid.* regd. No. 166 dated 4th *Muharram* 37th R.Y/23rd August 1693 A.D.
13. *Ibid.* regd. No. 1504/2 dated 25th *Shabban* 23rd R.Y. (Aurangzeb).
14. *Ibid.* dated 27th Rabi II 37th R.Y./6th November 1693 A.D.
15. R.A.J *Akhbarat*, *Waqai Pargana* Othal; Also regd. No. 1636 dated 16th *Ramzan* A.H. 1123/17th Oct. 1711 A.D.
16. A.N. Br. M. Add. 27, 247 fol 300b, tr. Bev. p. 916; *Darjun Nafais*, p. 500; *Iqbal Nama*, Ms. Rampur, p. 527.
17. *Ibid.* fols 310b, 396b; *Iqbal Nama*, Ms. Rampur, p. 687; *Jahangir Nama* by Mullah Hussain Kamgar, fols 61a-b.
18. R.A.J. *Akhbarat* regd. No . 1467/1 dated 6th Rabi II 23rd R.Y. (Aurangzeb).
19. *Mirat* I. p. 338.
20. *Kh. S.* N.A.I. P. 32; also f.n. 5
21. *B.G.* Ms. B.N. Paris, fols 61b, 284b.
22. *Kh. S.* N. A. I. P. 32; Ms. Aligh, fols 15b- 16a.
23. *Ibid.*
24. *Ibid.*
25. *Ibid;* also see portion related to the *Faujdar*.
26. See portion related to the *Faujdar*.
27. *Ibid.*
28. R.A.J. 'Maharaja' s letters', regd. no. 835 dated 39th R.Y. A.H. 1106/1693 A.D; *Ibid* regd no 840 dated 39th R.Y. A.H. 1106/A.D; *Ibid.* category no. 2 regd. no. 393 dated 20th *Rabi*, 38th R.Y. A.H. 1106/1693 A.D.

29. The Rajasthan Archives Jaipur are full of such distinct appointments. See category no 2 regd. no 393 dated 20th Rabi I 38th R.Y. A.H. 1106/A.D; S.N. Hydbd, fol 80a; Also for *Amin*, see f. now 14-16; Also portion related to *Karori*.
30. R.A.J. regd. no. 835 and 840 vide f.n. 17; *Mirat* I, 291.
31. See original *Chaknama* dated 9th *Rabi* II 10th R.Y. (Aurangzeb) vide f.n. 29b;
32. R.A.J. 'Misc. Persian Letters to State officials and Mughal court officials' regd no. 116 dated 8th Rajab 48th R.Y. (Aurangzeb) A.H. 1116/9th *Katak Samat* 1761/1704 A.D. quotes a *Parwana* regarding the appointment of *Amin* in the enumerated *Paibaqi Parganas* in the *Sarkars* of Alamgir Nagar and Chanderi (*Subha* Malwa) It also gives details of the duties of the *Amin*. Also 'Misc. Pers. Letters', regd. no. 363 dated 20th *Rajab* 37th R.Y. A.H. 1104/1750 *Samat*/1693 A./D. quotes a *Parwana* regarding the appointment of Abu Said as the *Mutsadi* and *Amin* of the *Khalsa Parganas* in Islamabad (*Chakla*).
33. *Ibid.* R.A.J. regd no. 116. The above quoted *Parwana* issued by the *Amin* himself informs the *Chaudharies, Qanungos, Muqaddams, Muzarian* and the *ryots* of the *Parganas* that he had appointed kanwal Nain to execute duties on his behalf and that he should be acknowledged as the *Amin*.
34. *Kh.S.* vide. f.n. 5; also f.n. 2.
35. See portion related to the *Faujdar*.
36. R.A.J. 'Misc. Persian Letters', regd. no 241 dated A.H. 1146/1790 *Samat*/ 1733 A.D.
37. M.I. Berlin, fol. 5b. Aurangzeb in his letter to Prince objected to the transfer of a *Diwan* to the job of an *Amin* or *Amin* in the *Jagir* lands. He commented that the duties of an *Amin* were far more difficult than that of a *Diwan*. A *Diwan* should not be transferred to the post of an *Amil* and *Faujdar* (*Raqaim Kariam*, Ms. Rampur, pp. 44-45).
38. M.I. Berlin fols 4b-6a; 13b.
39. *Murraqat-i Hasan*, pp. 328-329 quotes a *Parwana* dated 15th *Jamada* II 9th R.Y. A.H. 1026 regarding the appointment of Amaullah as the *Amin* of *Parganas* of Jehkahr etc. (*Subha* Bihar) and the duties to be Performed by him.
40. Udai Chand, *Farhang-i-Kardani okar-amozi*, AD 1699 (F.K.), Ms. Edinburgh, fols 39a-39b; Jagat Rai Shujai Kayath Saksena *Farhang-i Kardang* Ms. Aligh, A.D. 1679; Ms. Aligh, fol. 29a..
41. *Kh.S,* N.A.I. pp. 20-22; Ms. Aligh, fols 10a-11b.
42. An original *Chaknama* confirming 40 *bighas* of *Madad-i-Maash* land on Musamat Nur Bibi in village Nadla.
43. An Original *Chaknama* dated 9th *Rabi* II 10th R.Y. (Aurangzeb) confirming 4 *bighas* of garden land in *Madad-i Maash* on Saiyyadan s/o Saiyyad Khuballah in *Qasba* Ajmer (*Subah* Ajmer); also f.n. 27.
44. *Ibid.* pp. 36-41, Ms. Aligh, fols 17b-20a.

8. *Chaudhari* : The Place of *Chaudhari* in the *Pargana* Administration under the Mughals (1556-1707)

The office and the place of the *Chaudhari* in the land revenue administration of the *Pargana* has not received adequate attention so far. Moreland has discussed about the nature of that office relying on indirect evidence-a Parwana, two *Nishans* and two *Farmans* of the Mughal period concerning the position of the *Deshmukh* in Deccan *Subahs*.[1] Moreover the position explained for the *Deshmukh* is true, with certain reservations, only for the Chief Chaudhari of the entire *Pargana* in Northern India and completely ignores the working of the *Chaudhari's* office in the divisions of the *Pargana*. Dr. P. Sargan for want of contemporary evidence at his disposal has dealt with the position of the *Chaudhari* in the *Pargana* is justified. He has based his surmises either or the old traditions of village administration or on the 19th century sources.[5] Dr. Qureshi has not dealt with this office in his discussion on the *Pargana* officials under Akbar. However, with detailed examination of sources of Akbar's reign followed by recently discovered revenue literature and various *Dastur ul amls* of the 17th Century, a more reliable and comprehensive picture about the position and obligations of *Chaudhari* in the *Pargana* administration can be constructed.[7]

Inherited from the earlier administration, the *Chaudhari* with a semi-official status played an extremely important role in the working of the Mughal revenue administration of the *Pargana*. His post was more or less hereditary though subject to confirmation at every vacancy and by every succeeding monarch.[8] Even as such, the continuation of the job was always consistant with efficiency and proper discharge of the duties. In case of failure of a male succession, the vacancy could be filled by the *Subah* authorities subject to the confirmation of the Monarch.[9]

The term *Chaudhari* was generic. There was the Chief *Chaudhari* incharge of all the mints (*Dabul Zarab*) of the Empire.[10] A *Chaudhari* of every individual mint, a *Chaduhar* of a market (*Ganj*)[11] in a port, a city, *Pargana* or *Qasba*, who was responsible for recording all the sale-proceedds, customs and commercial transactions in his jurisdiction.[12] But as the land revenue official in the *Pargana*, the *Chaudhari* was the head of the village *Muqaddams* (Headmen), and had multifarious revenue duties. There was the Chief *Chaudhari* for the entire *Pargana* who had under him a few field.

Chaudhris for groups of villages, a field *Chaudhari* being incharge of a circle each. The *Chaudhari* of the whole *Pargana* was named '*Chaudhari-i-kalan*' i.e. the Chief *Chaudhari* though popularly know as '*Chaudhari-i-Pargana*.'[13] The filed *Chaudhari* was ordinarily associated with a named *Tappah* (fiscal division of *Pargana*[14]) or *Qasba* (large village[15]), though usually designed simply as *Chaudhari*. The distinction between the two- The Chief *Chaudhari* and the field *Chaudhari* in the *Pargana* has to be made in the context of narration. *Ain* simply refers to the *Chaudhari* with his counterpart in Berar in the *Deshmukh*[16] without mentioning the territorial jurisidiction of either of them. This has misled Moreland to conclude that there was only one *Chaudhari* in the *Pargana*[17] though facts prove the case to be quite otherwise. *Akbar Nama* in the 27th regnal year reforms by Todar Mal in the 2nd clause refers to various *Chaudharis* working under *Amil-i-Khalsa* (of *Pargana.*)[18] *Makhzan-ul-Ihetsab*, a comprehensive *Dastur-ul-aml* of the 17th century while narrating the land revenue administration of the last years of Shahjahan and the first three years of Aurangzeb's reign describes the procedure of assessment and land revenue collection to be made in a *Pargana* and distinctly refers to a number of *Chaudharies* and the various obligations to be discharged by them.[19] Apart from it, all appointment orders of the *Pargana* officials and the assignment of the *Jagir* within the *Pargana* were intimated to the *Chaudharis, Qanungos,* and *Muqaddams* of the *Pargana.*[20] If there was only one *Chaudhari* in the *Pargana*, he would not be addressed in plural language.[21] The existence of various *Chaudharies* in one *Pargana* is also confirmed by other original documents of Aurangzeb's reign.[22] There was, of course no uniformity about the number of *Chaudharis* to be appointed for each *Pargana* as that would depend on the size of the *Pargana* and the local tradition of allocation of village- grouping with assigned amount of revenue to be realised by each *Chaudhari.*[23] On an average, a large *Pargana* would have 4 to 5 *Chaudhari*[24] though in some cases, the number on record goes upto thirteen.[25] As against this a *Farman* of Aurangzeb's reign quoting an order embodied in a previous *Hasbulhukm* fixes the number of *Chaudharis* and *Qanungos* in a *Pargana* at two each.[26] At the same time, the *Farman* indicates the appointment of a large number of these officials in practice and forbids the same. It seems in the context that the *Hasbulhukm* referred to in the *Farman* was intended for operation in the *Subah* Gujrat only. This may have justification in the fact that in Gujrat, the *Chaudharies* were assisted by the *Desais* with somewhat similar duties and that the office of the latter did not exist in any of the other provinces in Northern India. Moreover, the above *Farman* itself deals with the problems of *Subah* Gujrat only and refers to the *Hasbulhukm* in the context of the special condition prevalent in the port of Kambayat (*Sarkar* Ahmadabad).

A *Chaudhari* would be appointed for one full *Tappah* and a group of villages from another *Tappah* or for a group of named villages drawn from two different *Tappahs*. His headquarters would be essentially located in a *Qasba*, which was also the seat of the *Tappah* itself associated with his jurisdiction. The number of set villages composing a division under his jurisdiction in a large *Pargana* varied (from to)[27] There were no uniform circles though a *Chaudhari* (i.e. *Chaudhership*) of a circle contined with more or less herediatary claims. All this is borne out by the original '*Fahrist-i-Tapphajat*' i.e. the *Tappah*, village habitation and *Mauza* (village) documents or *Pargana* Bhagalpur, *Sarkar* Monghyr, *Subah* Behar dated Fasli year 1179 (1769 A.D). They lie linked together with the original '*Raqba-bandi*' (measurement and area statement) documents dated *Fasli* year 1001 (1591 A.D.) pertaining to the same *Pargana* and named *Tappahs* and are available at the Secretariat Record Office, Patna (Bihar)[28]. The essential difference between the two is that whereas the documents of Akbar's reign pertain to the details '*Arazi*' (measurement figures) of the named *Tappahs* and *Mauzas* of *Pargana* Bhagalpur, the latter run *Chaudhriwise* with poritions of named *Tappahs* and a number of *Dehats* put under each named *Chaudhari*. A *Chaudhari* has sometimes one full *Tappah* and a few more villages from another *Tappah* shown under his name. But usually, portions of two to three *Tappahs* with specified number of villages are put under his charge. For example, *Chaudhari* Udhai Kand has one full *Tappah* of Alwar Abad and a portion from *Tappah* Akbar Nagar, *Chaudhuri* Jai Narain has one full *Tappah* of Azimpur and a portion from *Tappah* Sikandarpur but *Chaudhari* Khushal has only portions from two *Tappahs*, 14 *Mahals*[29] and 34 *Mauzas* from Wahilkeh, 1 *Mahal* and 3 *Mauzas* from Azim Nagar. Similarly, *Chaudhari* Nand Lal has portions from three *Tappahs* 7 *Mahals,* 7 *Mauzas* from Sikandpur, 3 *Mahals* and 5 *Mauzas* from Akbar Nagar, 7 *Mahals* and 15 *Mauzas* from Awarq pur. Though the sheets (total pages 203) of the year 1179 Fasli (1771 AD) pertain to the later Mughal period, their importance cannot be under-estimated keeping in view the fact that they fall in continuity with the '*Raqba-bandi*' documents of Akbar's reign with regard to the details of the same *Tappahs* of the same *Pargana*.[30] Despite the fact that in the later Mughal times, in Bengal, the jurisdiction of the *Chaudhari* increased at random, instances of *Chaudhership* for the circle of a *Pargana* or for one *Tappah* only with hereditary claims as descended from the earlier period can be traced.[31]

As to his obligations, the *Chaudhari* was the head of the *Muqaddams* of village under his jurisdiction and had somewhat similar duties on a large scale. As a part of his general duties, he was to assist all the higher *Pargana* and *Sarkar* officers in the discharge of their administrative duties[32]. He had to safeguard the interests of the *ryots*, to protect the peasantry against the high handedness of the turbulent elements and keep informing the higher authorities of any chaotic situations.[33] He would, with the help of the *Qanungo* and *Muqaddams* prepare a list of the names of all undesirable and obstructive bad characters and forward them to the higher authorities for appropriate action to be taken against them. As against this, such of the persons who worked for the welfare of the *ryots* and economy of the State exchequer were to be duly recommended by him for the award of *Inam*.[34] He had to augment agriculture by encouraging the peasantry and bringing the maximum of the waste land under cultivation.[35]

As to his specific revenue duties, assisted by the *Muqaddams*, he had to help the *Amin* (assessment officer) in the proper assessment of the holdings of the cultivators in the villages under his jurisdiciotn.[36] He was to get in advance a note (*Parwana*) from the *Amin* about the latter's tour programme for assessment in his area.[37] Helped by the *Muqaddams*, he had to remain with *Amin* throughout assessment work in every village of his area.[38] The '*Jama-bandi*' embodying assessment was to be made in his presence and with his consent.[39] He, along with with *Muqaddams*, represented the interests of both the *ryots* and the *State*. As such, under the rules, his consent and deed of acceptance to assessment made on the *ryots* by the *Amin* was essential.[40] *Baharistan-i-Ghaibi* of Jahangir's reign mentions the assessment made by Khawaja Muhammad Tahir in the newly conquered territory of Jessore and that the '*Nuskha-i-Jamma*' (Assessment document) prepared by the *Khwaja* was signed by the *Chaudharis* and *Qanungos* before it was submitted to Islam Khan (the Governor of Bengal)[41]. Besides this, the same source narrates that on the refusal of Sher Khan Fath-Jang to accept the *Jagir* of Tajpur Purnea owing to lack of correct assessment where, upon Khawaja Todar Mal being appointed as the special *Amin* prepared a new '*Jamma*' (assessment document) bearing the signature of the *Qanungos* and with the deed of its acceptance by *Chaudharis*.[42] He had to attest the measurement documents upon which the assessment of the *Kankut* (appraisment) was based.[43]

Above all, his most important function was the collection of the land revenue in his area for which he was even legally bound both by his appointment order and a yearly deed.[44] *Farhang-i-Kardani*, a 17th century *Dastrurulaml* quotes an acceptance deed taken from the *Chaudhari* of the *Pargana* after the assessment is complete, and require him to collect the land revenue, with specified amount on the basis of the assessment made both for *Rabi* and *Kharif* crops and to deposite the same in three installments as stated in the deed.[45] He was fully responsible for the collection to be done by the *Muqaddams* under him.[46] *Makhazan-ul-Ehetsab* explains in details the arrangement made by the *Amil* (collector) for land revenue collection in the *Pargana*, as to how the *Chakladars*,

Sitadars (small field unit official) were to assist the *Tappadars* (in charge of *Tappahs*) and *Muqaddams* in the collection of the land revenue of the villages and depositing the same in installments in the treasury. [47] All this was reduced in agreement bonds executed by the foregoing officials with the attestation of *Qanungos* and *Chaudharis*, who bore under legal bond full responsibility for the depositing of the regular installments in the treasury in his supervision. [48] He was also responsible for the the realisation of *Peshkash* from the *Zimindars*[49] and dues from the *Jagirdars* in his territory. [50] In the *Pargana* revenue documents, the number of the villages along with their revenue figures was put under the name of a *Chaudhary* presumably showing his responsibility for collection of their revenue.[51] Any differences occurring between the amount assessed and realised due to any adjustment in the original assessment and consequent remittance conceded to the *ryots* owing to their inability for further payment, had all to be attested by him.[52] He had also to attest any remission on account of drought, trampling of the crops and natural calamity.[53] He had the special responsibility of the advancement of '*Taqavi*' (agricultural loans) to the cultivators and their recovery in regular installments.[54] He had to stand security by signing a bond for the production of the *Muqaddams* or *Zimindars* or other persons needed in connection with the collection of the land revenue.[55] The *Pargana Chaudhari* had to shoulder all these responsibilities on a larger scale for the entire *Pargana*. The '*Taujih*' (ledger of realisation and the balance of the *Pargana* had to be finalised by the *Shiqdar* (*Pargana* officer) and his *Karkun* (assisant) at the *Chabotra* (administrative headquarters), only in the presence and with the attestation of the *Chaudharis, Qanungos*, and the *Muqaddams*.[56] The *Pargana Chaudhari* was signatory to the important *Pargana* revenue documents of assessment, realisations and balance i.e. '*Sayaha Taskish Jama*', acceptance deeds of assessment and '*Tumarjama*' of the land revenue and customs, *Pargana 'Taujih'*, and '*Awarija*'[57] As distinct from the land revenue, the *Chaudhari* of the *Pargana* or its circle was equally responsible for the collection of custom duties and other legitimate *cesses* in his jurisdiction.

The *Chaudhari* was one of the main addresses in all orders of appointment of the *Pargana* officials and as such had to show full co-operation to the latter.[58] He was always informed of any *Jagir* or *Zimindari* assignments in his jurisdiciton[59] and along with the *Patwari, Qanungo* and *Muqadams* had to attest their assignment '*Chakhamahs*' (territorial demarcations) and relevant documents.[60] He had also to help the assignees in the realisation of the land revenue in accordance with the regulations. The revenue literature of Shah Jahan's reign fixed direct responsibility of the *Chaudhari* for land revenue realisation in the *Jagir*.[61] '*Maktubat-i-*

khan Jahan Muzaffar Khan' in a letter written on behalf of the *Jagirdar* (Muzaffar Khan) to *Chaudhari* Lakhi Dass points out that in the revenue of the villages Jailini and Narari (*Chakla* Hisar) deposited in the treasury, a difference of Rs. 3/- only has occurred on account of difference in the exchange of old Indian Rupee and the Shahjahani currency.[62] It states that even though such accounts (of exchange) are difficult to reckon, the *Chaudhari* should settle the accounts in Shahjahani currency and that he should be extremely careful in keeping the account of the realisations and should also note down if there is any difference in the revenues as compared with the previous years. Another letter written to Khwaja Nand Lal (*Amil* of the *Jaqir* of Khan Jahan Muzaffar Khan *Faujdar* and *Dewan* of *Chakla* Hissar, *Subah* Delhi) states that it had been represented (to the *Jagirdar*) by some of the persons from the villages of Karnwalay and Kaliher (*Pargana* Hissar) that whereas the real assessment valuation of these villages was Rs. 125/-, they had actually been assessed for Rs. 50/ [63]. It further required that the latter amount be collected and for the balance, *Chaudhari* Bahar and the *Zimindar* of *Pargana* Hissar be directed to get the reassessment done and thereafter its entries be made in the relevant '*Jamma*' documents. The same may be realised and despatched (to the *Jagirdar*). In Jaipur Archives, of the numerous original *Parwanas* of Aurangzeb's reign, one from Jumlatul Mulk Asad Kha (*Dewan-i-Khalsa* of the Central Government) directed towards the *Chaudharis, Quanugos* and *Muqaddams* etc. of *Tappah* Khaeiled, *Pargana* Bajwaraha, *Sarkar* and *Subah* Akbarabad states that 92566 *dams* of the said *Pargana* were assigned to Raja Bishan Singh (of Amber) on the death of Raja Man Singh and that they should help in the collection in accordance with the regulations, and should see that the same amount was handed over to the Raja.[64]. All documents concerning the realisation and arrears in the *Jagir* had to be attested by him before the revenues were remitted to the assignees.[65] In case of any oppression upon the *ryots* by the *Amils* of the *Jagirdar,* the *Chaudhari*, along with the *Qanungos* and *Muqaddams*, would at once lodge a complaint to the *Jagirdar* and the *Pargana* authorities.[66]

Apart from his revenue duties, his evidence and attestation was essential in all legal transactions concerning sale or mortgage of the land. This is borne out by the original *Bainama* (sale deed) of Aurgangzeb's reign, executed by Brinda Ban in favour of *Vakil* Kanwar Raj Singh (of Amber) for gardens of 15 *bighas* in village Khampura, *Pargana* Shajahanbad, (*Subah* Shajahanbad) duly stamped in the Qazi's Court and attested in evidence by Mukesh Dass, *Chaudhari* and *Qanungo* and also attested by Mohan Dass, *Chaudhari* and *Qanungo* of *Pargana* (Shahjahanbad).[67]

As to the *Chaudhari's* relation with the *Qanungo*, Elliot has incorrectly remarked, "No material difference existed between the work done by the *Conoongeo* and the *Chowdrie*"[68] Though the *Chaudhari* had various functions akin to that of the *Qanungo*, the two officials had distinctly independent charges of their respective jobs. The *Qanungo* with his vast professional training was essentially a technical expert in revenue matters and a keeper of the revenue records in his jurisdiciton[69] over which the *Chaudhari* had no jurisdiction. Quite distinctly from the *Chaudhari*, the *Qanungo* had to furnish the *Pargana* officals with required information and relevant revenue document, of '*Taqsim*' (record of both cultivable and uncultivable area) '*Dasturulaml*' (schedule of rates) and other survey and realisation documents pertaining to the previous years.[70] More than the *Chaudhari*, he had to attest the survey and assessment documents of '*Khasra', Muntkhib', 'Jamabandi'*, prepared by the *Patwaries* and *Muqaddams* in the villages in his circle.[71] The *Pargana Qanungo*, apart from the document verified jointly with the *Pargana Chaudhari* was responsible for the custody of all land records filed in his office viz; the list of the villages, *Tappahs*, and their revenues along with the names of the *Chaudharis* responsible for collection; the list of the jurisdictions and revenues under the various *Zimindars*, along with the security bonds of the latter executed by the *Chaudharies*, the documents of '*Mawzna Deh Sala*' (record of assessment of ten years) and '*Taqsim*' of every village, the '*Tumar*' documents of the previous realisation, arrears, '*Jamma Wasilbaqi*' stamped by *Amil, Sihya Wasibaqi, Goshware, Jama Kharch* and *Tumar Jama*.[72] Besides this, he had to despatch regularly to the central government the document of the '*Taqsim*' and the '*Muwazana Deh Sala*' showing also the maximum realisation year (*San-i-Kamil*) and areas of every village, along with the '*Dasturulaml*' pertaining to the land realisations and customs, the regulations of the treasury, and the actual realisation of the previous years concerning both the *Khalsa* and the *Jagir* lands in his *Pargana*.[73] Along with the *Amin*, his responsibility for conducting the technical work of survey and assessment was far more significant.[74]

Far from serving as a check upon each other as suggested by Elliott. the two officials were complimentary in relation to each other. Jointly as the representatives of the Government and the *ryots*, and with their permanent tenure as against the frequently transferable *Pargana* officials and the assignees[75], they helped the latter in the discharge of their duties.[76] They equally served as a check on them against any financial or procedural irregularity.[77] They also conjointly acted as counterweight against any undue oppression upon the *ryots* by the assignees of the land and the *Zimindars*.[78] Within the division of the same *Pargana*, usually the two field officials had separate circles for their territorial jurisdiction,[79] though for the reign of Shah Jahan, there is evidence to show that the offices of the *Pargana Chaudhari* and the *Pargana Qanungo* in the *Pargana* were combined in the same person.[80]

As to this remunerations, the *Chaudhari* was entitled to perquisities named *Nankar-i-Chaudhari'* which would be paid either in cash or by way of rent-free grant of waste land. In Jaipur Archives, a *Yaddasht* embodying area statement of Aurangzeb in the detailed area figures of village Shah Jahan Bhanu Das show waste land given in rent free grant to the *Chaudhari* Bhanu Dass in accordance with the settled practice.[81] As against this, *Intkhab-i-dastrurlaml* in *Wajiblarz* (code of regulations) quotes the *Nankar* of the *Chaudharis* and *Qanungos* in cash and quotes the advance payment paid in cash both for the *Kharif* and *Rabi* crops.[82] Usually, he was paid some advance and the rate of payment on the revenue collection would depend on the traditional practice in the *Pargana*. The *Intknab-i-Dasurulaml* in its *Wajibularz* states that the *Nankar* of the *Chaudharis* and *Qanungos* in the *Pargana* is fixed in accordance with its *Amil-i Mamul* accustomed practice and that is is paid in advance by the *ryots* at the end of the year, i.e. after the *Rabi* crop.[83] The amount of advance quoted is Rs. 375/- apportioned at Rs. 250/- for the *Kharif* and the balance for the *Rabi* crop. The rate of payment for the collection made would be determined on the basis of the past few years practice after the perusal of the *Sanads* given by the higher officials.[84] In another instance, while giving the details of the revenues of the different villages deposited in the treasury, it shows Rs. 185/- as the revenue for village Rampur and as against this Rs. 5/- are shown as the joint emoulments of the *Chaudharies*[85] which gives 2.7% of the realisation in the village. *Makhzan-ul-Ihetsab* while conforming many of the above facts, distinctly notes that the advance was paid at the end of the *Rabi* crop and also points out the rate of the collection at 2.5% both for the *Chaudhari* and the *Qanungo*.[86] As known from the Jaipur Archives of the *Muqaddam's* case, the advance was to be adjusted in the favour of the *ryots* at the time of the revenue collection.[87] He was also entitled to some cash incidental charges.

The nature of the '*Chaudhari's* office, whether of the *Pargana* or a circle in the *Pargana*, with all its status and obligations, as explained, remained the same till the end of Aurangzeb's reign. Like various other offices, it underwent a change only in the later times, though still retaining some of its traits in its obligations. The *Chaudhari* acquired different characteristics in different parts of the century. By the 18th and 19th centuries, in Bengal he had become a *Taluqdar* with *Zimindari* rights in the contemporary sense and could even legally sell villages with all its rights from his *Taluqa*.[88] This is confirmed by an attested copy of the sale bond executed by Korhari Bose, *Chaudhari* of portion of the *Pargana* Chaotipur Ra, *Sarkar* Salimabad, *Chakla* Hugli, dated A.H. 1172 (1758 A.D.). In some cases, even his jurisdiction of *Chaudhership* had extended to numerous *Parganas*.[89] In Allahabad, Duncan noted him as an official only with revenue duties though mostly in a dilapidated condition and with shelved status of his former self.[90] In Oudh, as Elliott found him, he retained his position as revenue official though being fastly eclipsed by the *Qanungo* in official and social status as land owner.[91] In Ajmer, he stuck to his position as a revenue official and at some places, his office was combined with that of the *Qanungo*. [92] He was entitled to his *Rassum* (emoluments) *Choudhership* and *Qanungoi* in kind, which according to the 'Cavendish Enquires' had dwindled from age to age and most of his original perquistes having been usurped by the *Istamrars*[93] (hereditary revenue farmers). In the territories of Delhi, he continued with his original revenue duties and status, though his jurisdiction was curtailed to only one village.[94] In the Panjab under the Sikhs, he retained his original position, duties and status[95]. In the Deccan states, his counterpart, the *Deshmukh* became a *Zimindar* with over extending rights of '*Talukdari*' still retaining his revenue duties in theory along with its prequisities and various illegal cesses realised tyrinically from the *ryots*.[96]

References

1. Morleand; 'The *Pargana* Headman (Chaudhry) in the Mogul Empire (J.R.A.S of G. Brt. and Ireland. Oct. 1938. pp. 511-521.

(A) *Parwana*, dated A.H. I027, 13th regnal year of Jahangir adds ten Chawar (plough-land) of land to Desai and Deshmukh of *Pargana* Pathri.

(B) (i) *Nishan*, dated A.H. 1059, 23rd regnal year of Shah Jahan settles the succession of *Deshmukh* of the *taraf* (division) Anwal in *Pargana* Balgarh, *Subha* Telingana and reminde him of his duties.

(ii) *Nishan*, dated 19th regnal year of Shah Jahan confirms the hereditary succession of *Deshmukhi* of *Pargana* Pathri.

(c) **(i)** *Farman*, dated 30th regnal year of Aurangzeb makes an appointment as *Deshmukh* of *Pargana* Narsi, *Sarkar* Basim, *Subah* Berar reminds the *Deshmukh* of his duties and orders the local officials to recognized him.

(ii) *Farman*, dated A.H. 1100 confirming as earlier *Farman* of 5th regnal year of Aurangzeb narrates that *Pargana* Pathri had been devided between the *Deshmukhs* by Khan Khana Abdur Rahim where he held it in that arrangement had continued in force and that the practice of one offered a pedhah a faruar confined the partition; confirms it, enumerates his duties, and orders the local officials to comply and collect the *peshkash*.

2. *Ain*: Br. M. Add. 6552 fol 195a. ' And in this country (*Subah* Berar), Choudhry is known as *Deshmukh*. Also Jarret, ii. 237 Moreland: 'The *Pargana* Headman (*Choudhry*)', p. 512.
3. Moreland, p. 511, admits his failure to trace this office in any administrative literature.
4. Saran, '*Provincial Government of the Mughals'*, Appendix B. pp. 458-460.
5. *Ibid*, pp. 458-459. Dr. Saran has associated the *Chaudhari* with two different sets of village-grouping i.e. of 12 and 84 and traces them to the Rajput period. He states that this Hindu tradition permeated throughout the medieaval age and as such was noticed by EIlot in the 19th century, vide his '*Memoirs of the Races of N.W. Province of India'*, vol. II. Pp. 47-48. He further confirms that this practice has continued till the present day. But such village-grouping of *Chaudhri's* circle is not at all warranted by the revenue literature of the Mughal age.
6. Qureshi, I.H. ' *The Pargna officials under Akbar'*. *Islamic Culture,* vol. XVI, No. I., Jan, I942, pp. 87-93.
7. Dr. Saran in 'Provincial Government, p. 459, while tracing it to the Rajput times suggests two fold source of its etemology, as 'a corruption of the Sanskrit '*Chaturdhurin*' and as 'a corruption of the *Chitradhar'* (vide *Ab-i-Hayat*, p.35. by Maulana Moh. Husain Azad). In the Sultanate period, the office existed under Balban and Alaud Din Khilji: Tripathi '*Some Aspects of Muslim Administration*' pp. 252, 257 respectively. For *Chaudhry's* office in Shershah's and Humayun's administration, see *Tarikh-i-Daudi,* No. I34, Lytton collection, M.U. Aligarh, p. 179.
8. Usually, hereditary offices like *Muqaddams, Desais* (in Gujrat and Deccan *Subahs*), *Chaudhris, Qanungos*, and the grants of the *Madad-i-Maash* and some of the hereditary *Zimindaries* were confirmed by the royal authorities

in every reign. The practice of confirmation of these offices on the payment of *Peshkash* can be traced only in the reign of Aurangzeb. All the same, it is suggestive of the fact that the confirmation of these hereditary offices was usually taken of granted, it could be lawfully withdrawn at the discretion of the Monarch. Also for Deshmukh in Deccan, documents quoted by Moreland vide *Nishan* (i) of Shah Jahan's reign settles the disputed succession to *Deshmukhi*. The Viceroy had allowed an adoptive son of half-share, but the Emperor overruled this, and accepted the natural son as sole *Deshumukh*. *Nishan* (2) of Shah Jahan's reign also confirms the hereditary succession to the son of the death of his father. Also see 'Aurangzeb's *Farman* (ii).

9. An 18th cent. Ms. Orient Quart. 258, Berlin fols I6-I7a, while tracing the I7th cent. History of *Chaudhry* of *Parganas* Othaba and Satsika, *Sarkar* Salimabad, *Subah* Bengal confirms the re-grant of *Chaudheriship* to new families on the failure of male line of succession of the previous families. Also *Farman* (i) of Aurangzeb's reign quoted by Moreland makes fresh appointment of *Deshmukh*.
10. A.N. Br. M. Add OR 27, 247, fol 294b, also *Swanih-i-Akbari*, Khuda Baksh Library, Patna, Ms. No 556, fol I89b.
11. Binia (Rajasthan) uncatalogued Records, Personal Library of Raja of Binai.
12. *The English Factories in India* (1618-1621) pp. 269, 273-74. The editor Foster vide pp. I98, 269 has inaccurately associated '*Chowtry*' with the name of a resting place. The deciphering of '*Chowtry*' with *Chaudhari* an officer of the market is clear in the context of narrations.
13. *Makhzan-ul-Ihetsab*, Ms. Orient, fol 2I7 Berlin, fol. 5b. In this course of my research tour in Germany, I discovered a new Persian manuscript entitled *Makhzan-ul-Ihetsab Maruf Dasturulaml*, No. Ms. Orient. Fol. 217, Berlin. This manuscript consists of two independent portions, *Makhzan-ul-Ihetsab* and *Majmulat-i-Dasturulaml*. The former named *Makhzan-ul-Ihetsab,* though transcribed in 1211 H. (1796 A.D) is a version of an original *Dasturulaml* compiled in the early years of Aurangzeb's reign illustrating the working of the land revenue administration prevelant in the last years of Shah Jahan's and the first three years of Aurangzeb's reigns. Although in major portions of details and illustrations, it is evidently a version of another official *Dasturulaml* entitled '*Dasturulaml-i-Mujmil*' popularly known as '*Inkhab-i-Dasturulaml*' compiled at the order of Aurangzeb in the 3rd year of his reign, of which a transcribed copy, dated 1786 A.D., is available in the British Museum No.Rieu 1. 404; Add 6599, the former incorporates a detailed portion dealing with the role played by various officials in the land revenue administration of the *Pargana*, which cannot be traced in the latter British Museum Manuscript. It bears different introduction and is an absolutely complete document.
14. A *Tappah* was a purely fiscal unit of a *Pargana*, composed of numerous villages within its jurisdiction. For details, see my article on 'Raqba bandi' documents of Akbar's reign, *Indian Historical Records Commission Proceedings,* Vol. XXXVI, Part II, Chandigarh Session, February, 1961, pp. 55-60.

15. The *Qasba* at times comprised only one large village but would usually consist of few *mauzas* within its circle. See my above article on 'Raqba bandi' documents of Akbar's reign as per details on the above, p. 59.
16. Curiously like *Ain, Maalumat-Ufaq*, No: 248, Edinburgh, fol. 9a, also equates *Chaudhry* in the North with *Deshmukh* in Deccan. But at the same time, it comments, "The Headman of the city is called *Chaudhry*, the *Patel* in the fortune country of Hindustan (i.e. Northern India) is named *Chaudhri* and is known as *Deshmukh* in the country of Deccan". Here the synonimity of the *Chaudhri* with the *Patel* is done in a loose sense as the latter was the headman of the village and known as *Muqaddam* in the North. For *Subah* Serar, *Ain* states, 'The *Muqaddam* is called *Patel'*. (Br. M.Add. 6552, fol 195a; Jarrett ii. p. 237). Also an 18th Century Deccan *Dasturulaml* No. 678, O.R.O. Hydrabad fol 7b, states, 'In Telangana language, *Muqaddam* is known as *Patel'*.
17. Moreland in this respect followed the previous scholars, viz Elliot, '*Chronicles of Oonao*, p.112., F.D. Ascoli, '*Early Revenue History of Bengal and the fifth Report'* p. 22 who are equally wrong. On the contrary, Dr. Tapan Kumar Ray Chaudhuri vide '*Bengal under Akbar and Jahangir*', p. 27 has very inaccurately put *Chaudhari* as the headman of a village. Dr. Tara Chand in his latest writings, has been contradictory and wrong. In his '*History of Freedom Movement in India'*. Vol. I, 1961, p. 122, he has put one *Chaudhary* for a *Pargana*, whereas in his lectures on (All India Radio Patel Memorial Lectures), still under print, IInd lecture, p.23 of original manuscript), he has equated *Chaudhari* with *Muqaddam* and *Patel*, the village headmen.
18. *Akbar Namah*, Br. M.O.R. 27, 247 fol 33Ib.
"The Karori and the Amil of Khals (of Paigana) have two clerks, one *Karkun* and the other named Khas Nawis. The latter (two clerks) being in connivance with the *Chaudharis, Qanungos, Muqaddams*, and *Kalen* taran of every village (of the *Pargana*) are responsible for heavy expenditure. If in place of these two dishonest men only one trustworthy and right acting official were to be appointed, the expenditure thus incurred would be decreased and the ryots would be at peace."
19. *Makhzan ul Inetsab*, Berlin, fol 4b-7a.
20. *Dasturulaml* No. 748, C.R.O. Hydrabad, (Shah Jahan's reign). pp. 9, 12-13. *Farhaug-i-Kardani* (Aurangzeb's reign, No. 83, Edinburgh fols 39a-40b; also *Dur-al'ulum* (Aurangzeb's reign), Bodlein Library, Oxford, O.R.Walker 104 fols 136b-137b; also Jaipur, Rajasthan Archives, mad (category) No. 4, reg: 829, dated A.N. 1123 (17II A.D.)
21. Moreover, even in the Deccan, the documents quoted by Moreland, Nishan (i) of Shan Jahan's reign confirms the *Deshmukhi* of a division of *Pargana*. The *Deshmukhi* of the *taraf* itself had been further divided by the Viceroy into two shares between the natural and the adopted sons of the deceased, which was over-ruled by the Emperor in favour of the natural son for the sole *Deshmukhi* of the *taraf*.
22. *Durr-al'Ulum*, Bodlein, Oxford, fols 65a-65; also a *Farman* quoted in *Mirat-i-Ahmed*, Persian Text vol. I, p. 263.

23. *Intkhab-i-Dasturulam* Br.M.Add. 6599 fol 409; *Makhzanul Inetsab* Berlin, fol 27b.
24. *Yadasht-i-Fahrist-i-Dehat wa Tappah* 'i.e. statement of villages and *Tappahs* of *Pargana* Bhagalpur, dated year *Fasli* II79 (1771 A.D) puts five *Chaudhries* in the *Pargana* associated with different *Tappahs* and villages. Also see reference 30 and 31. (*old 29 and 30*).
25. *Durr-al 'Ulum*, Bod. Oxford, fols 65a-65b. On complaint from *ryots* of village Hassapur, *Pargana* Palwal (*Sarkar* and *Subah* Delhi) against *Chaudhry* Piha of the same village for having unlawfully taken the *Ijera* of the said village from the *Amil* and forcibly squandered the amount of Rs. 800/-for the *kharif* besides revenues of the *Rabi* crops and having misappropriated the State revenues the amount of Rs.1300/-, the *Hasb-ul-Hukm* of the *Wazir* ordered the appointment of two honest named *Chaudhries*, Manda and Hindal along with two *Qanungos* out of thirteen *Chaudhries* of the said *Pargana* for taking accounts and realising the amount from the corrupt *Chaudhry* Piha, ousting him from the village and that the amount be despatched to the Royal treasury.
26. *Mirat*. Vol. I. p. 263.
27. '*Fahrist-i-Dehat Mauza wa Mahal*' i.e. List of villages and Mahals of *Pargana* Bhagalpur (*Sarkar* Monghyr, *Subah* Bihar) dated year *Fasli* 1181 (1773 A.D.), p. 208 (Secretariat Record Office, Patna) enumerates 548 villages and *Mahals* in the *Pargana*. Chaudhries Har Narain and Ajit Singh have 199 *Mauzas* and *Mahals* under their jurisdiction whereas Chaudhry Har Hari Singh has 97 *Mauzas* and *Mahals* in his circle, pp. 210-225. A *Chaudhri's* family had always more or less hereditary and traditional jurisdiction of villages unless reshuffled under the stress of administrative expediency.
28. See my article on the '*Raqba bandi Documents of Akbar's Reign*', I.H.R.C. Proceedings, 1961, pp. 55-61.
29. Though a *Mahal* usually denoted a fiscal unit, here it stands for a *Qasba* market specialized in a particular crop-commodity.
30. The importance of these sheets, presumably in direct continuation with similar document of *Tappahs* and *Dehats* associated with *Chaudhries* for the Mughal Age (from Akbar onwards) was realised by even early British revenue officers. This is evident from and order noted in the hand of the collector C.S. Skinner dated April 29th, 1862 A.D. which runs, "To prevent any further confusion in future, Mr. Dy. Collector Renny will sign each sheet of this this first *Dehat* of Bhagalpoor of 1179 F.S." and they all bear the initials of 'AGR'.
31. *Muskha-i-Majmuat*, Ms. Or quart 258, Berlin, fol 125b, (Ms. 18th century quotes, and attested copy of a Sale Bond dated A.H.1172 (1761A.D.) which mentions Kor Hari Bose as the *Chaudhry* of '*Qismat-i-Pargana*' (division of *Pargana*) Chahotipur Ram. The same Ms. On fol 128b mentions anothor sale-bond dated A.H. 1161 (1750 A.D) executed by Nar Narien, *Chaudhry* of *Tappah* Sahiknaney, *Pargana* Sultan Partap (*Subah* Bengal).
32. See reference No 19.
33. A.N: Br.. M.Add. O.R.27, 247 fol. 332b.
34. *Ibid*, fol 332b.

35. This is emphasised in all the four documents of appointment of *Deshmukh* quoted previously. Moreland takes these obligations as a part of the executive powers of the *Chaudhries*. Far from being specifically executive powers, such duties of looking after the *ryots* are general instructions and form a part of set terminology issued in orders of appointment for all administrative and revenue officials inclusive of the *Jagirdars* and *Zimindars*. (See Moreland's view in 'The *Pargana* Headman '*Chaudhri*' J.H.A.S GB and *Ibid*., p. 518); *Dasturulaml* of Jawahar Mal Baikus, 954/4 *Subah* Allah Collection, M.U. Aligarh. fol. 43a.
36. *Makhzan ul Ihetsab*, Berlin, fol 4b-5b emphasises the vital role played by the *Chaudhries* in the assessment work of the *Amin*.
37. *Ibid*, fol 4b.
38. *Ibid*, fol 5ab.
39. *Ibid*, fol 5a.
40. *Baharistan-i-Ghaibi* (Jahangir's reign) no. Suppl. Pars. 252. Bibliotheque, Nationale, Paris, fol 61b *Murraqat-i-Hasan*, No: 217, State Library Rampur, 328. A *Parwana* dated A.H. I026 (9th regnal year of Shah Jahan) appointing Sheikh Aman Ullah as *Amin* of *Parganas* of Jaukajri (*Sarkar* Bahadrak, Orissa, *Subah* Bengal) enjoins him to prepare the '*Tumar*' of '*Taskhish Jama*' (assessment document) of these *Parganas* bearing the signatures of the *Zimindar, Chaudhries* and *Qanungos*. Also see *Makhzn-ul-Ihetsab*, Berlin fol 25a. Also *Farhaug-i-Kardani* (Aurangzeb's reign) No: 85/3I5, Abdus Salam Collection, M.U. Aligarh, fol 29a; *Khulasat'us Siyaq* (Aurangzeb's reign) Sulaman Collection No. 74, M.U. Aligarh, fol 10a.
41. *Baharistan-i-Ghaibi*,B.N.Paris, fol 61b.
42. *Ibid*, fol. 61b.
43. *Intkhab-i Dasturulaml*, Br. M. Riou 404, Add 6599, fol 41b; *Dasturulaml* No. 748 C.R.O. Hyderabad, p.14 mentions his attestation even for '*Sayaha-Zabit-i-Mauza*' i.e. for the entire village measurement document.
44. *Farhaug-i-Kardani*, Aligarh fol 34a; Also documents of the *Deshmukh's* appointment *Nishan* (i) dated A.H.1059; *Farman* dated A.H.1100.
45. *Ibid.* fol 34e.
46. *Makhzan-ul Ihetsab*, Berlin fol 6a.
47. *Ibid*, fol 6a.
48. *Ibid*, fol 6a.
49. In the Mughal age, the term *Zimindar* had varied meaning. It applied as much to the hereditary *Rajas* and *Rais* as to the feudal landlords and the administrative cum revenue officials. It has to be interpreted in the context of narration. The *Chaudhari* in his official capacity had to deal with the latter two categories.
50. *Chaudhari* in his official capacity had to deal with the latter two categories. *Intkhab-I Dasturaml*, Br. M. Add. 6599, fol 40b.
51. *Ibid*, fols 40b, 46b; *Makhzan ul-Ihetsab*, Berlin, fol 27b.
52. *Siyaq Nama* (Aurangzeb's reign) No. 858, C.R.O. Hydrabad.
53. *Intkhab-i-Dasturulaml*, Br. M. Add. 6599 fol 45b quotes '*Tumar Afat Khushki*' i.e. assessment of the damages to crops due to natural calamity and drought for three villages with a total assessed amount of Rs.520/-Two *Mahals* and two villages are shown with Chaudhry Gokal Dass, out of which two *Mahals*

are without damage and two named villages, Ram Pur and Shanker Pur are damaged to the extent of Rs. 100/ and Rs. 200/- respectively. Similarly, two *Mahals* and two villages are shown with Chaudhry Sangram, out of which two *Mahals* and one village remain undamaged and one village is damaged to the extent of Rs. 220/-

54. *Dur-al'Ulum,* Bod. Oxford fol 43. A *Hasbul Hukm* records a complaint made by the *Chaudhry* of Shah Ganj, *Subah* Lahore that the *ryots* of some of the villages of *Pargana* Itbarabad, *Doaba* Jullunder owed him the *Taqavi* loans but were reluctant to make the same payment. It orders the *ryots* of the above villages for the payment of *Taqavi* in installments.
55. *Makhzan-ul-Ihetsab*, Berlin fol 5b.
56. *Ibid*, fol 5b.
57. R.A. Jaipur, reg No. 1371, year 1090 *Fasli*, 28th year of Aurangzeb (1683 AD), a copy (ubcatalogued) dated 1098 *Fasli* (1688 AD) gives details of '*Tumar Wasalat Jumal Mal-i Jihat wa Sair-i-Jihat wa Kul Habutat'* of *Pargana* Tonk (Rajasthan) duly stamped by Qazi Abdur Rahim. *Siyaq Nama* No. 858 C.R.O. Hyderabad, fol 195b: *Sayaha Tashkhish Jama'* is a document which shows that total amount of the village assessment for either of the crops *Kharif* and *Rabi* along with a comparative statement of the previous year's assessmsent with increase or decrease if '*Tumar Jama'* records a general *Pargana* statement of income from various sources, land revenue, customs and *Mahsul* levied in the market on various articles, like cloth, ghee, oils, grains, horses, camels etc. '*Taujih*' records the land revenue realised and the balance due from every cultivator. '*Awarjia*' records the agricultural accounts especially the loans forwarded to the cultivators shown in '*Awaraija-i-Taqavi*'.
58. See F.N.20.
59. *Farman* Br. M. OR 1757, fol 39a-50b. A copy of original *Farman* concerning the grant of *Madad-i-Maash Jagir* dated A.H. 966 (1558 A.D.), an earliest traceable *Farman* of Akbar's reign. Also *Dasturulaml* No: 748, O.R.O. Hyderabad pp. 7, 13, 19. Also Jaipur Archives (Aurangzeb's reign), a *Dastak*, Misc, Persian letters Reg. 623, dated A.H.1117 (1705 A.D.) informs Kirat Singh that according to the '*Taqsim Namah*' (comarcation document) the villages of *Pargana* Amjhere, were given to Kishan Singh in jagir. It desires him to direct the *Chaudhris* to hand over the charge of the *Mauzis* to the *Gumashta* (Agent) of Kishan Singh (*Jagirdar*).
60. An original *Chaknama* (found with Sheikh Fiaz Ali, Khadim Darga Sharif, Ajmer) of a *Madad-i-Maash* grant, dated A.H. 1075, 10th regnal year of Aurangzeb with the stamp of *Qazi* Amanat Khan. It mentions the grant of four *bighas* of waste land in *Qasba* Ajmer to Sayyaiddain in *Madad-i-Maash* and directs the *Munsif* and his *Gumashta* to get it measured and demarcated with the help of *Chaudhri* Gowardan and Sayal Singh, *Qanungo*. Also *Dasturulaml* No: 748 C.R.O. Hyderabad p.19 gives a draft of *Chaknama* dated 11th regnal year of Shah Jahan's reign).
61. '*Maktubat-i-Khan Jahan Muzaffar Khan wa Gwaliar Namah*' Br. M. Rieu iii 837 Add. 16, 859 contain various letters written by Jalal Hissari and Balkrishan Brahman Hissari, which depict the agrarian life and working of the land revenue administration in *Chakla* Hissar, *Subah* Delhi in the reign of Shah Jahan.

62. *Ibid*, fol 27a-27b.
63. *Ibid*, fol 163a.
64. Jaipur, Rajasthan Archives, a *Parwana*, Misc. Persian Letters, Reg. No: 142 dated 12th of Ramzan A.H. 1099 (1688 A.D). Another *Parwana*, category no. 3 Reg. 407, dateless (Aurangzeb's reign) from Saiyed Abdulla Khan directed to the *Chaudhries, Qanungos* and *Muqaddams* informs them that *Pargana* Malma was in the *Zimindari* of the Maharaja (of Amber) since long and also directs them to the *Gumashtas* (agents) of the Maharaja and to hand over the collection of the *Zimindari* to the latter.
65. Jaipur, R.A. the original '*Tumar Jamma*' documents (uncatalogued) comprising the assessment and realization of land revenues and customs from *Pargana* Tonk in the *Jagir* of Raja Bishan Singh for the *Rabi* crop of the year 1098 *Fasli* (1693 A.D.) *Qanungos* along with the stamp of the *Qazi*. For the enumerated villages not included in the '*Tumar Jama*' realizations, the *Chaudhris* and the *Qanungos* had verified that they did not receive the accounts of their realisations from the *Muqaddams*. Also, '*Tumar Waslat*' i.e. document of realisations, Reg. No: 1371, dated 28th regnal year of Aurangzeb, *Fasli* year 1090 (1683 A.D.) states the realisations of village Nosna Nakaran situated in *Subah* Malwa in the *Jagir* of Sultan Hussain, after having been stamped by *Qazi* Kasarud Din and only verified by the *Chaudharis* and the *Qanungos*. Another document, *Misc. Persian Letters*, Reg. 630 dated 36th regnal year of Alamgir, *Fasli* 1097 i.e., A.H. 1103 (1192 AD) a reminder (on behalf of the *Jagirdar*) to Panna Majau (*Amil*) asks for the dispatch of the revenues of *Pargana* Pakasu along with the *Tumar* of the same having been stamped by the *Qazi* and verified by the *Chaudhari* and *Qanungos*. Another *Parwana*, Misc. Persian letters, Reg. No: 1165, dated A.H. 1104, from Jumlatul Mulk to Mir Ali directing him to send the revenues of *Pargana* Toda Bhim (*Sarkar* and *Subah* Agra) which was in the *Jagir* of Kamaluddin, regarding the current years to the Royal Court at once. It further requires that the accounts of realisation should be exact and verified by the *Chaudharis* and *Qanungos*.
66. *Waqai-i-Sarkar Ranthanbor* No: 2411, C.R.C. Hyderabad (22nd regnal year of Aurangzeb, p.386 records a report made by the *Chaudhari* and the *Qanungos* of *Pargana* Jiteran (*Chakla* Meerut) about the oppression of the Rajput on the *ryots* followed by disturbance and with a request for the dispatch of *Amin* and *Karori* over there for the resettlement of the *ryots* for the *Kharif* crop. Also Jaipur, R.A. letters to the Maharaja, Reg. No: 2188, dated the 12th of Ramzan, A.H. 1129 (1717 A.D.) A combined petition was submitted by the *Chaudharis, Qanungos* and *Muqaddams* of *Pargana* Ujjain (*Sarkar* Ujjain, *Subah* Malwa) to the Maharaja (of Amber and the *Jagirdar* of the *Pargana*) stating the undue oppression on the *ryots* by Hari Singh and Suran Chand, the *Amils* (of Maharaja) by making a very rigid assessment on the cultivators. The petitioners depict the depressed condition of the latter and suggest the appointment of another *Amil* named Himat Rai after the dismissal of the previous ones and also suggests comprehensive measures to be taken for the ameorlation of the condition of the *ryots*. Although the above petition refers to the conditions prevelant nearly ten years after Aurangzeb's

death, it is indictive of the duties and obligations of the *Chaudharis, Qanungos* and *Muqaddams* as a legacy from the earlier times.

67. Jaipur, R.A. *Bainama*, i.e. Sale Deed case No. 7, dated A.H. 1071 (1661 A.D.).
68. Elliot, *Chronicles of Onao*, a District in Oudh, Allahabad Mission Press, 1862, p.112.
69. *Siyaq Nama* No: 858, C.R.O. Hyderabad, fol 59a; *Khulasat'us Siyaq*, Aligarh, fols. 9b, 10a.
70. *Makhzab ul Ihetsab*, Berlin, fol 5a; *Khulasat'us Siyaq*, Aligarh, fol 14b.
71. *Ibid*, fols 5a-6a, *Waqai-i-Sarkar Ranthambor* pp. 163, 170, (Aurangzeb's reign) brings out the important role played by the *Qanungos* immediately after the annexation of Jodhpur in *Subah* Ajmer and relevant documents prepared by them. Also *Baharistan-i-Ghaibi*, B.N. Paris, fol 312b, *Khulastaus Siyaq*, Aligarh, fol 12a-12b; Also Ms.Or. Oct, 113, Berlin, fol 2, though an 18th cent. Ms. gives an account of agrarian development of Shah Jahan's reign.
72. '*Khasra*' or '*Nuskhe-i-Zabt*' comprises field wise area of the village, showing in respect of each field the name of its cultivator, the linear dimensions and total area, failed crop areas and the balance, and the crops growing at the time of survey. '*Muntkhib*' is a '*Khasra*' document for the entire village showing pagewise grand total area of the field as well as area detail of the crops. '*Jamabandi*' may also be complied 'asamiwise' (after every cultivator) named as '*Khatauni*' (*Khulasat'us Siyaq*, Aligarh, fols 12a-12b *Diwan-i-Panand,* Ms. Hyderabad, fols 8a-11b).
73. *Goshwara* is a statement showing the name of every village, the total cultivated area with crop details alongwith its '*Jamabandi*' and total '*Jamma*' assessed. Sihya '*Wasilbaqi*' is a *Pargana* statement showing the total revenue realisation based on the complication of the monthly assessment and realisation statements prepared at the end of every crop-*Kharif* and *Rabi* ('*Jama Kharch*' records yearly comprehensive statement of the total income and expenditure of the entire *Pargana*. ('*Jama Wasilbaqi*' shows village wise and for the entire *Pargana*, the accounts relating to the present assessment, dues from the cultivators, adjustment of the '*Taqaqvi*' loans for both the crops and the total balance of realisations.) '*Tumar Jama*' records a general *Pargana* statement of income from various sources, i.e., land revenue, '*Mal-i-Jihat*' and '*Sair-i-Jihat*', i.e., *Mahsul* levied in the market on articles like cloth, ghee, oils, grains, horses, camels etc. (*Diwan-i-Pasand*, fols 12b-38b; *Khulasat'us Siyaq*, fols 13b-14a.) or *Makhzan ul Ihetsab*, fols 24a-28a.
74. *Ibid.* fol 24a.
75. *Bibliotheque Nationale*, Paris, Ms. No. Suppl. 482, fols 91a-91b quotes a copy of *Farman* of Shah Jahan's reign which explains in details the duties of a *Pargana Qanungo.* This is the only *Farman* of its type traceable in the entire Mughal revenue literature.
76. Eliot, *Chronicles of Oonao*, p. 112. It is not within the scope of this paper to discuss in details the position and obligations of the *Qanungo* in the *Pargana* administration under the Mughals. All the same, it is essential to dispel Elliot's view that the original intention of the double appointments

(i.e., *Chaudhari* and *Qanungo)* was that of one should be a check on the other. A compromise deed, dated 9th Post. Samat year 1750, Hijri II 5, (37th year of Aurangzeb's reign) registered no. 65 Rajasthan Archives, Jaipur, executed under the seal of Qazi Mohammad Mustafa of *Pargana* Jalandhar, Doaba Pet Jalandhar (*Subah* Lahore) records a signed statement of the name *Chaudhris* and thirty five named *Muqaddams* to the effect that under Bhola, the *Qanungo* connected with their villages, the realisations of the land revenue is in accordance with the regulations and the *ryots* being satisfied, they have no grievances against him and promise to recognise him as their *Qanungo*. Moreover, Elliot's statement that the *Chaudhari* was selected from Muslim landed class to give political influence to a Mohammedan over a Hindoo is quite inept and is disapproved by the existence of Hindu *Chaudhari* in the *Pargana*. The above quoted compromise deed Regd. No. 65, R.A. Jaipur bears the signatures of two Hindu *Chaudharis*, Chattar and Chander Bhan. Also see '*Maktnabat-i-Khan Jahan*' Sr. N. fol. 27a-27b. and reference No. 52. Also original Bianamahs, Jaipur, R.A. case No. 7 dated A.H. 1071 (1661 A.D.) and Reg. No. 1721, case No. 9, dated A.H. 1704 (1664 A.D.) which mention the Hindu *Chaudhari* Mohandas and Behlidas respectively. On the other hand, the *Qanungo*, though, usually selected from the Hindu *Kaisth* class, could as well be a Muslim from the *Khwaja* community. See *Muntakhab al-Lubab* Pers. Text *Bib. Indica* Vol. I, pp. 156-157. Elliot's description regarding these offices is true in general for the early 19th century but not for the Mughal age till the death of Aurangzeb.

77. Ms. or. Quart. 258 Berlin fol 184a (an early 18th cent. Ms.) notes the advantage of fixed tenure of the *Qanungo* and the *Chaudharis* against the transferable Governors, *Faujdars,* and other revenue officers and serving as a connecting link in the revenue administration as emphasised in Akbar's reign.
78. See references 36-38, 43-45, 55-56, 54-55, 61-64. Also Ms. Or. Oct. 113 Berlin fols 1-2, though on 18th century Ms. which describing the agrarian policy of Shah Jahan's reign clearly underlines the respective functions of the *Chaudhari* and the *Qanungos* in the new *Zimindari* colonies.
79. *Waqai Sarkar Ranthambore*, Ms. Hyderabad, p. 38 (Aurangzeb's reign).
80. See reference No. 67 (old 66). Also Ms. Or. fol 270, Berlin fol 43a.
81. Though Aurangzeb's *Farman* (See reference 26) fixes the number of *Chaudharis* and the *Qanungos* at two each in a *Pargana* for the part of Karbayat (*Sarkar* Ahmedabad, *Subah* Gujrat) *Dur-ul'Ulum* Bod. Oxford fol 65b (See reference 21) puts 13 *Chaudharis* and 27 *Qanungos* in *Pargana* Palwal (*Sarkar* Delhi, *Subah* Delhi).
82. See reference 68, also Jaipur, R.A. Reg. No. 1721, case no. 9, dated A.H. 1704 (1664 AD).
83. *Ibid.* '*Yaddasht Haqiqat-i Arazi Mawazna Pargana Rewari*' uncatalogued sheet no. 7. Also *Parwana* (i) dated A.H. 1027 (Jehangir's reign) regarding appointment of *Deshmukh* in *Pargana* in Deccan grants on addition of ten Cheawar *Qalbas* or plough-land of waste land in *Inam* in addition to existing grant, and in case of all such rent free grants, orders the local officials to give in particular free of all cesses and demands of revenue.
84. *Intakhab-i-Dasturulaml*, Br. M. fol 53a.

85. *Ibid.* fol 53a. also *Farhauq-i-Kardani,* Aligarh fol 29b emphasises the role of emoluments based on '*Dastur wa Istmarar-i-qadim* (an ancient and permanent practice), to be paid in advance by the *ryots* at the end of the year. Also confined by the documents naming the *Deshmukh's* appointment in Deccan, Nishan ii (Shah Jahan's reign) and *Farman II* (Aurangzeb's reign) which describe the payment made according to *Mamul-i-qadim*' (Ancient practice).
86. *Ibid.*, fol 53a.
87. *Ibid.*, fol 42b.
88. *Makhzan ul Ihetsab*, Berlin, fol 74b. *Dasturulaml* of Baikas, Aligarh, fol 43a, in a *sanad* of appointment of a *Chaudhari* in the first half of the 18th century, put the rate of fixation of his '*Rasum*' (emoluments) at 1% of the collections made. At the same time, a *Parwana,* fols 45a-43b for *Nankar* assignment bestows one full village in '*Inam*' (rent free grant) on hereditary basis.
89. Jaipur, R.A. A *Pargana* document (uncatalogued) of '*Mal-i-Jihat*', sheet No. 37, year 1101 H. Rabi.
90. *Nuskha-i-Majbuhat* Ms. Or. Quart 258, Berlin, fols 125b-129a.
91. *Ibid.*, fols 16a-16b; also Ramsbothan's *Land Revenue History of Bengal, Amini Report*, pp. 103-110.
92. *Selections from Deccan Records* (Benares, 1973, p. 41).
93. Elliot, *Chronicles of Onao,*, Chapter V, pp. 111-113.
94. *'Cavendish Enquiries'* of District Ajmer (1829A.D.), for Binai, p. 5.
95. *Ibid.*, p. 3.
96. *Records of Delhi,* Residency and Agency, 1887, p. 232; Robert Cust, *The Rvenue Manual,* 188, p. 62; *Dasturulaml*, No. 676, O.R.O. Hyderabad, fol. 6a-6b. Moreland's estimate of the *Chaudharis* position in the 18th and 19th centuries based only upon the early British records is true in general. (The *Pargana* Headman-*Chaudhari* pp. 519-521.

9. *Desai* : The Position of *Desai* in the *Pargana* Administration of *Subah* Gujrat under the Mughals

The nature of *Desai's* office in the *Pargana* administration of the Mughal *Subah* of Gujrat has not received any attention so far. Sir J.N. Sarkar, Moreland, Dr. P. Saran and Prof. S.R. Sharma do not say anything about this office and its working in their respective works on the Mughal administration.[1] Even though in all other respects the patterns of *Pargana* administration in Gujrat was similar to other *Subahs* in Nothern India, the existence of the office of the *Desai* as the government official and as the representative of the *ryots* was exclusive to Gujrat. It was, of course, also prevalent in the administration of some of the Deccan *Subahs*.[2] For the Province of Gujrat, it finds very frequent mention in the official documents, viz *Farmans, Nishans, Hasbulhukm, Parwanas*, the daily reports of the *Waqai nawis, Dasturul amals* and *Mirat-i Ahmadi*. The English Factory record and the Dutch documents equally refer to this important official in the local administration. As the other local officials like *Patwari, Muqaddam, Chaudhari, Qanungo* and *Shiqdar* also find description in the foregoing document[3], the *Desai's* office cannot be identified with any of these. All the same, on the basis of the above sources, it is possible to construct a tentative picture about the position of *Desai* in the *Pargana* administration of *Subah* Gujrat.

Though the title of *Desai* can be traced to the pre-Mughal times in the Bijapur state and the territories of the Hindu Chiefs on the Malabar const[4] in the Mughal *Subah* of Gujrat, it owes its inception to Todar Mal of Akbar's reign, who during his measurement reforms and reorganization of the land revenue administration appointed *Desais* in all the *Mahals*[5], The *Desai*' office existed both in the *Khalsa* and the *Jagir* lands.[6] He also functioned in the areas under the jurisdiction of a certain class of *Zamindars*.[7] The *Desai* was appointed by a *Parwana* issued by the Provincial Authorities and had territorial jurisdiction over a circle of villages[8] or at times even a full *Pargana*.[9] His status in the *Pargana* was next to the *Shiqdar* but higher then the other revenue officials like *Muqaddams, Chaudharis* and the *Qanungos* who worked under him.[10]

As to his main functions, as a resident revenue official, he had to work for the increase of agricultural produce as well as for the welfare of the *ryots*.[11] He was essentially an assessment official and was responsible for the proper assessment and fixation of '*Jama*' of the cultivated areas of the villages under him in accordance with the regulations and the detailed classification of the land. A *Parwana* dated 1003 AH/1594 AD issued by Nawab Sadiq Mohmmad Khan to Khwaja Mohammad Maasum of *Pargana* Supa, *Sarkar* Surat, states that he had received a complaint from some of the villages against the *Desai* of the above *Pargana* reporting that the latter contrary to the established practice, had not accomplished proper assessment of the cultivated fields of the villages and had done only summary assessment of the villages based on the past record. He had also illegally realised the village expenses (*Malba*) and forcibly arrested twenty two persons. The same *Desai* had also omitted the assessment of his own cultivated lands amounting to Rs. three thousand *Mahmudis*[12] which had not been deposited in the treasury. The *Parwana* directs the addressee to summon the above *Desai* and admonish him to carry out fresh assessment of the disputed villages, based on the inspection of the cultivated areas and the '*Hasil*' (Produce), to afford remission to the *ryots* of the villages in accordance with the established practice, to realise the imprisoned persons, to deposit land revenue of his personal cultivated land and to avoid such irregularities in future.[13] Another *Parwana*, dated 9th year of Shah Jahan's reign, directs the *Desais* of the *Parganas* Balsar and *Pargana* (*Sarkar* Surat) to concede to the *ryots* half the remission on the excess produce on the hard land.[14] Still another *Parwana* of the same reign show the *Desai's* direct control over the assessment of the filed of the cultivators through the *Muqaddams* and the fixation of the '*Jama*' (assessed demand) on the holdings of the cultivators.[15] In coordination with the *Muqaddams* under him, the *Desai* was responsible for the advancement of the *Taccavi* (agricultural loans) to the deserving *ryots* and their subsequent recovery in installments in accordance with the established practice.[16] He as well had to safeguard the *ryots* against any over-realisation of the land revenue by either the revenue officials of the *Khalsa* administration or the agents of the *Jagirdars* and was required to bring any irregularity on this account to the notice of the higher authorities. *Mirat-i Ahmadi* while quoting Akbar's *Farman* regarding the remission of '*Zakat*' issued in A.H. 999/1590 A.D. states that during the administration of *Khan-i Azam*, *Desais*, *Muqaddams* and *ryots* of most of the *Parganas* submitted a petition to the Royal Court that the agents (*Gumshtas*) of the *Nazims* and *Jagirdars* expropriated the entire income of the *Zamindars* by exacting illegal cesses after the revenue collections were made. This had led to insurrection on the part of the Rajputs, the Kolis and the Muslims and consequent plundering of the produce and devastation of the cultivated fields by the latter. As this had resulted in the decrease of the Government revenue, the *Diwan* of the *Subah* was enjoined by the aforesaid *Farman* to make proper arrangements for the realisation of the land revenue through the agencies of the *Desais* and the *Muqaddams* both in the *Khalsa* and the *Jagir* lands.[17] As such, the *Desai* had to safeguard the interests of the *ryots* and even of the petty *Zimindars* against any undue coercion on the part of the local Government officers and the assignees. He had to tour every area in his jurisdiction and to keep a watchful eye on the revenue officials.[18] He was equally responsible along with the *Muqaddams* under him for the proper collection of the land revenue in accordance with the regulations.[19] He had the special responsibility of preventing the migration of any of the *ryots* or tenants of other places and in case of any such occurrence, he had to induce the migrator to settle in his homeland and also to afford him all facilities for resettlement. A *Parwana* dated 9th regnal year of Shahjahan's reign addressed to the *Mutsaddis* and the *Desais* of *Parganas* Kamraj and Balesar (*Sarkar* Surat) states that Kamchu and Kanwar, the tenants of the village Bankanirah, *Pargana* Balesar had migrated to a village in *Pargana* Kamraj and that Narain, the tenant of village Kalyan of the latter *Pargana*, had shifted to another village situated in the former *Pargana*. It further directs the above mentioned *Desais* to settle the tenants in their respective homes.[20] Another *Parwana* of the same reign narrates the position of a tenant who had migrated thrice. Ashaq, the tenant of a village Kacholi, *Pargana* Chaurasi (*Sarkar* Champner) shifted for a few years to Daman. From there, he came to *Pargana* Balsar (*Sarkar* Surat) and cultivated the land for two years. As the *Desai* of the latter *Pargana* insisted on entering him in the ledger of permanent occupants of holdings and thereby to assess him accordingly, the above mentioned tenant further shifted to village Rajwara, *Pargana* Chikhli (*Sarkar* Surat) and remained there for two month. Thereafter, on the consolation and assurance for sympathetic consideration afforded by the *Desai* of *Pargana* Chaurasi, he opted to go back and settled in his own home village, As the *Muqaddam* of Bajwara and the *Desai* of Balsar claimed and pressed for the repatriation of the above mentioned tenant to their respective territories, the above *Parwana* directs the latter officials not to insist for it and to all the tenants to settle in his home village.[21]

The *Desai* exercised full control over the *Muqaddams* in his circle.[22] Like the *Muqddams, Chaudharies* and the *Qanungos*, he was always informed of fresh appointments of the officials, the assignees and the declared descendants of the '*Madad-i-Maash*' holders in the *Pargana.*[23] The *Desai* had as well a jurisdiction over the commercial dealing in his territorial circle. He was responsible for the enforcement of the State regulation for the trade and commerce, As such, he acted under the authority of the *Faujdar* of his area.[24] For the proper discharge of his duties, he was provided with a staff of the horseman (*Sawars*) and footmen (*Piyadas*)[25]. He was responsible to the *Shiqdar* of the *Pargana, Amin* and *Faujdar* of his area and the *Diwans* of the *Sarkars* and the *Subah.*[26]

The office of the *Desai* was more or less hereditary though on the relinquishment of the charge by the previous incumbent or his removal on ground of inefficiency, another competent willing hand could be appointed for the job. A *Parwana* of late Shahjahan's period quotes a vacancy of a *Desai's* post in *Pargana* Biyadra *Sarkar* Sorath) on the relinquishment of a charge by an inefficient incumbent and requires the *Muqaddams* and the *ryots* for the suggestion of a voluntary offer by a competent hand for the job who would discharge the duties of the office enumerated therein .[27] This shows how exacting and responsible was the *Desai's* job and was not therefore always coveted and contested. Usually, the *Desai* himself was land-owner with local influence over the *ryots*,[28] Though at times, with his official position, he felt tempted to misuse his authority to coerce the *ryots*, taken as a whole, the contemporary sources emphasise the successful working of his office in the *Pargana* administration.

As to his remuneration, like the *Muqaddam*, the *Desai* was also entitled to commission on the revenue collections made in his circle. After Gujrat's conquest, during the Ist Governorship of Aziz Kokaltash, Tódar Mal effected an assessment and '*Jama*' of the Province in 903 A.H./1573 A.D.[30] and during his settlement operation also fixed the *Desai's* share at 2.5% of the revenue collections made in the latter's circle.[31] This is confirmed by Akbar's *Farman* on the remission of *Zakat* dated A.H. 999/1590 A.D. issued during the 2nd tenure of *Khan-i Azam* Azia Kokaltash's Governorship. It notes that laxity of land administration in Gujrat and directs the *Diwan-i Subah* to permit the *Desais* and the *Muqaddams* to retain collectively 5% of the revenue collections to be shared equally. This was to hold good both for the *Khalsa* and the *Jagir* lands.[32] But it seems that a little later, within the 2nd tenure of Aziz Kokaltash's Governorship, the share of the *Desai* was cut down to 6.25% only. *Mirat-i Ahmadi* in its supplement states that since Todar Mal's time, *ryots* had to pay 2.5% of the realisations as the *Desai's* dues, but in the time of *Khan-i Azam*, half the dues, i.e. 1.25% were cancelled, and half of the remaining half, i.e. 6.25% (ten *annas* against every hundred rupees realised), was taken over by the Government and remitted to the Royal treasury in favour of *Diwan-i Subah*. The balance of 0.625% of the realisations (*Annas* ten : Rs. 100) was retained by *Desais*.[33] This statement is further confirmed by the Mirat's list of '*Peshkas*' amount paid by the *Desais* of the various *Parganas*[34] when arithmatically worked out against the revenue of the same *Parganas* stated earlier.[35]

References

1. Sarkar, *Mughal Adminstration*; Moreland, *The Agrarian System of Moslem India*, Dr. P. Saran, *The Provincial Government of the Mughals*; Sharma, S.R., *Mughal Government Administration.*
2. For *Subah* Khandesh, see *Selected Waqai of the Deccan 1660-1671 A.D.*, pp. 134, Published by the Central Records office (CRO) Hyderabad Government, 1953 and edited by Dr. Yusuf Husain.
3. For these officials in Gujrat, see Ms. Suppl. 482 Bibliotheque Nationale, Paris, *Patwari* fol. 151b; *Muqaddam* fols. 119b, 152b-154a; Chaudhari fols, 151b, 174a; *Qanungo* fols, 91a, 148a; *Shiqdar*, fols. 158b-159a. Also seen the *English Factories in India. Muqaddam*, 1618-21, p. 74; 1622-23, pp. 125, 215; *Patel,* 1622-23, p. 212; *Qanungo*, 1618-21, p. 120; *Choudhari*, 1618-21, pp. 120, 273; *Shiqdar*, 1618-21, pp. 273-307.
4. The term *Desai* is Marhati in language (*Dasturulaml* no. 767, p. 6 , C.R.O. Hyderabad). *The English Factories in India* (1655-60 A.D.) in the *Deccan Factories*, 1660 A.D. p. 356 mentions the office of *Desai* at Rajapur who attested the inventory and the bill of the English factors. Rajapur vide p. 353 was with Rustam Zaman, who controlled the district round Rajapur in the names of the Bijapur monarch. *The English Factories* (1661-64 AD), for the Malabar Coast, 1663 A.D. p. 282 , mention the Bijapur king's order of the Governor of the Ponda, a Bijapur frontier post (ten miles S.S.E. of Goa city) to join hands with the 'Cuddall Jessyes' (*Desais* of Kudal. Kudal is situated 13 miles south of Savantvadi) for fighting against Shivaji and routhing him from Rajapur and Sarrapatan. *The English Factories* (1668-69) for the Malabar Coast, 1669 A.D. mention a quarrel between the Governor and the *Desai* of Karwar-a part under the rule of a Hindu chief named 'Sunda Rajah' (vide p. 268) who ruled in the name of the 'King of Carnopolly.' It seems that the *Desai* in the Bijapur state and the Malabar Coast had under his territorial jurisdiction a *Pargana* and had multifarious functions inclusive of the executive powers for the regulations of trade and commerce, the attestation of the commercial documents as well as the police and the military powers for the enforcement of law and order. *The Bombay Gazetter*, vol. X, p. 465, describing Kudal (mentioned above in *the English Factories* 1661-64, p. 242) says, "under the Bijapur kings its Brahaman ruler was, with the title of *Desai* of Kudal, contained as the head of twelve sub-division, each governed by a *Naik.*"
5. *Mirat-i Ahmadi*, Persian text, Gaelawar's Oriental Series, supplement, p. 28.
6. *Ibid.* I., p. 173.
7. *Ibid.* Supl. p. 233 states that in the reign of Sultans of Gujrat, the *Zimindar* of Rajpipala as feudatory chief had one fourth of land in Pargana of Nandod with 16 *Parganas* near Nandurbar. When his territory was conquered by Akbar, the *Zimindar* met Raja Todar Mal and explained his position. He was allowed with his previous possession on the coniditon of serving with 1,000 horses. *Desais, Qaziz* and *Waqai Niagars* (reporters) were appointed in his territory by the Government. Also, pp. 228-239 give detailed table of the '*Peshkash*' (tribute) paid by the *Desais* as well as the *Zimindars* in the

Zimindari Parganas of *Subah* Gujrat.

8. Ms no. Suppl 482. *Bibliotheque Nationale,* Paris vide *Parwanas* fols, 171b-172a; fol. 173a; fols 160b-161a.
9. *Ibid*, fols. 173b-174a; fol. 166b.
10. *Ibid.*
11. *Ibid*, fols. 173b-174a. vide a *Parwana* dated Rabinlawwal A.H. 1056/1646 A.D.
12. The exchange rate of '*Mahmudis*' to a rupee varied from 2-1/4 to 2-1/2 '*Muhmudis*' against one Rupee, vide *The English Factories*, 1642-45, p. 96.
13. Ms B.N. Paris, fols. 170b-171b. vide *Parwana* 9th *Muharram* A.H. 1003/ 24th September, 1594 A.D.
14. *Ibid.*, fols. 153b-154a.
15. *Ibid.* Fol. 166b.
16. *Ibid.* fol. 171b.
17. Mirat. I, pp. 171-173.
18. Ms. B.N. Paris, fol. 152a, vide a *Parwana* dated 12th *Muharram*, A.H. 1047/ 6th June, 1637 A.D.
19. *Mirat*, I, p. 171.
20. Ms. B.N. Paris, fols. 163b-164a.
21. *Ibid.* fol. 166b
22. *Ibid.*
23. *Ibid.* fol.173a vide a *Parwana* dated 2nd *Muharram* A.H. 1056/10th February, 1646 A.D.
24. *The English Factories in India*, 1634-36, pp. 287-88 narrate a complaint against the administration of Masih Uz-Zaman, the *Faujdar* of Surat, who had wrongfully imprisoned the *Desais* for favouring the English Factors. *The English Factories*, 1634-36, 'John Drake at Mandu to' President and Council at Surat, Sept. 7 (P.S. 9th Sept.) 1636, pp. 287-88, state, "...The King, hearing of Monu Vassee (Mana Vaisya) and the rest of *Desyds* (*Desais*) imprisonment at Surat by the Huckeeme, is much displeased, and Meir Moza contended, who hath still hopes of that place; and likewise tells me hee hath on our behalf procured the like *Firmaen* as the Dutch have required for their good usuage in Bengala." Also see a Dutch letter from Surat summarised in the Dagh Register, 1636 p. 271.
25. Ms. B.N. Paris, fols. 153a vide a *Parwana* dated 9th regnal year of Shahjahan.
26. *Ibid.*, fols. 160b-161a vide a *Parwana* dated 26th Rebiulawwal, A.H. 1056/ 12th May, 1646 A.D.; Also Mirat I, p. 171.
27. *Ibid*, fols 173b-174a vide a *Parwana* dated Rabiulawwal A.H. 1056/1646 A.D. (*Pargana* Biyadra *Sarkar* Sorath. Vide *Mirat*, Suppl. p. 224, Jarrett. *Ain*, II, p. 263 inaccurately puts it as Banward).
28. *Ibid.* fols 170b-171b. A *Parwana* dated 9th Muharram A.H. 1003/24th September, 1594 A.D. quoted earlier in the main text shows that the *Desai* of *Pargana* Supa (*Sarkar* Surat) owned large holding of his own cultivated lands on which three thousand Mahmudis could be assessed as land revenue which he had deliberately omitted to enter in the revenue documents and had evaded payment.

29. *Ibid.*
30. *Mirat,* I, pp. 131-132.
31. Ibid. Supplement, p. 229.
32. *Ibid.* I. p. 173.
33. *Ibid.* Supplement p. 220.
34. *Ibid.* pp. 188-228.
35. *Ibid.* pp. 228-239.

10. Karkun

The Karkun was a full-fledged *Pargana* officer[1] and occupied an important position in the *Pargana* administration, being only next to the *Shiqdar*.[2] He was the General Assistant to the *Shiqdar* and the registrar of his office. He peformed many of the duties of the *Bitikchi* (assessment officer) and stood in the same relation to the *Shiqdar* as the *Bitikchi* to the *Amil Guzar* or *Karori*.[3] He was a revenue expert with full understanding of the technical details of the land administration in respect of documentation, assessment of the State demand and the realisation of the land revenue.[4] As such, he was indispensible to the *Shiqdar* in his revenue duties and the vital part of his establishment.[5] His position remained the same throughout the Mughal age.[6]

Generally speaking, he had to discharge the same duties in the revenue administration of the *Pargana* as the *Shiqdar* and likewise in the *Pargana* of his appointment, he was always enjoined to look after the welfare of the *ryots*, the augmentation of the agriculture and the prosperity of the *Pargana* on the whole.[7] As to his specific obligations, he had to accomplish the survey and asessment of every cultivator village wise, hand in hand with the *Patawari*, *Muqaddam, Munsif* (assessment official), the *Qanungo* and the *Jaribkash* (Suryeyor).[8] He had to set down the transactions of the village assessments separately from those of the *Patwari* and the *Muqaddam*.[9] After the completion of the assessment accounts of the entire village (*Muntakhib*) along with the *Patwari*.[10] He had to accompany the *Shiqdar* and the Assessment Officer for village to village inspection and survey of the cultivated and uncultivated lands and to help the latter in the assessment of the State demand on the cultivators.[11] He was signitory to the *Siyah Tashkhish* and to the *Taujih* to be prepared at the *Chaubutra*.[12] He had to equally help the *Shiqdar* in the realisation of the land revenue.[13] As registrar of the *Pargana* officer, along with the *Qanungo*, he had to finalise and sign *Pargana* documents of realisation and expenditure viz. *Tumar*, *Dhakhil Tumar Jamma*, and the *Jamma*.

In all matters involving expenditure in the Pargana,[14] he had to show full integrity and thriftiness.[15] He had an active share in the management of the *Pargana* treasury. He had to give his consent to the location of the treasury room.[16] He had to put up his own lock on the main door of the treasury and to get it unlocked in his own presence.[17] He had to sit in the treasury along with the *Shiqdar* during the periods of realisation of the land revenue.[18] Along with the *Fotahdar*, he had the joint responsibility for the issue of receipts to the cultivators for direct deposits made by them in the treasury.[19] His consent was essential for any emergency disbursement from the *Pargana* treasury. To serve as a counter check against the *Fotahdar*, he had to prepare his own day-ledger of the deposits made in the treasury.[20] Every month, he had to forward the day-ledgers of realisations and expenditures after his personal signature[21] and duly attested by the *Shiqdar*, the *Chaudharies, Qanunogs* and the *Muqaddams*.[22] Likewise, he had also to despatch the income and expenditure documents (*Tumar Jamma, Mujmil wa Kharch Jamma*) prepared on yearly basis.[23]

References

1. Intkhab-i-Insha Harkarn, Ms. Rampur, P. 58; Ms. Supl. 482 N.B. Paris, fol. 169a; *Mahazai-Shahjahani*, p.22; *Durul Ulm*, Bod. Oxford 137a-137b. The *Karkun* was essentially attached with the *Shiqdar*. In rare cases, as already explained for the latter, he also could have lesser territorial jurisdiction than a full *Pargana*.
2. Surprisingly, Dr. Qureshi (*Pargana* officials under Akbar) and Dr. Saran (Provincial Government) have not attached any importance to this official and have dismissed him only as an official subordinate to *Shiqdar*.
3. See discussion on *Karori* and the *Bitikchi*. *Akbar Nama* (Br, M, Add, O, R,27,247, fol, 33Ib) mentions even the *Karkun* as one of the *Bitikchis* and *Ain-i-Akbari* (Br. M.Add. 7652, fols, 143a-144; Hamilition Berlin, fols. 121a-122a states many of the common duties of the *Karkun* and the *Bitikchi*.
4. *Insha-i-Harkarn*, p.58; Ms. Suppl. 482, N.B. Paris, fol. 169a; *Durul Ulm*, Bod. Oxford, fols. 137a-b.
5. *Makhzanual Ihetsab*, Berlin fols, 4b-7a.
6. *Ain-i-Akbari* and *Akbar Nama* make only incidental references to the office of the *karkun* with regard to the village assessment and the management of the *Pargana* treasury. But *Intkhabat-i-Insha-i-Harkarn*, p.58, Ms. Suppl. 482 N.B. Paris, fol. 169a and Durululm Bod. Oxford, fols, 137a-137b quote appointment *Parwanas* for the *Pargana Karkun* for the reigns of Jahangir, Shah Jahan and Aurengzeb respectively with the same duties. The R.A. Jaipur of Aurangzeb's reign corroborate the same.
7. *Ibid. Parwanas* quoted in the above Mss.
8. *Khullastus Siyaq*, Aligarh, fol. 12b gives an assessment draft (*Zabt*) of a village conducted and attested by the *Munsif*, the *Karkun*, the *Qanungo* and the *Jaribkash*.
9. *Ain*, Br. M. Add. 7652, fol. 143a; Hamiltion, Berlin, fol. 120b.
10. *Ibid.*
11. *Makhzen ul Ihetsab*, Berlin, fols. 5a-5b.
12. *Ibid.*
13. *Ibid.* fols. 6a-6b, Ms. Suppl. 482 N.B. Paris, fol. 174a.
14. *Khullastus Siyaq*, Ms. Aligarh fols, 27a, 27b. 28b.
15. *Insha-i-Harkarn*, p.58.
16. *Ain*, Br. M. Add. 7652, fol. 144b, Hamiltion 1 Berlin, fol. 122a
17. *Ibid.*: also *Makhzanul Ihetsab*, Berlin, fol. 6a.
18. *Ibid.*
19. A.N. Br. M. Add. O.R. 27,247, fols, 332a-332b.
20. *Ain*, Br. M. Add. 7652, fol. 144b; Ms. Hamilton, Berlin, fol. 122a.
21. *Ibid.*, fols, 143a, 144b; fols. 122a, 122a respectively.
22. Whereas *Ain* (Br. M. Ad 7652, fol. 143a, Hamiltion, Berlin, fol.121a and *Insha-i-Harkarn* (p.58) require such despatches every month, Durululm, Bod. Oxford, fol. 137b enjoins such despatches to be made bi-monthly and consolidated ledger every two months. This shows a slight change in procedure form the reigns of Akbar and Jahangir to that of Aurangzeb. Ms.Suppl. 482

N.B. Paris, fol. 169a (Shah Jahan's reign) states that day-ledgers of receipts of land revenue (*mal-i-Jihat*), Octroi Customs (*Sair Jihat*) etc. were to be despatched to the authorities.

23. *Durululm*. Bod. Oxford. fol. 137b; *Insha-i-Harkarn*, p.58.

11. Fotahdar

The *Khazanadar* or the treasurer of the *Pargana* treasury (*Fotah Khanna*) was popularly known and officially designated as the *Fotahdar*.[1] As custodian and the keeper of the treasury, he was responsible for its safety, the cash receipts, the maintenance of the treasury records, and disbursement or transfer of money with appropriate sanction. As for the safety of the treasury, it had to be essentially located near the residence of the administrator of the *Pargana*[2] and had a double lock system sealed separately by the latter and the *Fotahdar* himself.[3] It was to opened by him in joint presence of the administrator and his *Karkun*.[4] He had to keep the money in sealed bags and deposit it in a strong room within the knowledge of the *Shiqdar* and the *Karkun*.[5] He would accept in the treasury all the deposits made by the *Amil* and his agents on account of land revenue and customs realisations from the *ryots*,[6] which if denied would make the collectors responsible for any discrepancy.[7] In such a case, the original ledger (*Kaghaz-i-Kham*) of the *Patwari* with entries of such receipts from the *ryots* shall be accepted as final regardless of any commission in the *Taujih* (Balance Sheet) prepared by the revenue officials.[8] He would also receive money directly form the cultivators and issue receipts for the same[9] failing which he was accountable to the *Karori* for such an omission and had to make good the loss on account of any discrepancy if the *ryots* asserted having made the payment but were denied the receipts for the same.[10] He would accept money only within the knowledge of the *Amil* and the *Karkun* and was not to receive any unauthorised payment.[11] He would accept any type of official currency, even of the previous regimes without any rebate and was not to demand any special type of coin.[12] In exchange of coinage, he would take merely the equivalent of the deficiency in coin-weight[13] in according with the schedules of rates and weights of different coins and extreme marginal differences in exchange were to be adjusted in favour of the *ryots* paying the revenue.[14] He had to be extremely cautious and methodical in the maintenance of the accounts. He had to prepare his own day-ledger of the *Karkun* and get it attested by the Collector.[15] For the money received from the cultivators, in order to avoid any future discrepancy, he would get his ledger (*Bahi*) attested by the *Patwari* concerned.[16] When two lacs of *dams* were collected or at the end of every month,[17] he would despatch the money along with the account of the daily receipts and expenditure duly attested by the Collector to the main treasury or the Royal Court.[18] He had no personal authority of disbursement of any money without the previous sanction of the *Diwan*.[19] But in case of an emergency expenditure, he had to act under the authority of the *Karkun* and the *Shiqdar* and report the case to the higher authorities for appropriate sanction.[20] He had also to keep full accounts of the pooled expenditure (*Malba*) of the various village and *Pargana* officials.[21] He had to keep a keen watch on the treasury clerk (*Gumashta*) and was accountable for the conduct of the latter.[22]

References

1. *Ain*, Br. M. Add. 7652, fol. 144a; Hamiltion, Berlin, fol 121b. *Ain* puts him under the heading of the *Ain-i-Khazanadar* and comments that in the popular language of the day, he is known as *Fotahdar*. In *Ain-i-Bitikchi*, (Br. M. Fol. 144a, Hamilton. Berlin, fol. 121b) it also calls him *Khazanchi* and *Gaujwar*. But *Akbar Nama* (Br. M. Add. O.R. 27, 247, fols 332a-b) always desingates him only as the *Fotahdar*. *Ain-i-Akbari* has described his duties not only in *Ain-i-Khazanddar* but also in *Ain-i-Amal Guzar* and *Ain-i-Bitikchi*.
2. *Ibid.* As against this, Makhzanul Ihetsab, Berlin, fol 6a, 17th century Ms. suggests that the treasury was located within the residential premises of the Shiqdar.
3. *Ibid.*, fols. 143b, 121a respectively. *Makhazanul Ihetsab*, Berlin, fol, 6a states that of the two locks on the treasury gate, on was locked by the *Shiqdar*, another by the *Karkun*. Here *Ain's* version seems to be more plausible though it is possible that the practive may have changed by the time of Shahjahan's reign.
4. *Ibid.*, fols 144b, 122a respectively. *Makhzanul Ihetsab*, Berlin, fol. 6a.
5. *Ibid.*
6. A.N. (Br. M. Add. 27,247,fol. 332a) 9th clause of 27th year reforms of Todar Mal; *Insha-i-Harkarn*, p.56.
7. A.N. *Ibid.*
8. *Ibid.*
9. *Ibid.*, 7th clause.
10. *Ibid.*
11. *Ain*, fols. 144b, 122a respectively.
12. *Ibid.*, fols 144a-b; 121b-122a
13. *Ibid.*
14. A.N. Br. M. Add. 27,247, fol. 332b.
15. *Ain*, fls 144b; 122 a respectively. *Insha-i-Harkarn*,p. 56; Dururulm, Bod. Oxford, fol. 137b..
16. *Ibid.*
17. *Ibid.*, fols. 143b, 121a respectively. As against *Ain's* version of despatch of two 'lacs' of dams, *Insha-i-Harkarn* p. 56 suggests the despatch of money every month.
18. *Ibid.*
19. *Ibid.*, fols 144b, 122a respectively. Dururulm, Bod. Oxford, fol 137b states that he could not spend a single *dam* without authorised sanction.
20. *Ibid.*
21. Dururulm, Bod. Oxford, fol. 137b.
22. *Insha-i-Harkarn*, p.56

IV. The *Thanadar*

For the purposes of police and revenue adminstration, regular Thanas were set up in the *Parganas* of every *Subah.* It is significant to note that during the mughal age, the *Thanas* served as the real and regular sanction behind the land revenue administration. A *Thana* served as a military-cum-police post with a specified number of contingent of *Sawar* (Cavalry) and *Piyada* (Footmen). The practice of establishment of *Thanas,* both for military and revenue purposes is on record throughout the Mughal age.[1] In fact, the designation of *Thanedar* as the officer in charge of a *Thana* was a general one. A *Mansabdar* could be appointed as a *Thanadar* of a *Dehat Thana* or a *Thana* at the *Pargana* headquarters or a strategic frontier post with a much larger jurisdiction than a *Pargana.* The *Mansab* and the status of the *Thanedar* varied according to the strategic nature and the territorial jurisdiction of the *Thana.*[2] A high *Mansabdar* posted as *Thanadar* at a *Thana* with strategic position would have various other *Mansabdars* under him. At times, the *Thandari* duties were performed by a *Qiladar* who was not only the Commander of the fort but also the administartive officer of the *Mahals* attached to the fort.[3] Not withstanding this variation in the nature and jurisdiction of a *Thana* in the settled territories of the *Subahs*, the *Pargana* and the *Dehat Thanas* formed the main sanction behind the machinery of land revenue collection. Immediately after the conquest of a territory, military posts at strategic places named *Thanas* were established both for further conquest and the administrative consolidation of the territory already under occupation.[4] Baharistan gives a detailed picture of the creation of *Thanas* for such purposes in the newly conquered territories in Bengal, Kuch Bihar and Assam in the reign of Jahangir.[5] The *Thanadar,* who was a Royal *Mansabdar,* was appointed as incharge of the garrison of the *Thana*[6] Apart from safeguarding the passage and the provisions of the regular Army for further expansion,[7] a *Thanadar* had to pacify the people and to establish regular peaceful administration in the locality, to maintain law and order and especially to suppress any recurrence of refractory tendencies, to have proper control over the local *Zamindars*,[8] and finally to help the *Karori* in the realisation of land revenue from the ryots.[9] He could not leave station without proper sanction of the higher authorities.[10] Though appointed by the Central Government, the *Thanadar* was responsible to the *Subahdar* and in case of any misdemeanour could be removed from office by the latter with an intimation to the Royal Court.[11] The *Subahdar* was competent to make stop gap arangements for the appointment of a *Thanadar* subject to the final Royal approval.[12] The *Subahdar* or the Provinical *Diwan* could also make recommendations for the *Thanadari* appointments which were usually approved by the Royal Court.[13] The *Thanader* of an important and highly Strategic Center with jurisdiction over wide territories was also designated as the *Sardar*.[14] In fact, Bharistan presents the administrative structure of the freqently conquered territories still awaiting regular and proper set-up already in vogue in the peacefully settled portions of the Mughal Empire. As such, it is difficult to work out the exact relationship between a *Thanadar*, *Sardar* and a *Faujdar*[15] though all the three were State *Mansabdars* and performed more or less the same functions in different regions. The term *Sardar* just denoted an administrative officer whose jurisdiction could vary in territorial extent.[16] In fact, the designation of *Sardar* of a territory though sparingly used, remained in vogue right from Akbar's reign[17] to that of Auranagzeb.[18] It seems that ordinarily, a *Sardar* enjoyed higher status than that of a *Thanadar* and was more of an administrator like a *Faujdar* of a territory.

The *Ain* mentions the office of the *Thanadar* only incidentally as one of the signatories to the attestation of the survey and measurement documents of the villages prepared by the staff of the *Bitikchi*.[19] It is difficult to make out the nature of the *Thanadar's* office simply from the *Ain* where he appears to be a petty official-perhaps a *Dehat-Thanadar* of few villages. The real significance of the role of a *Thanadar* in the Revenue Administration of a Mughal *Pargana* can be known from the *Akhbarat* of Rajasthan Archives and the original documents of some of the *Parganas* in Subah Malwa of Aurangzeb's reign. Regular *Thanas* were set up in the *Parganas* of a *Sarkar* division.[20] It seems that the *Pargana* headquarters themselves formed the seats of the main *Thanas*.[21] Every main *Thana* of a *Pargana* was further subdivided into various small *Thana* circles named as *Thanas* of *Dehats* (villages) or popularly known as *Thanas*.[22] Each *Thana-i-Dehat* had a number of villages in its jurisdiction. The number of such *Thanas* varied from *Pargana* to *Pargana* depending on the geographical and strategical position of the villages, the nature of the inhabitants and *Zamindars* whether revenue paying (*raiyati*) or recalcitrant (*Zur Talb*). Every *Thana* had its strategic importance and was situated very near the turbulent *Zamindars* or tribal populations.[23] The jurisdiction of a *Thana* though well defined, was always subject to reshuffling from time to time as the situation demanded. In fact, regular *Thanabandi* (fixation of *Thanas*) documents were prepared periodically along with the *Jamabandi* (revenues) documents of the *Parganas* of a *Subah*.[24] The demarcation of *Thana* boundries was done by a specially appointed officer of the Central Government in consultation with the *Faujdar* of a divison of *Parganas*.[25] A *Thanadar* was an officer-in-charge of the *Thana* headquarters and exercised jurisdiction over all the *Dehat-Thanas* in the *Pargana*.[26] Sometimes, a *Thanadar* would be appointed with jurisdiction over a number of *Mahals*.[27] But it seems that in such a case though officially designated as *Thanadar*, the latter would virtually be a *Faujdar* discharging all *Faujdari* obligations as well and would exercise authority over all the *Thanas* situated at the *Pargana* headquarters and their village circles. On the other hand, an official could also be designated both as *Faujdar* and *Thanadar* of a particular station.[28] A number of *Sawars* (Cavalry) and *Piyadas* (Footmen) were stationed both at the *Thana* headquarters and the *Dehat-Thanas*.[29] The *Pargana Thanadar* was always a small *Mansabdar* with a rank usually ranging from 100 *Zat* to 400 *Zat* with additional *Sawars* depending on the status of the officer.[30]At times, he was also assisted by a *Naib-Thandar*.[31] The *Dehat-Thanadar* was also a petty *Mansabdar* who was also appointed directly by the Central Government.[32] At times in the *Dehat-Thanas*, only *Sawars* were posted as guards and no *Thanadars* were appointed.[33]

For the proper working of the main *Thanas*, it is essential to bear in mind a regular distinction between the *Khalsa* and the *Jagir Parganas*. In *Khalsa Parganas* where the jurisdiction of a *Faujdar* cum *Karori* extended over more than one *Pargana*, a *Thanadar* was stationed at the main *Pargana Thana* who was responsible to the former. But where the jurisdiction of the *Faujdar* himself was just over one *Pargana*, no separate *Pargana Thanadar* was appointed as the *Faujdar* of the *Pargana* himself exercised the *Thanadari* powers.[34] He maintained his troops both at the main *Pargana* and the *Dehat Thanas*. He was in-charge of all the *Thanas* in his jurisdiction and was responsible to the *Faujdar* of the *Parganas* of his division.[35] On the contrary, in the *Jagir Parganas*, the office of a *Thanadar* was an essential feature of the *Pargana* administration. He was responsible to the *Faujdar* and *Amin* of the *Jagir Parganas* of his division. At times, the offices of the *Thandar* and *Amin*[36] or the *Thanadar* and *Amin-i-Peshkash*[37] of the *Pargana* were combined in one and the same person. In case of transfer of a *Pargana* from *Jagir* to *Khalsa*, the *Thanadar* would also the transferred to be replaced by a *Faujdar* and *Karori* of the *Pargana*.[38] At the same time, it is quite clear that despite the existence of regular circles of the *Khalsa* and the *Jagir Parganas*, there were mixed *Parganas* as well, wherein some villages were in *Khalsa* while others were assigned in *Tankhwah Jagir*. In such cases, a *Thanadar* would administer the *Jagir* villages whereas the control over the *Khalsa* villages would go to some other *Thanadar* or *Faujdar* of the *Khalsa Pargana*. This may well account for the varied jurisdiction of a *Faujdar* over full one or more *Parganas* along with one or more *Thanas* from different *Parganas*.[39]

As regards his duties, a *Thanadar* had to execute a bond (*Iqrarnamah*) to the effect that he would suppress the insurgents, populate the *Pargana*, guard the main roads for traffic, and would see that no illegal cesses were collected in his area.[40] The *Thanadar* held his own court at the *Pargana* headquarters.[41] On any special instructions from the *Faujdar* of his division, he had to help the *Khalsa* or *Paibaqi* officials[42] or the *Amils* of the *Jagirdar*,[43] depending on the teritory of his posting, in suppressing the recalcitrants and realising land revenue from them. Even for the normal administration, he had to show full cooperation in the realisation of the revenues. In a *Jagir Pargana*, along with the other officials viz. the *Shiqdar*, *Chaudharis*, *Qanungos*, etc. the *Thanadar* too had to attend the court of the *Jagirdar* or his *Amil*.[44] At the time of the realisation of revenues of either of the crops, *Kharif* or *Rabi*, the *Amil* in consultation with the *Thanadar* and other *Pargana* officials would fix approximately three instalments for collection and for this purpose would serve demand notices to the *Muqaddams*.[45] Meetings of the *Amil* and the *Thanadar* with other *Pargana* officials and the representatives of the *waqainawis an Sawanihnawis* (News Writers) would take place at regular intervals to consider the revenue problems of the *Pargana*.[46] In his own court which was attended by the *Waqainingar, Chaudharies* and *Qanungos*, the *Thanadar* would take full purview of the revenues collected by the *Muqaddams* and other administrative matters of the villages in the *Pargana*.[47] At times, even the *Qazi* would attend his court for the purposes of consultation.[48] He had to see that the *Chaudharies* and the *Qaunungos* attended the court of the *Amil* whenever called upon to do so and for this purpose he had to issue directions to them.[49]

On receipt of any complaint or direction from the higher authorities regarding the revenues of the *Jagir*, he would summon the *Chaudharies*, *Qanuongos* and *Muqaddams* to enquire if they had submitted full accounts of the revenues realised (*Siha Amdni*) to the *Amil* of the *Jagirdar* after having been attested by the *Gumashats* (collecting agents) of the latter.[50] He had to verify from the *Muqaddams* the amount of the payment made to the local village *Sawars* and *Paiyadas* for the collection of the revenues.[51]

He maintained full accounts of the fees (*Talbana*) charged for the deployment of his *Sawars* by the *Jagirdar, Muqaddams, Waqainawis* and the *Amin* for the purposes of revenue collection or other official business.[52] He had to remit the above amount (*Talbana*) and other fines collected from the *Muqaddams* to the Royal treasury.[53] In a *Jagir Pargana*, his most important duty was to collect *Peshkash* and other dues (*mutalba*) which the *Jagirdars* owed to the State.[54] He had to submit a detailed statement (*Fard*) of all such income and expenditure incurred in the *Pargana* to the Royal treasury.[55]

For *Subah* Gujrat, Mirat-i-Ahmadi enumerates a number of *Thanas*[56] described as *Zamianah* or *Painam* of the *Faujdar* i.e. *Thana's* accredited to a particular *Faujdar's* division whose *Sawar* rank is also given. In such a case, the *Faujdar* was competent to assign a number of *Sawars* in various *Thanas* under him. Besides, there are a number of *Thanas* described as *Huzuri* or *Huzuri Mashruti* with specified ranks of *Sawars* to be maintained. Thirdly, some *Thanas* are described both as *Huzuri* as well as *Painam* or *Zamianah* while others show only the latter. In some cases, no *Thanas* are given. *Mirat* gives only a general picture underlying the relation between the *Thanas* and the *Faujdar* of the division. It is completely silent on the role of the *Thandar*.

Thus it is clear form the working or the *Thandar's* office that as representative of the Central Government and subordinate to the *Faujdar* of his division, the *Thanadar* was not only the custodian of law and order but also safeguarded the revenue interests of the State in the *Pargana* administration. He ensured the smooth working of the local administration and acted as a check against any unauthorised financial practice on the part of the *Jagirdar* or his staff and the semi-officials of the *Pargana*. He especially protected the interests of the *ryots* against any illegal realisation of the cesses (*Abwab*).

References

1. Under AKbar Sarfaraz Khan Chugta was promoted to the *Thanadari* of Bijapur, *Sarkar* Pattan *Subah* Gujrat. (M.U. II p. 421); Jaimal s/o Rupsi, who was nephew of Raja Bahra Mal, was appointed as *Thanadar* of Marot (*Subah* Ajmer. (*Ibid.* II p. 109). Under Jahangir, See f.n. 5.
2. *Ibid.* Under Akbar, Sarfaraz Khan Chugta held the *Mansab* of 1000/500 (Original and additional); Abdur Rashim Beg was appointed the *Thanadar* in the hills of Madariyah (*Subah* Malwa) in 1566/67 A.D. with 500 *Sawars* (*Tabqat*, II. p. 329); Under Jahangir, after the conquest of Kamrup (*Subah* Bengal) *Thanadars* were the appointed at different *Thanas* with different number of forces in command. (B.G. I to Borah, p. 403); Under Aurangzeb, Fateh Ullah Khan Alamgir Shahi, the *Thanadar* of Lohgar (Kabul) held the rank of 3000 Z 1200 S (M.U. III, p. 47); Maharaja Jaswant Singh was appointed as the *Thanadar* of Jamrud in the 14th R.Y (Aurangzeb) with the rank of 7000 Z 7000 S. (*Ibid.* p. 603).
3. Waqai R, pp. 4-5; S.D.A.R., pp. 53, 139. Ordinary, the *Qiladar* was subordinate and responsible to the *Faujdar* of the division (*Ibid.* pp. 135, 137-138) but at times, the offices of the *Qiladar* and the *Faujdar* were combined in the same person vide *Akhbarat*, 9th *Safar*, 36th R.Y. (Aurangzeb), 22nd *Safar* (*Ibid.*).
4. For example, Akbar established *Thanas* in *Subah* Malwa in 1566-67. Qazi Khan Badakshi, Shareef Khan Atkah, Majahid Khan and Subahn Quli were posted at Mauhi with 3000 *Sawars* and Abdur Rahim Beg with 500 *Sawars* was posted in the hills of Madariyah. *Thanas* were established through the Province of Malwa. (*Tabqat*, II pp. 322, 329, 390).
5. After the conquest of Kamrup, (Subah Bengal) Yusuf Barlas was posted at Barnagar with a force 100 horsemen and 200 match lockmen, Mirza Sahib Arghun was posted to the *Thana* of Dhamdhama with 250 horsemen and 400 match lockmen, Mir Abdur-Razzaq Shriazi and Seth Hridayram were posted to the *Thana* of Pandu with 100 horesemen, 500 match lockmen and the whole of fleet of the *Zamindars*. (B.G.I. tr. Borha, p. 403); also for other *Thanas* in the territories of Bengal, Kuch Bihar, *Ibid.*, pp. 9, 341, 352.
6. *B.G.* tr. Borah, pp. 9, 341, 352, 403.
7. *Ibid.* II, pp. 516-17.
8. *Ibid.*, I, pp. 341, 352, II, pp. 516-517.
9. *Ibid.*, I, pp. 341, 352, 403.
10. *Ibid.* pp. 271-272.
11. *Ibid.*
12. *Ibid.*
13. R.A.J. *Akhbarat*, dated 12th Rajab 44th R.Y. (Aurangzeb) quotes two recommendations of Lutf Ullah Khan, the Nazim of Bijapur (Deccan) for *Thanadari* appointments which were approved by the King. Also Mirat Suppl. pp. 6, 189.
14. B.G. tr. Borah II, p. 586. Qulij Khan, the *Thanadar* of Hajo was not on good terms with the *Subahdar* of Bengal, Ibrahim Khan Fath Jang. The latter reported against him to the Royal Court for excessive drinking and having

removed him from office after having become useless appointed Shaykh Kamal who was confirmed by the Central Government in the *Sardarship* of the aforesaid *Thana.* Later on, Qulij Khan was excused and reappointed at the '*Thana* of Haja to hold the office of the *Jagirdar* and the *Sardar* of the territory of Kuch.' (*Ibid.* II, p. 586.) Mirza Nathan was appointed the *Sardar* of Sylhat after the death of Shaykh Sulayman, the *Thanadar* of Sylhat (*Ibid.* p. 633). Still later, the *Sardarship* of Jessor was offered to Mirza Nasthan. (*Ibid.* p. 637.) Also see pp. 658, 675.

15. For *Faujdar's* Office and Jurisdiction, *Ibid.* I, pp. 89, 218, 274, 328.
16. See f.n. 14; Also *Ibid.* II, pp. 673-75. When a quarrel took place between Shitab Khan, the assignee of *Pargana* of Khantaghat and Mir Safi, the *Diwan* of Kuch over the revenues of the aforesaid *Pargana,* Mirza Bahram, the *Sardar* of Kuch, asserted his authority for investigation and to report against the defaulting party as the trouble maker to the *Subahdar*. (B.G. Ms. B.N. Paris, fols. 285a-286b). Whereas the earlier appointment over Hajo was that of a *Sardar* (Vide f.n.9), later on Saiyid Mufattih was appointed as the *Subahdar* of Hajo and Kuch (*Ibid.* II, p. 113).
17. *A.N.* II, p. 14 mentiones the appointment of Abdullah Khan to the *Sardarship* of Sarkar Kalpi.
18. *Mirat-i-Alam*, Ms. Aligh. fol. 111a.
19. *Ain*, Br. M. Add 7652, fo9l. 144a; Ms. Hamilton, Berlin, fol 120b.
20. R.A.J. Category, no. 3, reg no. 408 (Aurangzeb's reign) '*Thana bandi wa Jamabandi-i- Parganat-i- Malwa* i.e. *Thanabandi* and *Jawabandi* documents of Malwa; also *Ibid.* reg no. 880 '*Fard-i-Thanajat*' of *Parganas* of *Subah* Malwa.
21. *Ibid.*; Also compare the *Mahals* of *Sarkar* Sarath (Kathiawad, *Subah* Gujrat) in *Ain*, J. II, pp. 263-64 with the *Thanas* in the division of Soruth vide '*Thanas* of Saurashtra in the last decade of Aurangzeb's Reign, 1697-1707, p. 319 by K. H. Kamdar, *I.H.C. Proceedings*, Gauhati, 1959. Despite the fact that some of the *Mahal* circles and the names may have changed from the date of the *Ain's* compilation, surprisingly majority of the *Mahal* names of the *Ain* are also put as *Thanas* under Aurangzeb; Also S.D.A.R., pp. 119-120. Dr. Noman Siddiqi's analysis (vide the *Faujdar* and *Faujdari* under the Mughals, pp. 7-9) of the *Thana* as a part of the *Faujdari* circle irrespective of the *Pargana* administration is absolutely incorrect.
22. R.A.J. *Akhbarat* regd. no. 1594 dated 15th of Shahban 23rd R.Y. quotes the promotion of Ajab Singh, S/o. Sajja Singh Rathore, *Thanadar* of Mauza Bayawar from the rank of 100 Z 50 S to additional 100 S; also category no. 3 regd. no. 723 (Aurangzeb's reign) quotes the appointment of Awduet Rai as the *Thanadar* of *Pargana* Othal *Sarkar* Ujjain (*Subah* Malwa) and at the same time quotes the Royal Order for the creation of '*Thana-i-Dehat*' i.e., the village *Thanas* in the *Pargana*. Also S.D.A.R., p. 86 clearly mentions the *Thanadar* of village Dharpur (*Subah* Berar); also Mirat.
23. Also see K.H. Kadar, '*Thanas* of Saurashtra in the Last Decade of Aurangzeb's Reign, 1697-1707' *I.H.C. Proceedings*, Gauhati, 1959, pp. 319-320. Prof. Kamdar, who has given details of 84 *Thanas* in *Sarkar* Sorath (*Subah* Gujrat),

comments that a *Thana* was intended to "Keep peace, and to control the turbulent chiefs, *Kathis*, *Girasies* and refractory populations, as for instance *Kolis*, *Ahirs*, *Mers,* etc. Evidently, the station had a strategic importance and it was situated very near the turbulent Chiefs, or populations, as for instance, Gariadhar, Dhank, Majewadi Ambaran, etc."

24. See f.n. 20.
25. R.A.J. *Akhbarat,* dated 17th 26th R.Y. (Aurangzeb); also Category no. 3 regd. no. 880 vide f.n. 20.
26. R.A.J. Category no. 3 regd. no. 723 vide f.n. 22.
27. R.A.J. *Akhbarat,* dated 12th Rajab, 44th R.Y. (Aurangzeb) quotes an appointment of Shamsuddin as *Thanadar* of Sundri, comprising five *Mahals* (*Subah* Bijapur, Deccan).
28. *Ibid.* date4d 9th Rabi I, 9th R.Y. (*Ibid*) quotes the appointment of Khwaja Muqim as the *Faujdar* anda *Thanadar* of Poona. (*Subah* Gujrat).
29. *Ibid.*; also for Aurangabad (Deccan *Subah*), see 'S.D.A.R.' Pers. text, pp. 46, 53.
30. R.A.J. *Akhbarat* regd. no. 1594 dated 15th Shaban 23rd R.Y. (Aurangzeb) regd. no. 1719/1 dated 1st Zilhaj 24th R.Y. (*Ibid*); regd. no. 1847 dated 11th Rabi II 24th R.Y. (*Ibid*); no. 1839/1 dated 3rd Rabi II 24th R.Y. (*Ibid*); regd. no. 1729 dated 11th Zilhaj 24th R.Y. (*Ibid*), dated 28th Zilhaj 10th R.Y. (*Ibid*).
31. *Ibid. Waqai Pargana* Othal, regd. no. 707, dated 15th Jamada II, 49th R.Y. (*Ibid*).
32. *Ibid. Akhbarat,* regd. no. 1594, dated 15th Shaban 23rd R.Y. (*Ibid*) Ajab Singh, *Thanadar* of *Mauza* Bayawar with 100 Z 50 S.
33. *Ibid.* Category no. 3 regd. no. 723 vide f.n. 22; also f.n. 28.
34. *Ibid.* Category no. 3 regd. no. 783 (Aurangzeb) quotes a *Parwana* addressed to the *Thanadar* of *Pargana* Shahjahanpur that the *Pargana* had been transferred to the *Khalsa* and that the *Aminship* and *Faujdari* of that place as granted to Rai Sahab Singh. The *Parwana* directs him to hand over the charge of the *Parwana* to the latter and to attend the Royal Court; Also R.A.J. *Akhbarat*, dated 9th Rabi I, 9th R.Y. (*Ibid*), vests the *Faujdari* and *Thanadari* powers of Poona (*Subah* Gujrat) with Khwaja Muqim.
35. *Ibid.* Category no. 4 regd. 405 dated 19th Jamada, I, A.H. 117/1705 A.D.; *Nigar Nama*, Bod. Oxfd. fols. 66b-67a, 75b-77b, Ms. N.A.I., fols. 54b-55a, 60b-61b.
36. *Nigar Nama,* Bod. Oxfd, fols. 84a-b; Ms. N.A.I. fols. 65a-b.
37. R.A.J. *Akhbarat* dated 30th , 37th R.Y. quotes the appointment of Mohammad Hadi as the *Thanadar* and *Amin-i-Peshkash* of Burhanpur with 300 Z 150 S.
38. See f.n. 33.
39. *Mirat*, Suppl.
40. R.A.J. Misc. Persian Letters reg. no. 655 dated 1113 Fasli/1703 A.D. An *Iqarnamah* (Bond executed by Puran Mal, the *Thanadar* of *Pargana* Othal, *Sarkar* Ujjain, *Subah* Malwa).
41. R.A.J. *Akhbarat, Waqia Pargana* 13th-14th (*Subah* Malwa) reg. no. 630 dated Jamada II 49th R.Y. A.H. 117/21st-22nd September, 1705 A.D. mentions Udhai Singh *Thanadar* of *Pagana* Bhorasah *Sarkar* Sarangpur *Subah* holding

his court. Similarly, *Waqai Pargana* Othal *Sarkar* Ujjain *Subah* Malwa regd. no. 654 dated 12th Rabi II, 49th R.Y./1705 A.D. mention Ajab Singh *Thanadar* holding his Court.

42. R.A.J. Category no. 2, regd. no. 939 dated 5th Jamada I, A.H. 1117/1705 A.D./1762 Samat.
43. *Ibid.* Category no. 4, regd. n o. 2855 dated 19th Rabi II, A.H. 1124/1712 A.D.
44. R.A.J. *Waqai Pargana* Othal, *Sarkar* Ujjain regd. no. 688 dated 24th Jamada I, 49th R.Y. (Aurgangzeb) states that Puran Mal *Thanadar* along with other officials attended the Court of Sakat Singh, the *Amil* of Nawab Nawzish Khan.
45. *Ibid.*
46. *Ibid.* regd. no. 679 dated 15th Jamada II, 49th R.Y. A.H. 1117/24th August, 1705 A.D.
47. *Ibid.* regd. no. 656 dated 19th Rabi II, 49th R.Y. A.H. 1117/39th July 1705 A.D.
48. *Ibid.* regd. no. 654 dated 12th Rabi II, 49th R.Y. A.H. 1117/1705 A.D.
49. *Ibid.*
50. *Ibid.*
51. R.A.J. *Waqia Pargana* Bhorsah *Sarkar* Sarangpur, regd. no. 635 dated 23rd Jamada I, 49th R.Y. A.H. 1117/1705 A.D.
52. *Ibid.* regd. no. 644, dated 7th Rajab 49th R.Y. (Aurangzeb).
53. *Ibid.* The *Waqai* reports that Udhai Singh, the *Thanadar* of *Pargana* Othal went personally to Ujjain treasury and deposited Rs. 279/- which he had realised from the *Jagirs* as *Talbana,* etc. The details of the amount realised from different sources are given in the document.
54. *Ibid.* also regd. no. 630 dated 13th Jamada I, 49th R.Y. A.H. 1117/21st September 1705 A.D. states that the *Thandar* Udhai Singh of *Pargana* Bhorasah *Sarkar* Sarangpur did not accept the terms of payment of *Peshkash* by the *Amil* of Ibrahim Khan and directed him to deposit the amount of *Peshkash* within a day or two.
55. *Ibid.*
56. *Mirat,* Suppl. pp. 194, 196, 199-200.

Index